First World War
and Army of Occupation
War Diary
France, Belgium and Germany

27 DIVISION
81 Infantry Brigade
Headquarters
11 February 1914 - 30 September 1915

WO95/2263/1

The Naval & Military Press Ltd
www.nmarchive.com
Published in association with The National Archives

Published by

The Naval & Military Press Ltd

Unit 10 Ridgewood Industrial Park,
Uckfield, East Sussex,
TN22 5QE England
Tel: +44 (0) 1825 749494

www.naval-military-press.com

www.nmarchive.com

This diary has been reprinted in facsimile from the original. Any imperfections are inevitably reproduced and the quality may fall short of modern type and cartographic standards.

© **Crown Copyright**
Images reproduced by permission of The National Archives, London, England, 2015.

Contents

Document type	Place/Title	Date From	Date To
Heading	WO95/2263-1		
Heading	Headquarters, 81st Infantry Brigade (27th Division) December (19th to 31st) 1914		
War Diary	Magdalen Hill Camp Winchester	19/12/1914	19/12/1914
War Diary	No 2 Dock Gate Southampton	19/12/1914	19/12/1914
War Diary	Southampton	19/12/1914	19/12/1914
War Diary	Winchester	19/12/1914	19/12/1914
War Diary	Havre	20/12/1914	20/12/1914
War Diary	Atlantian	20/12/1914	20/12/1914
War Diary	No 1 Platform	20/12/1914	20/12/1914
War Diary	No 6 Platform	21/12/1914	21/12/1914
War Diary	Rouen	21/12/1914	21/12/1914
War Diary	St. Omer	22/12/1914	22/12/1914
War Diary	Aire	22/12/1914	25/12/1914
War Diary	N.E of Aire	26/12/1914	26/12/1914
War Diary	Aire	26/12/1914	26/12/1914
War Diary	3 Miles N.E. Aire	27/12/1914	27/12/1914
War Diary	Vicinity of Pecqueur	28/12/1914	28/12/1914
War Diary	H of Houleron	29/12/1914	29/12/1914
War Diary	3 Miles N E of Aire	30/12/1914	30/12/1914
War Diary	H of Houleron	31/12/1914	31/12/1914
Miscellaneous	Brigade Operation Orders Nos. 1 to 10.		
Operation(al) Order(s)	81st Infantry Brigade Order No. 1 By Brig. Genl. D.A. Macfarlane, D.S.O. Commdg. 81st Infy. Bde.	18/12/1914	18/12/1914
Miscellaneous	Instructions	18/12/1914	18/12/1914
Miscellaneous	Road Only.		
Operation(al) Order(s)	81st Infantry Brigade Order No. 2 By Brig. Genl. D.A. Macfarlane, D.S.O. Commdg. 81st Infy. Bde.	22/12/1914	22/12/1914
Miscellaneous	Brigade Order No. 3 By Brig. Genl. D.A. Macfarlane, D.S.O. Comdg 81st Infy. Bde.	23/12/1914	23/12/1914
Miscellaneous	Brigade Order No. 3 By Brig. Genl. D.A. Macfarlane, D.S.O. Comdg 81st Infy. Brigade.	24/12/1914	24/12/1914
Miscellaneous	Brigade Order No. 5 By Brig. Genl. D.A. Macfarlane, D.S.O. Commdg. 81st Infy. Bde. Aire.	25/12/1914	25/12/1914
War Diary	Brigade Order No. 6 By Brig. Genl. D.A. Macfarlane, D.S.O. Commdg. 81st Infy. Bde. Aire.	26/12/1914	26/12/1914
Miscellaneous	Brigade Order No. 7 By Brig. Genl. D.A. Macfarlane, D.S.O. Commdg. 81st Infy. Brigade	27/12/1914	27/12/1914
Miscellaneous	Brigade Order No. 8 By Brig. Genl. D.A. Macfarlane, D.S.O. Commdg. 81st Infy. Bde. Aire.	28/12/1914	28/12/1914
Miscellaneous	Brigade Order No. 9 By Brig. Genl. D.A. Macfarlane, D.S.O. Commdg. 81st Infy. Bde.	29/12/1914	29/12/1914
Miscellaneous	Brigade Order No. 10 By Brig. Genl. D.A. Macfarlane, D.S.O. Commdg. 81st Infy. Bde	30/12/1914	30/12/1914
Heading	War Diary B.H.Q. 81st Inf. Bde. January 1915		
Heading	27th Divisions 81st Bde H Q Vol II 1-31.1.15		
Heading	War Diary of Hd. Qrs 81st Inf Bde 27th Div. from Jan 1st to Jan 31st (Vol. 2)		
War Diary	H of Houleron	01/01/1915	01/01/1915
War Diary	Cross roads pt. 33 N. of the M of Boeseghem	02/01/1915	02/01/1915

War Diary	Northern Section of Trenches	03/01/1915	03/01/1915
War Diary	Aire	04/01/1915	06/01/1915
War Diary	Meteren	07/01/1915	07/01/1915
War Diary	Dickebusch	08/01/1915	13/01/1915
War Diary	Westoutre	14/01/1915	15/01/1915
War Diary	Dickebusch	16/01/1915	23/01/1915
War Diary	Westoutre	24/01/1915	30/01/1915
War Diary	Dickebusch	31/01/1915	31/01/1915
Miscellaneous	Divisional Operation Orders Nos. 7		
Operation(al) Order(s)	27th. Division Operation Order No. 7	10/01/1915	10/01/1915
Operation(al) Order(s)	27th. Division Operation Order No. 8	10/01/1915	10/01/1915
Operation(al) Order(s)	27th. Division Operation Order No. 9	11/01/1915	11/01/1915
Operation(al) Order(s)	27th. Division Operation Order No. 13	15/01/1915	15/01/1915
Operation(al) Order(s)	27th. Division Operation Order No. 15.	17/01/1915	17/01/1915
Miscellaneous	27th. Division Operation Order No. 16.	19/01/1915	19/01/1915
Miscellaneous	27th. Division Operation Order No. 17.	20/01/1915	20/01/1915
Miscellaneous	27th. Division Operation Order No. 18.	22/01/1916	22/01/1916
Miscellaneous	27th. Division Operation Order No. 22.	28/01/1915	28/01/1915
Miscellaneous	Brigade Operation Orders Nos. 11 to 32.		
Miscellaneous	Brigade Order No. 11 By Brig. Gen. D.A. Macfarlane, D.S.O. Commdg 81st Infy. Bde.	31/12/1914	31/12/1914
Miscellaneous	Brigade Order No. 12 By Brig. Gen. D.A. Macfarlane, D.S.O. Commdg 81st Infy. Bde.	01/01/1915	01/01/1915
Miscellaneous	Brigade Order No. 13 By Brig. Gen. D.A. Macfarlane, D.S.O. Commdg 81st Infy. Bde.	02/01/1916	02/01/1916
Miscellaneous	Brigade Order No. 14 By Brig. Gen. D.A. Macfarlane, D.S.O. Commdg 81st Infy. Bde.	03/01/1915	03/01/1915
Miscellaneous	Brigade Order No. 15 By Brig. Gen. D.A. Macfarlane, D.S.O. Commdg 81st Infy. Bde.	04/01/1915	04/01/1915
Miscellaneous	Brigade Order No. 16 By Brig. Gen. D.A. Macfarlane, D.S.O. Commdg 81st Infy. Bde.	05/01/1915	05/01/1915
Miscellaneous	81st Infy Brigade Order No. 17 By Brig Genl. D.A. Macfarlane D.S.O. Commdg 81st Infy Bde.	06/01/1915	06/01/1915
Miscellaneous	Brigade Order No. 18	08/01/1915	08/01/1915
Miscellaneous	Brigade Order No. 19 By Brig. Genl. D.A. Macfarlane, D.S.O. Commdg. 81st Infy. Bde.	09/01/1915	09/01/1915
Miscellaneous	81st Inf. Brigade Order No. 20	10/01/1915	10/01/1915
Miscellaneous	Brigade Order No. 21 By Brig. Genl. D.A. Macfarlane, D.S.O. Commdg. 81st Infy. Bde.	11/01/1915	11/01/1915
Miscellaneous	Brigade Order No. 22 By Brig. Genl. D.A. Macfarlane, D.S.O. Commdg. 81st Infy. Bde.	12/01/1915	12/01/1915
Operation(al) Order(s)	81st Infantry Bde Operation Order No. 23	14/01/1915	14/01/1915
Operation(al) Order(s)	81st Infy Bde Order No. 24	16/01/1915	16/01/1915
Operation(al) Order(s)	81st Inf Brigade Order No. 25	17/01/1915	17/01/1915
Operation(al) Order(s)	81st Infy Bde. Order No. 26		
Operation(al) Order(s)	81st Infantry Bde. Order No. 27.	21/01/1915	21/01/1915
Operation(al) Order(s)	81st Infantry Bde. Order No. 28.	22/01/1915	22/01/1915
Operation(al) Order(s)	81st Infy. Bde. Order No. 29.	28/01/1915	28/01/1915
Operation(al) Order(s)	81st Infy. Bde. Order No. 30.	29/01/1915	29/01/1915
Operation(al) Order(s)	81st Infy Bde Order No. 31	30/01/1915	30/01/1915
Operation(al) Order(s)	81st Infy. Bde. Order No. 32.	31/01/1915	31/01/1915
Miscellaneous	Instructions Regarding Taking Over Trenches And Their Relief.	20/01/1915	20/01/1915
Miscellaneous	Instructions For Commencing New Trenches Near St. Eloi.	21/01/1915	21/01/1915
Miscellaneous	A Form. Messages And Signals.	10/01/1915	10/01/1915

Miscellaneous	A Form. Messages And Signals.		
Miscellaneous	A Form. Messages And Signals.	08/01/1915	08/01/1915
Map			
Miscellaneous			
Map			
Miscellaneous	App I.		
Miscellaneous	Report On Sapping Operations	20/01/1915	21/01/1915
Diagram etc			
Heading	Headquarters, 81st Infantry Brigade (27th Division) February 1915		
War Diary	Dickebusch	01/02/1915	10/02/1915
War Diary	Westoutre and Reninghelst	11/02/1914	14/02/1914
War Diary	Westoutre	14/02/1915	14/02/1915
War Diary	Dickebusch	15/02/1915	27/02/1915
War Diary	Westoutre	28/02/1915	28/02/1915
Miscellaneous	Brigade Operation Orders Nos. 33 to 41.		
Operation(al) Order(s)	81st Infy. Bde. Order No. 33	01/02/1915	01/02/1915
Operation(al) Order(s)	81st Infy. Bde. Order No. 34	03/02/1915	03/02/1915
Miscellaneous	Amendment To Brigade Order No. 34 of 3rd Feb. 1915.		
Operation(al) Order(s)	81st Infy. Bde. Order No. 35	05/02/1915	05/02/1915
Operation(al) Order(s)	81st Infy. Bde. Order No. 36.	05/02/1915	05/02/1915
Operation(al) Order(s)	81st Infy. Bde. Order No. 38.	07/02/1915	07/02/1915
Operation(al) Order(s)	81st Infy. Bde. Order No. 37.	06/10/1915	06/10/1915
Operation(al) Order(s)	81st Infy. Bde. Order No. 39.	09/02/1915	09/02/1915
Operation(al) Order(s)	81st Infy. Bde. Order No. 40.	14/02/1915	14/02/1915
Operation(al) Order(s)	81st Infy. Bde. Order No. 41.	26/02/1915	26/02/1915
Miscellaneous	C Form (Duplicate). Messages And Signals.	14/02/1915	14/02/1915
Miscellaneous	B Form. Messages And Signals.	14/02/1915	14/02/1915
Miscellaneous	C Form (Triplicate) Messages And Signals.	14/02/1915	14/02/1915
Miscellaneous	C Form (Duplicate). Messages And Signals.	14/02/1915	14/02/1915
Miscellaneous	C Form (Triplicate) Messages And Signals.		
Miscellaneous	C Form (Original) Messages And Signals.		
Miscellaneous	B Form. Messages And Signals.	15/02/1915	15/02/1915
Miscellaneous	C Form (Quadruplicate). Messages And Signals.	15/02/1915	15/02/1915
Miscellaneous	B Form. Messages And Signals.	15/02/1915	15/02/1915
Miscellaneous	C Form (Duplicate) Messages And Signals.	17/05/1915	17/05/1915
Miscellaneous	C Form (Quadruplicate). Messages And Signals.	18/02/1915	18/02/1915
Miscellaneous	C Form (Duplicate). Messages And Signals.	18/02/1915	18/02/1915
Miscellaneous	C Form (Duplicate). Messages And Signals.		
Miscellaneous	B Form. Messages And Signals.	19/02/1915	19/02/1915
Miscellaneous	B Form. Messages And Signals.	23/02/1915	23/02/1915
Miscellaneous	B Form. Messages And Signals.	28/02/1915	28/02/1915
Miscellaneous	Reports on Saps		
Miscellaneous	C Form (Duplicate) Messages And Signals.	23/02/1915	23/02/1915
Miscellaneous	B Form Messages And Signals.	24/02/1915	24/02/1915
Miscellaneous	Messages And Signals.	24/02/1915	24/02/1915
Miscellaneous	C Form (Original) Messages And Signals.		
Miscellaneous			
Miscellaneous	B Form. Messages And Signals.	24/02/1915	24/02/1915
Miscellaneous		24/02/1915	24/02/1915
Miscellaneous	Reports on Trench No. 21	24/02/1915	24/02/1915
Miscellaneous	B Form. Messages And Signals.	25/02/1915	25/02/1915
Miscellaneous	C Form. (Duplicate). Messages And Signals.	26/02/1915	26/02/1915
Miscellaneous	C Form (Original). Messages And Signals.	27/02/1915	27/02/1915
Miscellaneous	C Form (Duplicate). Messages And Signals.	27/02/1915	27/02/1915
Miscellaneous			

Miscellaneous	B Form. Messages And Signals.		
Miscellaneous	C Form (Duplicate). Messages And Signals.	27/02/1915	27/02/1915
Miscellaneous	German Sap In Front of No. 17.	27/02/1915	27/02/1915
Miscellaneous	Headquarters 27th Division.	26/02/1915	26/02/1915
Diagram etc			
Miscellaneous	Headquarters, 27th Division.	20/02/1915	20/02/1915
Miscellaneous	All reference To Left or right of saps etc. refer to our own left or right.		
Diagram etc			
Miscellaneous	Extract from a report by Captain E.J.F. Johnston, 1st Battn.		
Diagram etc			
Miscellaneous	C Form (Duplicate). Messages And Signals.	21/02/1915	21/02/1915
Miscellaneous	Situation at St Eloi.	15/02/1915	15/02/1915
Diagram etc			
Miscellaneous		25/02/1915	25/02/1915
Miscellaneous			
Miscellaneous	Proposal for Brigade to take over		
Miscellaneous	A Form. Messages And Signals.		
Miscellaneous	81st Infantry Brigade. Right Section Of Defence App III	12/03/1915	12/03/1915
Miscellaneous	81st Infantry Brigade. The Role Of The Different Portions Of The Front Line And Policy With Regard To It.	08/02/1915	08/02/1915
Miscellaneous	81st Infantry Brigade.	08/02/1915	08/02/1915
Miscellaneous	Headquarters. 27th Division	06/03/1915	06/03/1915
Miscellaneous	Report On Proposed Scheme For Holding Right Section Permanently.	05/03/1915	05/03/1915
Miscellaneous	Officer Commanding.	04/03/1915	04/03/1915
Miscellaneous	B Form. Messages And Signals.	04/03/1915	04/03/1915
Miscellaneous	Report By Brigadier-General Commanding 81st Infantry Brigade On Proposal To Hold One Section Of Trenches By One Brigadier General Commanding 81sth Own Reliefs	03/03/1915	03/03/1915
Miscellaneous	Sketches of the Mound-St. Eloi.		
Diagram etc			
Heading	B.H.Q. 81st Infantry Brigade March 1915		
War Diary	Westoutre	01/03/1915	05/03/1915
War Diary	Dickebusch	06/03/1915	14/03/1915
War Diary	Class 2/Glastos-R Serts in Trenches)	14/03/1915	15/03/1915
War Diary	Dickebusch	16/03/1915	23/03/1915
War Diary	2 Eve Coten	24/03/1915	31/03/1915
Miscellaneous	Brigade Operation Orders Nos. 42 to 49.		
Operation(al) Order(s)	81st Infantry Brigade Order No. 42	04/03/1915	04/03/1915
Operation(al) Order(s)	81st Infy. Bde. Order No. 43.	04/03/1915	04/03/1915
Operation(al) Order(s)	81st Infy. Bde. Order No. 44.	05/03/1915	05/03/1915
Operation(al) Order(s)	81st Infantry Brigade Order No. 45.	08/03/1915	08/03/1915
Operation(al) Order(s)	81st Infy. Bde. Order No. 46.	08/03/1915	08/03/1915
Operation(al) Order(s)	81st I. Brigade Order No. 46	11/03/1915	11/03/1915
Operation(al) Order(s)	81st Bd Operation Order No 47.	13/03/1915	13/03/1915
Operation(al) Order(s)	81st Infantry Bde. Order No. 48.	19/03/1915	19/03/1915
Operation(al) Order(s)	81st Inf. Bde Order No. 49.	25/03/1915	25/03/1915
Miscellaneous	Maps		
Diagram etc			
Miscellaneous	2nd Camerons, 1st A. & S. Highrs.	16/03/1915	16/03/1915
Diagram etc			
Miscellaneous			

Diagram etc			
Miscellaneous			
Diagram etc			
Heading	B.H.Q. 81st Infantry Brigade. April 1915		
Heading	War Diary of Hd. Qrs. 81st. Infy Bde 27th Divn. from 1st April 1915 to 30th April 1915 (Volume V)		
War Diary		01/04/1915	30/04/1915
Miscellaneous	31st Infantry Brigade. March Table for 4th April, 1915	04/04/1915	04/04/1915
Miscellaneous	G.O.C. 81st Inf. Bde. App. I	14/04/1915	14/04/1915
Miscellaneous	First Subsidiary Line.	06/04/1915	06/04/1915
Miscellaneous	Second Subsidiary Line.	08/04/1915	08/04/1915
Miscellaneous	Headquarters, 81st Infantry Brigade.	07/04/1915	07/04/1915
Miscellaneous	Headquarters, 27th Division.	08/04/1915	08/04/1915
Miscellaneous	G.O.C. 81st Brigade.	11/04/1915	11/04/1915
Miscellaneous	Report on French Centre Sector	11/04/1915	11/04/1915
Miscellaneous	Report on Centre Section of Trenches 27th 81st	18/04/1915	18/04/1915
Miscellaneous	G.O.C., 81st Infantry Brigade.	14/04/1915	14/04/1915
Miscellaneous	27th Division.	13/04/1915	13/04/1915
Miscellaneous	Headquarters, 81st Infantry Brigade.	18/05/1915	18/05/1915
Miscellaneous	Report by G.O.C. 81st Infantry Brigade	22/04/1915	22/04/1915
Diagram etc			
Miscellaneous	App. 3		
Heading	B.H.Q. 81st Infantry Brigade. May 1915		
Miscellaneous	War Diary		
War Diary		01/05/1915	18/05/1915
Miscellaneous	27th Division		
War Diary		19/05/1915	31/05/1915
Miscellaneous	Casualties		
Miscellaneous	Casualties 7th Inf. Bde.		
Miscellaneous	Operation Orders		
Operation(al) Order(s)	81st Infantry Bde. Order No. 50		
Miscellaneous	81st Infantry Brigade Operation Order No. 51.		
Operation(al) Order(s)	81st Infantry Brigade Operation Order No. 52.	29/05/1915	29/05/1915
Operation(al) Order(s)	27th Division Operation Order No 46	02/05/1915	02/05/1915
Miscellaneous	81st Infantry Brigade Operation Order Z.		
Miscellaneous			
Miscellaneous	Report On Bridges		
Miscellaneous	Report on Bridges across yPRES canal in Square I.	03/05/1915	03/05/1915
Diagram etc	App 2		
Miscellaneous	Crossings Zillebeke Sketch Of G.H.Q. Line		
Miscellaneous	A Form. Messages And Signals.	08/05/1915	08/05/1915
Miscellaneous	Units 81st L.B.	09/05/1915	09/05/1915
Miscellaneous			
Miscellaneous	Maps		
Miscellaneous	Headquarters, 81st Infantry Brigade.	18/05/1915	18/05/1915
Diagram etc			
Miscellaneous	App 2		
Diagram etc	Appendix 63		
Heading	B.H.Q. 81st Infantry Brigade June 1915		
Heading	War Diary		
War Diary	Armentieres	01/06/1915	30/06/1915
Operation(al) Order(s)	81st Infantry Brigade Operation Order. No. 53.	26/06/1915	26/06/1915
Diagram etc			
Heading	B.H.Q. 81st Infantry Brigade July 1915		
War Diary	Armentieres	01/07/1915	31/07/1915
Miscellaneous	Headquarters, 27th Division.	09/07/1915	09/07/1915

Type	Description	From	To
Diagram etc			
Heading	B.H.Q. 81st Infantry Brigade August 1915		
War Diary	Armentieres	01/08/1915	02/08/1915
War Diary	Erquinghem	03/08/1915	16/08/1915
War Diary	Rue Marle Armentieres	17/08/1915	31/08/1915
Operation(al) Order(s)	81st Infantry Brigade Operation Order No. 53.	31/07/1915	31/07/1915
Operation(al) Order(s)	81st Infantry Brigade Operation Order No. 55.	14/08/1915	14/08/1915
Miscellaneous	Distribution Of Units.	15/08/1915	15/08/1915
Diagram etc			
Miscellaneous	81st Infantry Brigade.		
Miscellaneous			
Diagram etc			
Heading	B.H.Q. 81st Infantry Brigade. October 1915		
Miscellaneous	War Diary		
War Diary	Proyart	01/10/1915	04/10/1915
War Diary	Chuignolles	05/10/1915	24/10/1915
War Diary	Abancourt	25/10/1915	26/10/1915
War Diary	Boves	27/10/1915	27/10/1915
War Diary	Seux	27/10/1915	31/10/1915
Diagram etc			
Miscellaneous	Tracing of 81st Inf Bde Trenches 4 Oct 1915		
Operation(al) Order(s)	81st Infantry Brigade Operation Order No. 59. Appendix I.	30/09/1915	30/09/1915
Operation(al) Order(s)	81st Infantry Brigade Operation Order No. 59.	02/10/1915	02/10/1915
Operation(al) Order(s)	81st Infantry Brigade Operation Order No. 60. Appendix 2	21/10/1915	21/10/1915
Operation(al) Order(s)	81st Infantry Brigade Operation Order No. 60.	24/10/1915	24/10/1915
Miscellaneous	Time Table Of Relief		
Operation(al) Order(s)	81st Infantry Brigade-Operation Order No. 61 Appendix III	25/10/1914	25/10/1914
Miscellaneous	For Information Only		
Miscellaneous	The Following amendments are made in Operation Order No. 61		
Miscellaneous	The information only.		
Operation(al) Order(s)	81st Infantry Brigade Group Operation Order No. 62. Appendix IV	24/10/1915	24/10/1915
Miscellaneous			
Heading	B.H.Q. 81st Infantry Brigade. September 1915		
War Diary	Rue Marle Armentieres	01/09/1915	15/09/1915
War Diary	Steenwerck	16/09/1915	16/09/1915
War Diary	Vieux Berquin	17/09/1915	20/09/1915
War Diary	Abancourt	21/09/1915	26/09/1915
War Diary	Proyart	27/09/1915	30/09/1915
Miscellaneous	Distribution of Units. Appendix I		
Diagram etc			
Operation(al) Order(s)	81st Infantry Brigade Operation Order No 56. Appendix II	12/09/1915	12/09/1915
Operation(al) Order(s)	81st Infantry Brigade Operation Order No. 56.	14/09/1915	14/09/1915
Miscellaneous	Table Of Reliefs		
Operation(al) Order(s)	81st Infantry Brigade Operation Order No. 57 Appendix III		
Miscellaneous	March Table		
Operation(al) Order(s)	81st Infantry Brigade Operation Order No. 58. Appendix IV		
Miscellaneous	81st Infantry Brigade.		

WO 95/2263/1/1

Brigade arrived Havre
from England 20.12.14.

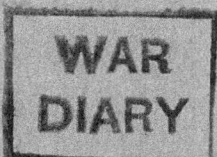

Headquarters,

81st INFANTRY BRIGADE.

(27th Division)

D E C E M B E R
(19th to 31st)

1 9 1 4

Attached:

Brigade Operation
Orders.

Army Form C. 2118.

WAR DIARY
or
INTELLIGENCE SUMMARY
(Erase heading not required.)

Instructions regarding War Diaries and Intelligence Summaries are contained in F. S. Regs., Part II. and the Staff Manual respectively. Title pages will be prepared in manuscript.

Hour, Date, Place	Summary of Events and Information	Remarks and references to Appendices
9 a.m. 19.XII.14 Magdalen Hill Camp Winchester	The 81st Infy Bde marched off in the following order:— Bde Hd Qrs 9 A.M. ½ A. & S. Hdrs. 9.5 A.M 2/Glouc R 9.15 A.M 1/Royal Scots 9.25 A.M 2/Cameron Hdrs 9.35 A.M Sr│bn Transport and Train followed immediately behind Units	Ref. 81st Infy Bde Order No.1
2.10 P.m. 19.XII.14 No 2 Dock Gate Southampton	Arrival of Hd Qrs.— The Troops were distributed as follows. Serial No. │ Unit │ Ship │ Berth 1. │ Bde Hd Qrs. │ "ATLANTIAN" │ 44 2. │ ½ A. & S. Hdrs. │ "NOVIAN" │ 26 3. │ 2/Glouc R │ "CITY OF CHESTER" │ 47 4. │ 1/R. Scots │ "CITY OF DUNKIRK" │ 39 5. │ 2/Cameron Hdrs. │ "ATLANTIAN" │ 44	Extract from embarkation Table
5 p.m. 19.XII.14 Southampton	Convoy started for HAVRE	

Army Form C. 2118.

WAR DIARY
or
INTELLIGENCE SUMMARY
(Erase heading not required.)

Instructions regarding War Diaries and Intelligence Summaries are contained in F. S. Regs., Part II. and the Staff Manual respectively. Title pages will be prepared in manuscript.

Hour, Date, Place	Summary of Events and Information	Remarks and references to Appendices
19·XII·14 WINCHESTER	Marching Out States.—	
	1/A. & S. Hdrs Officers 25 Other Ranks 925 W.O.+	Includes RG. 2 Officers Sick In H.T. Exclusive of
	2/Glouc. R. " 25 " 906 W.O.1	6 A but Tea joined ship at 3 p.m.
	1/R. Scots " 27 " 994 W.O.1	
	2/Cameron Hdrs. " 29 " 924 —	Officers includes 1 M.O. 1 Chaplain
	Hd. Qrs 81st Infy Bde	
	Officers 5	
	Other Ranks 29 RG. 24	

Army Form C. 2118.

WAR DIARY
or
INTELLIGENCE SUMMARY

(Erase heading not required.)

Instructions regarding War Diaries and Intelligence Summaries are contained in F. S. Regs, Part II. and the Staff Manual respectively. Title pages will be prepared in manuscript.

Hour, Date, Place	Summary of Events and Information	Remarks and references to Appendices
10am 20.XII.14 HAVRE	Orders received to entrain at No 6 Platform at 1AM on the 20.XII.14 the following Ration to be taken — On the Soldier — Iron Ration In Supply Wagon — 1 days Ration In Railway Trucks — 2 " "	This order cancelled by Telephone at 4pm 20.XII.14 Orders issued to entrain at No 1 Platform at 5AM 21.XII.14
4 P.M. 20.XII.14 S.S. "ATLANTIAN"	The 3 G.S. Wagons of Hd Qr Transport were loaded on floats only 2 of these Wagons arrived at appointed place (1 Wagon lost landed at different part of the Dock found at 9.30 P.M.)	Horses sent for this Wagon but owing to counter Orders was unable to reach Platform No 1 in time to catch Train — PG 20.XII.14
11 P.m. 20.XII.14 No 1 Platform	Verbal orders received from D.A.D.R.T. and D.A.Q.M.G. to return to No 6 Platform and entrain at 5 A.M. 21.XII.14	
5.15am 21.XII.14 No 6 Platform	Train left HAVRE Bde Hd Qrs deficient of 1 G.S. Wagon (for Tools) 4 Horses and 2 Drivers for this Wagon.	

WAR DIARY
or
INTELLIGENCE SUMMARY

(Erase heading not required.)

Army Form C. 2118.

Instructions regarding War Diaries and Intelligence Summaries are contained in F. S. Regs., Part II. and the Staff Manual respectively. Title pages will be prepared in manuscript.

Hour, Date, Place	Summary of Events and Information	Remarks and references to Appendices
1914		
9.30 am 21.XII.14 ROUEN	Waited here an hour. Men issued with hot coffee — Horses watered and fed.	
3.15 am 22.XII.14 ST OMER	Waited here 4½ hours	
8.30 am 22.XII.14 AIRE	Arrived proceeded to billets previously allotted by Staff Capt. Sent on by Motor from HAVRE — Roads from East and South picquetted by 3 Regts — Argylls who only arrived at 9PM in reserve North of AIRE.	Bde Order No 2
23rd Dec 11 am.	Brig. Gen. inspects Regt. in billets in morning. G.O.C. Div and Staff visited Bde HQ. Orders for alarm and Piquets by night revised.	Bde orders No 3.
24th Dec 10 am.	Bde Route March all available transport went with the Bde. All Ranks warned that operations are just as possible on Christmas day.	Bde Order No 4
25th Dec	Orders issued ref: sick in 91st Hy Bde. until arrival of Motor Ambulance — G.O.C. Inf Bde. visited the R.F.A at BLARINGHEM to ascertain what protective measures were necessary	

WAR DIARY
or
INTELLIGENCE SUMMARY

(Erase heading not required.)

Army Form C. 2118.

Instructions regarding War Diaries and Intelligence Summaries are contained in F.S. Regs, Part II. and the Staff Manual respectively. Title pages will be prepared in manuscript.

Hour, Date, Place	Summary of Events and Information	Remarks and references to Appendices
1914		
9 A.M. 26th Dec N.E. of AIRE	Brigadier Genl. reconnoitred the ground for proposed line of Trenches for the defence of AIRE	
6. P.M. 26th Dec AIRE	Conference of all C.M. ref. line of trenches and type of	
9.30 A.M. to 4.30pm 27 Dec 3 miles N.E. AIRE	Line of trenches commenced (Ref. map ST. OMER 4 - 1/80,000) from road junction due S. of the T. of STEEMBECQUE to bridge over the CANAL DE LA LYS. (N.E. of PECQUEUR) – Bns. worked in two reliefs –	Bde. Orders No 6
9.30 am to 4.30 pm 28th Dec Vicinity of PECQUEUR	Trenches continued on N. side of the CANAL DE LA LYS and new trenches commenced running from the R.R. PECQUEUR through the H in HOULERON to the CANAL D'AIRE	Bde. Order No 7
9.30 am to 4.30 pm 29th Dec H of HOULERON	Trenches continued – (High parapet necessary on account of wet and flooded (ogroma) ground Night picquets provided with lanterns and instructions issued for the examination of passes belonging to Motor Drivers proceeding to and from AIRE	Bde. Order No 8
9.30 am to 4.30 pm 30 Dec 3 Miles N.E. of AIRE	Cover trenches communication Trenches & latrines dug for trenches in Northern section (E. of BOESEGHEM)	Bde. Order No 9
9.30 am to 4.30 pm 31st Dec H of HOULERON	Improvement of Trenches continued parapets revetted with brushwood – Impossible to dig below ground level owing to flooded nature of country near CANAL D'AIRE	Bde. Order No 10.

BRIGADE OPERATION ORDERS

Nos. 1 to 10.

Copy No. 1

81st INFANTRY BRIGADE ORDER No. 1.
By
Brig. Genl. D.A. Macfarlane, D.S.O. Commdg. 81st Infy. Bde.

Magdalen Hill Camp,
Winchester,
18th Decr. 1914.

Reference 1" O.S. Map.

1.   The Brigade will march to Southampton Docks to-morrow, the 19th inst. for embarkation. (14 miles).
        Route - WINCHESTER HIGH STREET - SOUTHGATE STREET - OTTERBOURNE - CHANDLERSFORD to SOUTHAMPTON DOCKS.
        Detail of route through SOUTHAMPTON - AVENUE - St. MARY'S ROAD - ST. MARY'S ST. - THREE FIELD LANE - LATIMER ST. - NO. 2 DOCK GATE.

2.   Starting point - Road Junction at H of HOSPITAL.
        Order of march.

        1. Brigade Hd. Qrs.   9 a.m.
        2. 1st A. & S. Highrs.   9-5 a.m.
        3. 2nd Gloucester Regt.   9-15 a.m.
        4. 1st Royal Scots.   9-25 a.m.
        5. 2nd Cameron Highrs.   9-35 a.m.

        The 82nd Infantry Bde. follows at 9-50 a.m.

3.   Each unit will march complete with 1st Line Transport and Train wagons immediately behind it.
        The hours at which each unit will enter the dock gates is shown on attached embarkation table.
        One cyclist from each battalion will march with Bde. Headquarters.

4.   Medical. 2 Ambulance wagons march in rear of the 82nd Infantry Brigade.

5.   The unexpired portion of the day's ration will be carried on the man. One day's supplies only will be carried in the supply wagons.
        All supply wagons and all other possible vehicles will be loaded and parked on the ground West of camp in order of march at the following hours to-day.
        1st A. & S. Highrs.   3 p.m.
        2nd Gloucesters.   3-15 p.m.
        1st Rl. Scots.   3-30 p.m.
        2nd Cameron Highrs.   3-45 p.m.

        Officers Commdg. Battns. will arrange to guard their own wagons during the night.

6.   As the camp will be taken over immediately by another brigade, it will be left thoroughly clean, latrine and refuse pits being closed except what are required for the details.

Captain,
Brigade Major, 81st Inf. Bde.

INSTRUCTIONS.

1. Every vehicle including guns will be marked in chalk with the serial number allotted in attached embarkation table. Numbers to be placed on near side of vehicle and in such a position where it will not be obscured by wagon cover.

2. Each unit will be met at No.2 Dock Gate at the time stated in embarkation time table by a guide who who will conduct it to its berth.

3. Units on arrival at berth will close up as much as possible in order to make room for other units coming in behind.

4. On arrival at Dock Gates, G.O.C's Infantry Brigades and O.C. R.F.A.Brigade will detail one officer to lead each of their units to its berth and another officer to bring up the rear.

5. Any vehicles or men which are allowed to fall out on the line of march will be given instructions in writing to report to the Staff Officer at No.2 Dock Gate, Southampton. These instructions should contain the serial No. of the unit, name of ship and number of berth.

6. Maps of Southampton are herewith issued to G.O.G's Brigades and O.C. R.F.A.Brigade shewing route to be followed through the town. These maps are to be posted to G.S.O. 27th.Division, George Hotel, Winchester, immediately on arrival at Docks.

7. No officers or men will be allowed to leave the ship once troops have been embarked. Guards will be placed on all gangways to ensure that order being carried out.

V. Baumgartner Major

Winchester.
18th.Decr.1914.

~~Lt. Colonel~~ G.S.
27th. Division.

ROAD ONLY.

BY ROAD. UNITS COMPLETE WITH TRANSPORT.

SERIAL NO.	UNIT.	TIME AT WHICH UNITS WILL MEET UNIT AT NO.2 DOCK GATE.	SHIP.	BERTH.
1.	H.Q.81st.I.Bde.	2-0 p.m.	"ATLANTIAN"	44.
2.	1st.A.& S.H'grs.	2-10 p.m.	"NOVIAN".	26.
3.	2nd.Gloster Rgt.	2-20 p.m.	"CITY OF CHESTER".	47.
4.	1st.Roy.Scots.	2-30 p.m.	"CITY OF DUBLIN".	39.
5.	2nd.Cameron Hgrs.	2-40 p.m.	"ATLANTIAN".	44.
6.	H.Q.82nd.I.Bde.	2-50 p.m.	"MATHERAN".	33.
7.	2nd.D.C.L.I.	3-0 p.m.	"MOUNT TEMPLE".	36.
8.	2nd.R.I.Fusrs.	3-10 p.m.	"CITY OF BENARES".	43.
9.	2nd.Leinsters.	3-20 p.m.	"LAKE MICHIGAN".	46.
10.	1st.R.Irish.	3-30 p.m.	"MATHERAN".	33.
11.	H.Q.19th.Bde.R.F.A. 131st.Bty.R.F.A.	3-40 p.m.	"NOVIAN".	26.
12.	95th.Bty.R.F.A.	3-50 p.m.	"CITY OF CHESTER".	47.
13.	67th.Bty.R.F.A.	4-0 p.m.	"CITY OF DUBLIN".	39.
14.	19th.Bde.Am.Coln.	4-10 p.m.	"MOUNT TEMPLE".	36.
15.	98th.Bty.R.F.A.	4-20 p.m.	"CITY OF BENARES".	43.

BY RAIL.

16.	36th.Depot.Unit) of Supply.) 37th.Depot Unit) of Supply.)	4-30 p.m.	"CITY OF DUBLIN".	39.
17.	29th.Fd.Bakery) 13th.Rly Supply) Det.)	4-30 p.m.	"LAKE MICHIGAN".	46.
18.	27th.Fd.Butchery.	4-30 p.m.	"ATLANTIAN".	44.

Copy No. 2

81st INFANTRY BRIGADE ORDER No. 2
By
Brig. Genl. D.A. Macfarlane, D.S.O. Commdg. 81st Infy. Bde.

AIRE,
22nd Decr. 1914.

Reference Map St. OMER 4 - 1/80.000.

Battalion on duty - 1st Royal Scots up to 8 a.m. 23rd December, 1914.

1. FRONTAGE.

In case of alarm the 2nd Cameron Highlanders are responsible for the East of the Billeting Area from the road junction about 500 yds. North of the E. of Ft. GASSION to the CANAL de la LYS. The 2nd Gloucester Regt. thence by the N of NEUF PRE - E of AIRE to the track at the 2nd SS of MISSISIPI exclusive.

The 1st Royal Scots from this track inclusive to the stream at the last E of ESTRACELLE.

2. The roads within these fronts will be picquetted from 4-30 p.m. till 8 a.m. by the regiments concerned. The 1st Argyll and Sutherland Highlanders will be in reserve near the point where the 4 roads meet on St. OMER road just N. of AIRE.

The three Battalions furnishing outposts will each have an inlying picquet of ½ a company.

3. Special care is to be taken against fire while occupying barrack rooms the floors of which are covered with straw.

Fire picquets should be told off for each room or group of rooms and such local arrangements as are possible for water or earth in buckets should be made.

Leonard. Captain,

Bde. Major, 81st Infy. Bde.

Copy No. 1

BRIGADE ORDER No. 3
By
Brig. Genl. D.A. Macfarlane, D.S.O. Commdg. 81st Infy. Bde.

AIRE,
23rd decr. 1914.

Reference Map, St. OMER 4 - 1/80,000.

ARRANGEMENTS IN CASE OF ALARM WHILE AT AIRE AND DISPOSITIONS OF OUTPOSTS.
----

1. ALARM.

Attention is called to Divnl. and Brigade Standing Orders, page 23 and F.S.R. I, Sect. 49.

(a). In the case of alarm without actual attack, picquets will be reinforced by the inlying picquets, and patrols pushed out 1 mile to their front.

Battalions will remain on their Battalion Alarm Posts until orders are received by the Field Officer sent to Brigade Headquarters.

(b). In case of actual sudden attack on any part of the line, battalions will defend the fronts which correspond to the zones of responsibility for outposts (para. 2).

2. (a). Picquets will be furnished by Battalions from 4-30 p.m. till 8 a.m. on all roads leading to the 13de Billeting Area.

Picquets should not take up the actual positions to be occupied for the night till after dark.

Each picquet should be at least 1 section of not less than 8 men. Actual strength at discretion of Officers Commanding Battalions.

(b). Zones of responsibility in case of sudden alarm and for outpost picquets.

2nd Camerons - CANAL de NEUF - FOSSE to ECLSE on CANAL de LYS S. of Ft. GASSION (same as last night).

× 1st Argyll & Sutherland Highrs - Thence by E of AIRE to the 2nd SS of MISSISSIPI (exclusive).

1st Royal Scots- Thence to the 2nd E of ESTRACELLE

2nd Gloucesters - Thence up to and including the road AIRE - THEROUANNE near the C of MOULIN-LE-COMTE.

3. Brigade Order No. 1 of yesterday is cancelled.

× No part of the outposts will be sent into the Railway Stn or any buildings belonging to it.

L. Howard, Captain,
Brigade Major 81st Infy. Bde.

Copies Nos. 1 & 2..Bde. H.Q.
3...1st Rl. Scots.
4...2nd Gloucesters.
5...2nd Camerons.
6...1st A. & S.H.

Copy No. 2

BRIGADE ORDER No. 6
By
Brig. Genl. R.A. Macfarlane, C.V.O. Comndg. 81st Infy. Brigade.

Aire,
24th Decr. 1914.

1. All ranks are to be warned that although to-morrow is Christmas Day, operations are just as probable as on any other day.

2. SUPPLIES.

The Battalion on duty will send a fatigue party of 1 N.C.O. and 4 men to the band-stand opposite the Town Hall to report to the Supply Officer daily at 11 a.m.

Order for drawing rations to-morrow:-

2nd Warwick Highrs.   2 p.m.
2nd Gloucester Regt.   2-30 p.m.
1st R1. Scots.   3 p.m.
1st A. & S. Highrs.   3-30 p.m.

The order will in future be arranged in succession by the Supply Officer.

L. Holland
Captain,
Brigade Major 81st Inf. Bde.

Copy No. 2

BRIGADE ORDER No. 5
By
Brig. Genl. D.A. Macfarlane, D.S.O. Commdg. 81st Infy. Bde.
Aire,
25th Decr. 1914.

1. FIELD OFFICER OF THE DAY.

With reference to 81st Infy. Bde. Standing Orders, Sec XIV (c) the name of the Field Officer of the day will be reported to Bde. Hd. Qrs. by noon the day previous to his taking up his duties.
The order quoted above to be amended accordingly.

2. IRON RATIONS.

All units in the Brigade will notify the Supply Officer, 81st Infy. Bde. of any deficiencies in iron rations or regimental reserve as soon as possible to enable him to arrange for same to be completed.

3. ORDNANCE SERVICES.

With reference to Div. Administrative Order No. 1 of to-day O.'s C. Battns. will report whether their transport, harness and vehicles, including spare parts authorized in Field Service Manuals, are complete or otherwise.

4. ARMY ROUTINE ORDERS.

The following extracts from Army Routine Orders dated 24th inst. are published for information.:-

No. 475. COURTS MARTIAL.

Attention is called to the improper admissions in evidence of police reports, and other similar documentary evidence. It is pointed out that no written statement by any person must be produced in evidence or seen by the court at the trial unless it is tendered by the accused as part of his defence; and no written statement on behalf of the prosecution must be included in the summary or otherwise seen by any member of the court before or at the trial unless the person making the statement is to be called as a witness at the trial.

No. 479. BILLETS AND RATIONS

Reference Army Routine Order No. 230, when officers are billeted in hotels and rations are not drawn for them by the Formations to which they belong, the allowance mentioned in para 2 may be drawn.

No. 481. FORAGE

When obtainable from local resources, beetroot at the rate of 2 lbs. per horse may be added to the forage ration for all horses.

L. Holmes Captain,
Bde. Major 81st Inf. Bde.

NOTICES.

A Field Post Office is established with the Brigade and is located near Bde. Hd. Qrs. For the present the English Mail closes daily at 12 noon. All letters should be signed by an officer as well as bearing the censor stamp.

The following copies of telegrams addressed to Sir John French are published for information of all ranks.

Buckingham Palace, 24th Decr. 1914.
"The Queen and I send you and the troops under your command "our hearty good wishes for Christmas and the New Year"
GEORGE R.I.

Buckingham Palace, 24th Decr. 1914.
"I send ~~you~~ Christmas Greetings to you and all ranks of the troops under your command. No words of mine can express the great admiration which we all feel for the splendid endurance and bravery of our gallant soldiers and I wish you and them from the depths of my heart success in the just and righteous cause for which our country is fighting."
ALEXANDRA.

BRIGADE ORDER No. 6
By
Brig. Genl. D.A. Macfarlane, D.S.O. Commdg. 81st Infy. Bde.

Copy No. 2

Aire,
26th Decr. 1914.

Reference Map, St. Omer 4 - 1/80,000.

1. The Brigade will commence a line of trenches N.E. of AIRE to-morrow working in two reliefs under the following arrangements:-
½ Bn. 2nd Cameron Highrs. to be at the road junction due S. of the T of STEEMBECQUE about 1½ miles E. by N. of BOESEGHEM at 9 a.m.
½ Bn. 1st Argyll & Sutherland Highrs. and ½ Bn. 2nd Gloucester Regt., marching in the order named will march by BOESEGHEM Village and be at the cross roads about ¼ mile S. of the M of BOESEGHEM at 9-30 a.m.
½ Bn. 1st Royal Scots will march by NEUFPRE - PECQUEUR to reach the bridge over the CANAL de la LYS at 10 a.m.
½ 2nd Wessex Fd. Co. R.E. will proceed to the same point as 1st Argylls and 2nd Gloucesters ready to commence work at 10-30 a.m. Work will be carried on till 4-30 p.m. and officers commanding units will arrange for the working parties to be relieved by the other half of their units at ½ time so as to prevent any delay in the work.

2. All digging tools will be taken with the first party and about 120 picks and shovels from the Brigade Reserve will be available for each Battalion on the ground.

3. Machine gun teams and transport drivers will continue their training.

ROUTINE ORDERS.

4. Field Officer of the Day for the 27th inst. - Major F.C. Nisbet, 2nd Gloucester Regt.

5. TRANSPORT.
From the 27th inst. inclusive, the battalion on duty and the battalion next for duty will each place 4 train wagons daily at the disposal of the O.C. Train for general transport work of the Brigade.

6. BOUNDS.
The attention of all units is called to Page 34, Administrative Routine Orders, "Bounds".

7. SUPPLIES.
A list of any supplies which regiments pay for out of their Imprest Account must be given to the Supply Officer of the Brigade as soon as the purchase is made. The purchase of vegetables will be made by the Supply Officer.

8. MACHINE GUNS.
Machine gun officers should guard against the water in the barrel casing of the machine guns becoming frozen.
Until glycerine can be obtained the guns should be kept in the rooms where the men are sleeping.

Captain,
Bde. Major 81st Infy. Bde.

Copy No. 2

BRIGADE ORDER No.7
By
Brig. Genl. D.A. Macfarlane, D.S.O. Commdg. 81st Infy. Brigade

Aire,
27th Decr. 1914.

Field Officer of the Day for the 28th inst. - Major P.T.C. Baird, 2nd Cameron Highlanders.

1. The entrenching will be continued to-morrow. The 2nd Cameron Highlanders will complete the trench on the North side of the Canal de la LYS on the line which has been picketted out by the 2nd Wessex Field Company R.E.

The 1st Argyll & Sutherland Highlanders will march out by NEUFPRE and PECQUEUR to just short of the canal Bridge over the CANAL DE LA LYS.
The Officers Commanding of these two battalions will meet the Engineer Officer at the Canal Bridge at 9-30 a.m.
Tools should be distributed and the men ready for work by 9-40 a.m.
1 Brigade tool wagon will follow the Argyll & Sutherland Highlanders for these 2 battalions
Tools will be distributed at the Canal Bridge.
The 2nd Gloucesters and 1st Royal Scots with 1 Brigade tool wagon will march by NEUFPRE - PECQUEUR and thence EAST and halt about 500 yards EAST of the village just under the Q of PECQUEUR.
Tools to be distributed and men ready for work by 10 a.m.
The officers commanding of these two battalions will ride on and meet the Engineer Officer about the Canal Bridge at 9-45 a.m.
The 2nd Wessex Field Company R.E. will complete the trench they started to-day.
Reliefs as to-day.

L Howard Captain,
Bde. Major 81st Infy. Brigade.

Copies Nos 1 + 2 Bde Hq Qrs
3   1/Rl Scots
4   2/ Gloucesters
5   2/ Camerons
6   1/ A & S. Highrs
7   2/ Wessex Fd Co R.E.

Copy No. 1

BRIGADE ORDER No. 8
By
Brig. Genl. D.A. Macfarlane, D.S.O. Commdg. 81st Infy. Bde.

Aire,
28th Decr. 1914.

Field Officer of the Day for 28th Decr. 1914 - Capt. D.M. Porteous, 1st Argyll & Sutherland Highrs.

(1)   Work for to-morrow has been detailed on the ground.

Units will march so as to be ready to commence work at 9-30 a.m. Brigade tool wagons, one to follow the 1st Argyll & Sutherland Highlanders to PECQUEUR where tools will be distributed to the 1st Argyll & Sutherland Highlanders and 2nd Cameron Highlanders.

One to follow the 2nd Gloucesters to a point ½ way between PECQUEUR and LA ROUPIE where tools will be distributed to 1st Royal Scots and 2nd Gloucesters.

N.C.O.'s in charge of brigade tool wagons to be detailed by 1st Argyll & Sutherland Highlanders and 2nd Gloucesters.

The 2nd Wessex Field Co. R.E. will work under the supervision of Major Barnardiston, R.E. G.H.Q.

2.   The night picquets should be provided with lanterns (red if available). They should stop all motor cars proceeding to or from AIRE and examine the drivers' passes. If passes cannot be produced or if there are any suspicious circumstances, they will be conducted to Brigade Head Quarters for instructions

L. Howard Captain,
Bde. Major, 81st Infy. Bde.

Copies 1 & 2 Bde HQ
        3   1/Rl Scots
        4   2/Glosters
        5   2/Camerons
        6   1/A&SH
        7   2/Wessex Fd. Co.

Copy No. 1

BRIGADE ORDERS No 9.
By
Brig. Genl. D.A. Macfarlane, D.S.O. Commdg. 81st Infy. Bde.

29th Decr. 1914.

Field Officer of the Day for 30th inst. - Captain F.C. Tanner,
1st Royal Scots.

1. Instead of completing the trenches commenced to-day the work for to-morrow will be digging cover trenches, communication trenches and latrines for the Northern Section.

Each regiment will, as far as possible, complete the trenches which they started during the first day's digging but Officers Commanding Battalions will consult so as not to leave any gap.

2. The 1st Argyll & Sutherland Higrs. and 2nd Cameron Highrs. in this order, with one Brigade tool wagon, will march by the B of BOESEGHEM to the road junction ¼ mile S. of the T. in STEENBECQUE.

The 2nd Gloucesters and 1st Royal Scots in this order, with one Brigade tool wagon will march by BOESEGHEM village to the road junction ¼ mile S. of the M. of BOESEGHEM.

The O.C. 1st A. & S. Highrs. and 1st Royal Scots respectively will be responsible for the Brigade tool wagons on the march and select the place for the distribution of the tools.

ROUTINE ORDERS.

3. ~~AMBULANCE~~ *Ammunition* WAGONS. *Ammunition amended*

The Brigade Reserve ~~Ambulance~~ wagons will assemble at the entrance to FORT GASSION at 10 a.m. to-morrow and report to Lieut. Fowler, 2nd Cameron Highlanders.

4. BOUNDS.
The road from LES OUSEAUX to the VOIE ROMAINE W. of STEENBECQUE is placed out of bounds on account of typhoid fever.
The O.C. 1st R.F.A. Brigade will arrange to put up notice boards.

5. INOCULATION.
Opportunity should be taken of having all men inoculated who were not done at home.
Medical officers i/c units will report the numbers of men of units under their charge who have not been inoculated, to the O.C. 81st Field Ambulance.

6. FATIGUE PARTIES.
Until further notice the fatigue party of 1 N.C.O. and 4 men detailed by the Battalion on duty to report to the Supply officer at 7 a.m. will be increased to 1 N.C.O and 10 men.

Captain.
Bde. Major 81st Infy. Brigade.

Copy No. 2

BRIGADE ORDER NO. 10
by
Brig. Genl. R. MacFarlane, C.B.C. Comdg. 81st Infy. Bde.

30th Decr. 1914.

Field Officer of the Day for 31st Decr. 1914 — Capt. D.J.H. McMahon, 2nd Gloucester Regt.

1. WORK FOR TO-MORROW.

Work will be continued to-morrow on the right section of entrenchments which was commenced yesterday.

Battalions will march as follows:—

1st Argyll & Sutherland Highrs. and 2nd Cameron Highrs. by NEUFFRE.

2nd Gloucesters and 1st Royal Scots South of the CANAL D'AIRE.

Battalions responsible for Brigade tool wagons — 1st Argyll & Sutherland Highrs. and 1st Royal Scots.

Hours and reliefs as usual.

ROUTINE ORDERS.

2. RATIONS.

Any case of shortage in rations is to be reported to Brigade Headquarters, giving full details.

Captain,
Brigade Major 81st Infy. Bde.

27th Div.

WAR DIARY

B.H.Q. 81st INF. BDE.

JANUARY

1915

Apps.   Brigade Orders
        Divisional Operation Orders.
        Instructions re Trenches etc.

Index..........

SUBJECT.

No.	Contents.	Date.
	27th Division 81st Bde HQ Vol II 1 – 31.1.15	

Confidential

War Diary.
of
Hd. Qrs 81st Inf Bde 27th Div.

from Jan 1st to Jan 31st
(Vol. 2)

All references refer to map.
BELGIUM
Sheet 28
Scale 1/40,000

Army Form C. 2118.

WAR DIARY
or
INTELLIGENCE SUMMARY
(*Erase heading not required.*)

Instructions regarding War Diaries and Intelligence Summaries are contained in F. S. Regs., Part II. and the Staff Manual respectively. Title pages will be prepared in manuscript.

Hour, Date, Place	Summary of Events and Information	Remarks and references to Appendices
1915		
9.30 am to 4.30 pm 1st Jan. H of HOULERON	Improvement of Trenches cont'd — in the morning — At 2.30 pm the Bde was drawn up near the M of BOESEGHEM and inspected by the Field Marshal C-in-C	Bde Order No 11 PG
9.15 am Cross roads pt 33 N. of M of BOESEGHEM 2nd Jan.	Bde Genl. accompanied by OC. Bns & OC 2/Wessex FA Co R.E. proceeded to mark out the 2nd line of Trenches — Bns contd. digging on same section as 1.1.15	Bde. Orders No 12 PG
9.15 am to 12.30 pm. 3rd Jan. Northern Section of Trenches —	½ Bns. commenced digging 2nd line of Trenches — Remn: ½ Bns carried out rifle, Kit & other Bns. Inspections Washing &c. In the morning as many Officers & N.C.Os as were available were instructed in the art of throwing Hand Grenades — There uses and precautions necessary in handling them were fully explained —	Bde Order No 13 PG
4th Jan. AIRE	Bns. at disposal of C.M.	Bde Order No 14 PG
5th Jan. AIRE	Bns. at disposal of Cos. 1 Off & 25 men to be trained as Sappers to be known as Bn. Sappers. 6 NCos and men per platoon to be trained in the use of hand grenades and fire grenades —	Bde Order No 15 PG

Army Form C. 2118.

WAR DIARY
or
INTELLIGENCE SUMMARY
(Erase heading not required.)

Instructions regarding War Diaries and Intelligence Summaries are contained in F. S. Regs., Part II. and the Staff Manual respectively. Title pages will be prepared in manuscript.

Hour, Date, Place	Summary of Events and Information	Remarks and references to Appendices
9 am 6 Jan AIRE	The Bde Marched into the Billeting area CAESTRE – METEREN – STRAZEELE – BORRE Order of March Bde Hd. Qrs. 2/ Camn. Highrs. 3/ Wessex Fd Co. RE 1/ Arg. & Suth'd. Highrs. 2/ Glouc. R. 1/ R. Scots Echelon B 1st Line Trans. Train 21st Fd. Amb. Hd. Qrs arrived METEREN 4.30 pm.	Ref map. 1/40,000 Bde Orders No 16 JRG.
9 am 7 Jan. METEREN	The Bde Marched to DICKEBUSCH where it became a supporting line to the 80th Bde — Owing to heavy shell firing on the afternoon of the 6th Jan a message was received during the night 6/7th ordering the Bde to march via BAILLEUL–LOCRE–WESTOUTRE–REMINGHELST–OUDERDOM instead of BAILLEUL–LOCRE–LA CLYTTE–DICKEBUSCH owing to exposed	Ref 1/40,000

Army Form C. 2118.

WAR DIARY
or
INTELLIGENCE SUMMARY
(Erase heading not required.)

Instructions regarding War Diaries and Intelligence Summaries are contained in F. S. Regs., Part II. and the Staff Manual respectively. Title pages will be prepared in manuscript.

Hour, Date, Place	Summary of Events and Information	Remarks and references to Appendices
Jan. 7th	Portion of road LA CLYTTE – DICKEBUSCH. The Interpreter M. René Larüe died from heart failure during the march. The head of the Bde reached a point opposite S Edge of OUDERDOM – Here it was halted in full dark owing to heavy firing in the vicinity of DICKEBUSCH. Most of the transport were on the road all night.	Interpreter to Bde Hd Qrs Address René Larüe "Les Roses" VERNEUIL s/SEINE (S&O) FG
Jan. 8th DICKEBUSCH	Bns. at the disposal of CRA – Men employed in making gabions, fascines and improving roads near billets. Men's feet suffered on the march from AIRE owing to the roads being paved with cattle & horses. A.S.I. refm in Civy Syphon ½ mile E of DICKEBUSCH. Bns. at disposal of CRA – Transport Officers from Regts	FG
Jan. 9th DICKEBUSCH	went out with the respective Bn. Trans. Offs. of the 80th (whom they relieved next day) Bde. to ascertain how near Supply Waggons could be taken to the Trenches, method of loading same, and their distribution to the various Corps. in the firing line –	FG
Jan. 10th DICKEBUSCH	The following was the time table for the relief of the 80th Bde. 2/Cam'n. relieved 4th KRR.C leaving DICKEBUSCH between 4.30 p.m. & 5.30 p.m. 2/Glouc.R. " K.S.L.I. " " 5.40 p.m. " 6.30 p.m. 1/R. Scots " 3rd K.R.R.C. " " 6.35 p.m. " 7 p.m.	FG

WAR DIARY
or
INTELLIGENCE SUMMARY

Army Form C. 2118.

Hour, Date, Place	Summary of Events and Information	Remarks and references to Appendices
1915 Jan.10th DICKEBUSCH	1/Arg. & Suff. Hdrs. relieved the 4th Rifle Bde in support near ELZONWALLE leaving the cross roads Square H 29 (b) between 8.30 p.m. and 9 p.m. 220 Rds S.A.A. were carried on the man and about 50 Boxes per Bn. were taken over in the Trenches. Casualty Report up to 9 p.m. 10th inst. Nil. Wire sent to 27th Div ref relief of Bn in support at VIERSTRAAT. The Question of taking Packs into the Trenches was raised owing to the fact that all articles in the pack would get wet and the extra load was not advisable — The G.O.C 27 Div ordered Packs being taken into the Trenches —	Ref Map 1/40,000 Attached. Attached. Attached. 1 PG

Army Form C. 2118.

WAR DIARY
or
INTELLIGENCE SUMMARY

(Erase heading not required.)

Instructions regarding War Diaries and Intelligence Summaries are contained in F. S. Regs., Part II. and the Staff Manual respectively. Title pages will be prepared in manuscript.

Hour, Date, Place	Summary of Events and Information	Remarks and references to Appendices
1915		
11th Jan. DICKEBUSCH	Casualty Reports:— Killed Wounded Y R. Scots Nil 2 R&F 2/C,one.R Nil 3 R&F 2/Camh Hdrs. *2 died of exposure 4 R&F Y A & Sth. Hdrs. Nil Nil Machine Guns practically useless as they sank into the mud — Saturating morning rags — Telephones were not reliable — Some sniping occurred (Khaid Trenches and near Bn. Hd. Qrs — Germans clamped rifles to fire down roads and on suitable targets in day time — These rifles were fired automatically during the night — Conferences were held this day (re the drainage and improvement of Trenches)	*6396 Pte George King 8098 "Samuel Stallwood" A section of Lt. R Campbell's Company was trapped in an old French Communication Trench S of St ELOI. One man was lost (Pte King) the other died of exposure being dug out of the bog. RC

WAR DIARY
or
INTELLIGENCE SUMMARY

(Erase heading not required.)

Army Form C. 2118.

Hour, Date, Place	Summary of Events and Information	Remarks and references to Appendices
1915		
12 Jan. DICKEBUSCH.	Casualty Report—	
	Killed Wounded	
	1/R. Scots Nil 3 R & F	
	2/Glouc. R. Nil 8 R & F	
	2/Camn. Hdrs. * 1 died of exposure 5 R & F	
	1/Arg. & Suth. Hdrs. Nil Nil	* 7545 Pte James Bain
	The 81st Bde was relieved by the 82nd Bde as follows —	
	1/R. Scots and 2/Glouc R. at 4:30 p.m.	
	2/Camn. 5:30 p.m.	
	1/Arg. & Suth. Hdrs. were not relieved but remain in position under the orders of G.O.C. 82nd Bde until being relieved on the night 13th/14th instant	
	Bns. that were relieved occupied their old Billets in DICKEBUSCH.	

RG

WAR DIARY or INTELLIGENCE SUMMARY

Army Form C. 2118.

Hour, Date, Place	Summary of Events and Information	Remarks and references to Appendices
1915		
13 Jan.	The Bde proceeded to WESTOUTRE becoming Bde in Reserve (being relieved by the 80th Bde. at DICKEBUSCH) The Men suffered chiefly from exposure — While in the Trenches many men were up to their waists in liquid mud and a large number were unable to march.	JPG
14th Jan. WESTOUTRE	Every endeavour was made to wash the troops and dry their clothes — but proper arrangements had not yet been made.	JPG

WAR DIARY or INTELLIGENCE SUMMARY

Army Form C. 2118.

Hour, Date, Place	Summary of Events and Information	Remarks and references to Appendices
1915		
4 p.m. 15 Jan. WESTOUTRE	The Bde marched to DICKEBUSCH and became Bde in support in relief of the 80th Infy. Bde. — The following were unfit to march not having recovered from exposure in the trenches — 1/R. Scots 37 2/Glouc.R 39 2/Cavn Hdrs. 86	RG
16th Jan. DICKEBUSCH	During the morning Bns. were employed, cutting brushwood — collecting hop poles for road making — cleaning the Main Street of DICKEBUSCH — making fascines — cleaning and improving billeting lines — Instruction was given in grenade throwing —	RG

Army Form C. 2118.

WAR DIARY
or
INTELLIGENCE SUMMARY

(Erase heading not required.)

Instructions regarding War Diaries and Intelligence Summaries are contained in F. S. Regs., Part II. and the Staff Manual respectively. Title pages will be prepared in manuscript.

Hour, Date, Place	Summary of Events and Information	Remarks and references to Appendices
1915 16th Jan. DICKEBUSCH	At 4.30 p.m. the Bde commenced to relieve the 80th Bde as follows. 2/Glouc. R. relieved K.S.L.I. and part Rifle Bde in Central Section. 1/R. Scots " " 3rd K.R.R.C. " Right " Y.A.my & Suff. Hdrs. " P.P.C.L.I. and part 4th K.R.R.C. " Left " 2/Canian. Hdrs. in support. 2 Coys at VIERSTRAAT 2 " " DICKEBUSCH The 80th Bde going into their billets in DICKEBUSCH with one Bn in Close Support at PLAS ENZONVALLE (Attached to 81st Inf. Bde)	Ref 1/40,000 Map.

Army Form C. 2118.

WAR DIARY
or
INTELLIGENCE SUMMARY

(Erase heading not required.)

Hour, Date, Place	Summary of Events and Information	Remarks and references to Appendices
1915		
17th Jan. DICKEBUSCH	Casualty Report—	
	Killed Wounded	
	2/ Glouc. R Nil *2	* Includes 1 Officer 2nd Lieut. F. Braddell
	1/ R. Scots 1 Nil	
	1/ Arg. & Suth Hdrs. 1 Nil	
	2/ Cam'n Hdrs. Nil 1 (accidently)	
	On the evening of the 17 Jan. the 80th Bde in support were relieved by the 82nd Bde— The 80th Bde going into Reserve at WESTOUTRE.	
	One Bn. of the 82nd relieving the Bn of the 80th Bde (Attached 81st Inf Bde) at PLAS ENZONVALLE and three Bns taking the place of the three Bns 80th Bde at DICKEBUSCH. (a Bde in Support)	Ref. Div. Operation Order No 14.
		JRG

Army Form C. 2118.

WAR DIARY
or
INTELLIGENCE SUMMARY

(Erase heading not required.)

Hour, Date, Place	Summary of Events and Information	Remarks and references to Appendices
1915		
18th Jan. DICKEBUSCH.	The Three Bns of the 81st Infy Bde were relieved by the 82nd Infy Bde as follows :— 1/Argy & Suth. Hdrs. by R. Irish Regt who left DICKEBUSCH at 4.30 p.m. 2/Glouc R " D.C.L.I. " 5.15 p.m. 1/R. Scots " R. Irish Fus. " 4.30 p.m. 2/Cam´n remained at VIERSTRAAT. Bns occupied their old billets in DICKEBUSCH. Casualty Report Killed Wounded 1/R. Scots Nil 2 R.&F. 2/Glouc R Nil 4 R.&F. 2/Cam´n Hdrs Nil Nil 1/Argy & Suth Hdrs. 1 R.&F. *5 R.&F.	JRG *Includes 1 Officer Lt. A. McD. Ritchie

Army Form C. 2118.

WAR DIARY
or
INTELLIGENCE SUMMARY

(Erase heading not required.)

Instructions regarding War Diaries and Intelligence Summaries are contained in F. S. Regs., Part II. and the Staff Manual respectively. Title pages will be prepared in manuscript.

Hour, Date, Place	Summary of Events and Information				Remarks and references to Appendices
1915		Killed	Wounded	Missing	
19 Jan. DICKEBUSCH	Casualty Report—				
	Bde. Hd Qrs.	Nil	Nil	Nil	
	1/R. Scots	3	5	1	
	2/Glouc. R.	1	1	2	
	2/Cam'n Hdrs.	Nil	Nil	Nil	
	1/Arg. & Sutld. Hdrs.	1	4	Nil	

Army Form C. 2118.

WAR DIARY
or
INTELLIGENCE SUMMARY

(Erase heading not required.)

Instructions regarding War Diaries and Intelligence Summaries are contained in F.S. Regs, Part II. and the Staff Manual respectively. Title pages will be prepared in manuscript.

Hour, Date, Place	Summary of Events and Information	Remarks and references to Appendices
20th Jan. DICKEBUSCH	The Bde relieved the 92nd. Bde in the front line as follows.	
		BRASSERIE N Sq/d 5.B. S.W. corner Ref. 1/40,000.
	Relieve Section leave DICKEBUSCH	
	1. G. Argy.& Suth. Hdrs 1 Co. Cam'n Hdrs BRASSERIE 4:30 pm	
	Y.R. Scots {R.I. Fusrs. Right Section {4:40 pm to	
	{1. Co. Cam'n Hdrs VIERSTRAAT { 5:15 pm.	
	2/Glouc. R. D.C.L.I. Centre Section 4:45 pm.	
	2/ Cam'n Hdrs. R.I. Regt. Left Section 2 Coys 5:30pm	
	The Argy. & Suth. Hdrs. less 1 Coy. relieved the Leinster Regt at	R.G.
	ELZONWALLE	

Army Form C. 2118.

WAR DIARY
or
INTELLIGENCE SUMMARY

(Erase heading not required.)

Hour, Date, Place	Summary of Events and Information	Remarks and references to Appendices
21 Jan. DICKEBUSCH.	Owing to some of the trenches near ST ELOI becoming untenable owing to flooding new trenches have begun by the 1/Arg. & Suth. Hdrs. Casualty Report Killed Wounded Missing 1/R. Scots Nil Nil Nil 2/Glouc. R Nil 3 Nil 2/Cam'n Hdrs Nil 1 1 1/Arg. & Suth. Hdrs. Nil Nil Nil	JRG.

Army Form C. 2118.

WAR DIARY
or
INTELLIGENCE SUMMARY

(Erase heading not required.)

Instructions regarding War Diaries and Intelligence Summaries are contained in F. S. Regs., Part II. and the Staff Manual respectively. Title pages will be prepared in manuscript.

Hour, Date, Place	Summary of Events and Information	Remarks and references to Appendices
22 Jan. DICKEBUSCH	The Bde was relieved by the 82nd Bde as follows.	
	Leaving DICKEBUSCH at	
	D.C.L.I. relieve 2/Glouc.R 4.30 p.m.	
	R.I. Fus. " Y.R. Scots 4.35 p.m.	
	Leinster.R. " Y Argy.&Suth.Hdrs 5.30 p.m.	
	R.I. Regt. " 2/Camn Hdrs. 6.30 p.m.	
	The Bde returned to their old billets in DICKEBUSCH	
	Casualty Report	
	Killed Wounded Missing	
	Bde. Hd. Qrs. Nil Nil Nil	
	Y/R. Scots 2 * 1 Officer 2	* Lieut. G. M. V. Bidie.
	2/Glouc.R Nil 3 Nil	
	2/Camn Hdrs. 1 2 Nil	
	Y Argy.&Suth.Hdrs. 1 4 Nil	RG.

Army Form C. 2118.

WAR DIARY
or
INTELLIGENCE SUMMARY

(*Erase heading not required.*)

Instructions regarding War Diaries and Intelligence Summaries are contained in F. S. Regs., Part II. and the Staff Manual respectively. Title pages will be prepared in manuscript.

Hour, Date, Place	Summary of Events and Information	Remarks and references to Appendices
23rd Jan.	The Bde was relieved as "Brigade in Support" by the 80th Bde and marched to WESTOUTRE becoming the Divisional Reserve	1RG

Army Form C. 2118.

WAR DIARY
or
INTELLIGENCE SUMMARY

(Erase heading not required.)

Hour, Date, Place	Summary of Events and Information	Remarks and references to Appendices
1915 24 Jan to 28 Jan WESTOUTRE	The Btn remained at WESTOUTRE - The Bns being employed in improving roads - Arrangements were made for bathing men at BOESCHEPE and providing them with an entire change of under garments -	YRG

Army Form C. 2118.

WAR DIARY
or
INTELLIGENCE SUMMARY

(Erase heading not required.)

Instructions regarding War Diaries and Intelligence Summaries are contained in F. S. Regs., Part II. and the Staff Manual respectively. Title pages will be prepared in manuscript.

Hour, Date, Place	Summary of Events and Information	Remarks and references to Appendices
1915		
29 Jan WESTOUTRE	The Bde marched to DICKEBUSCH relieving the 82nd Bde and becoming Bde in Support	TRG.
30 Jan WESTOUTRE	The Bde relieved the 80th Bde in the front line as under:— Y R. Scots relieved 3rd K.R.R.C. 2/Glouc.R. " 4th Rifle Bde & K.S.L.I. Y Amy & Suff Hdrs in close support at ELZEENWALLE 2/ Camn Hdrs. remained at DICKEBUSCH as Bde. Reserve. Casualty Report Killed Wounded Y R. Scots 2 1 2/Glouc.R. 1 1 Y Amy & Suff Hdrs. Nil Nil 2/ Camn. Hdrs. Nil Nil	TRG.

Army Form C. 2118.

WAR DIARY
or
INTELLIGENCE SUMMARY

(Erase heading not required.)

Hour, Date, Place	Summary of Events and Information	Remarks and references to Appendices
1915 31 Jan. WESTOUTRE DICKEBUSCH	The following reliefs took place:— 2/Cam'n Hdrs. relieved 1/R.Scots leaving DICKEBUSCH at 5.5 p.m. 1/Arg. & Suth. Hdrs. " 2/Glouc.R. 1/R.Scots proceeded to ELZENWALLE in close support 2/Glouc.R. " " DICKEBUSCH as Bde Reserve. Casualty Report Killed Wounded 2/Cam'n Hdrs Nil Nil 1/Arg & Suth. Hdrs. Nil Nil 1/R.Scots 1 *2 2/Glouc.R. Nil Nil	* This includes 1 Officer RG

DIVISIONAL OPERATION ORDERS NOS.

7
8
9
13
15
16
17
18
22

SECRET

Copy No. 13

27th. Division Operation Order No.7

BOESCHEPE.
10th. January, 1915.

Reference 1/40,000 Map.

Relief.

1. On evening of 10th. instant the 80th. Infantry Brigade (less 1 battalion) will be withdrawn from the front line of trenches and close supports and replaced by the four battalions of the 81st. Infantry Brigade.

    Vierstraat

    The battalion of the 80th. Infantry Brigade now in close support about PLAS ENZONVALLE will stand fast and come under command of G.O.C. 81st. Brigade until relieved on night of 11th/12th. by a battalion of 82nd. Infantry Brigade.

    The remaining four battalions of the 80th. Infantry Brigade will take the places as "Brigade in support" now occupied by battalions of 81st. Infantry Brigade.

    The above relief will commence at 5 p.m. under arrangements in detail drawn up by G.O.C's 80th. and 81st. Infantry Brigades in consultation.

Officers proceeding in advance.

2. Officers of 81st. Infantry Brigade who proceeded to trenches night of 9th. January will meet and lead their battalions and companies to their positions in the front line.

    Similarly, officers of 80th. Infantry Brigade sent back to Brigade in support night of 9th/10th. will meet and lead their battalions to position to be occupied on relief of 81st. Brigade.

3. <u>No trench will on any account be evacuated until actually occupied by relieving troops.</u>

Articles to be handed over on relief.

4. Entrenching tools, ammunition, braziers, buckets and telephones, will be left in trenches and taken over by brigade in relief.

Rations.

5. One day's rations will be taken into the trenches: Water bottles full.

Ammunition.

6. At least 250 rounds S.A.A. per man will be carried to the trenches, <u>220 rounds</u> on the person and the remainder in boxes.

Operation Order No.7 continued.

Transport. 7. In order to prevent unnecessary movement of transport between position of Brigades in Divisional Reserve and DICKEBUSH -

    (a) The G.O.C. R.A. will arrange to establish a S.A.A.Column in a position of security near DICKEBUSCH from which brigades in front line and in support can refil.

    (b) The C.R.E. will arrange to park, near DICKEBUSCH, Brigade Tool Carts, which will stand as follows and not move on relief:-

        Inf.Brigade in front line, empty in R.E.Park.
        -----do----- support - loaded (unless tools are in use) in R.E.Park.
        -----do----- reserve - Billets of battalions.

[handwritten margin note:] We hand over our full Tools to the at Westoutre with wagons. When we leave for Divl Reserve we take our horses and leave our carts. Bns will not hand over wagons & Tools except what are taken with [illegible]

Issued at 8.30 a.m. 10.1.15

H.L. Reed
Lieut.Colonel G.S.
27th. Division.

SECRET

Copy No. 13

27th. Division Operation Order No.8

Reference 1/40000 Map.

BOESCHEPE.
10th. January, 1915.

RELIEF. 1. On evening of 11th. instant the battalions of the 80th. Infantry Brigade in support about DICKEBUSCH and the battalion about PLAS ENZONVALLE [VIERSTRAAT] attached to 81st. Infantry Brigade in position will be relieved by battalions of the 82nd. Infantry Brigade from Divisional Reserve, three battalions taking the place of the four battalions 80th. Infantry Brigade as Brigade in support, under G.O.C. 82nd Infantry Brigade, and one battalion taking the place of battalion about VIERSTRAAT, and on arrival there coming under orders of G.O.C. 81st. Infantry Brigade.

    The 80th. Infantry Brigade on being relieved will proceed to billets now occupied by 82nd. Infantry Brigade, and form the Divisional Reserve.

TRANSPORT. 2. All 2nd. Line Regimental Transport of 80th. Infantry Brigade will be moved back on morning of 11th. via OUDERDOM - ZEVECOTEN. Supply wagons to join train at HEKSKEN, blanket and baggage wagons to battalion Headquarters of billets direct. Clear of cross roads S.E. corner of H 32 by 10 a.m.

    Similarly, 2nd. Line Transport wagons of 82nd. Infantry Brigade will move to positions vacated by those of 80th. Infantry Brigade, via WESTOUTRE - CROSS ROADS M 17 - LA CLYTTE. This transport, less Supply Wagons, will clear WESTOUTRE at 9-30 a.m., and will march, by battalions, at 200 yards interval, under command of Brigade Transport Officer.

    Supply vehicles of all battalions [82nd Inf Brigade] will proceed by road running N.E. out of BOESCHEPE to road triangle in square G 26 - thence to HEKSKEN by usual route and await orders to refil. After refilling they will proceed to DICKEBUSCH by route followed by remainder of transport. An officer will be detailed to take charge of those wagons and lead them to their destinations.

<u>Brigade Tool Carts, except those of one battalion 80th. Infantry Brigade, will not move, 80th. and 82nd. Infantry Brigades exchanging.</u>

Officers proceeding in advance. 3. Officers of 82nd. Infantry Brigade sent [transport &] forward on evening of 9th. will meet and lead their battalions to positions to be occupied under arrangements to be made by G.O.C. 82nd. Infantry Brigade. Those officers will have acquainted themselves of exact locations of billets, regimental transport, etc. A Signal Officer of 82nd. Infantry Brigade will, on morning of 11th, proceed to DICKEBUSCH and acquaint himself with communications of 80th. Infantry Brigade.

    Similarly, officers of 80th. Infantry Brigade sent back on 10th. instant, will meet and lead (a) Regimental Transport, (b) battalions, to their billets, as Brigade in Reserve.

Operation Order No.8 continued.

4. The 82nd. Infantry Brigade will march via WESTOUTRE - CROSS ROADS M 17 - LA CLYTTE to DICKEBUSCH. The march will be timed so that head of column passes LA CLYTTE at 5 p.m. The battalions will enter DICKEBUSCH in order of relief, EAST to WEST, thus, battalion proceeding to N.E. end of DICKEBUSCH will lead.

5. No battalion of 80th. Infantry Brigade is to move until actually relieved. On relief battalions of 80th. Infantry Brigade will march independently via CROSS ROADS S.E. Corner of H 32 - OUDERDOM - ZEVECOTEN - RENNINGHELST - billets. *Clear of Dickebusch at least one hour before dawn.*

H. L. Reed
Lt. Colonel G.S.
27th. Division.

Issued at 5.30 pm.
10.1.14

Copy No. 11

27th. Division Operation Order No.9

BOESCHEPE.
11th. January, 1915.

Reference 1/40,000 Map

RELIEF.
1. On evening of 12th. instant the 82nd. Infantry Brigade will relieve the 81st. Infantry Brigade as "Brigade in front line" under G.O.C. 82nd. Infantry Brigade. The battalion of 81st. Infantry Brigade in close support on left flank about PLAS ENZONVALLE will stand fast and come under orders of G.O.C. 82nd. Infantry Brigade

The remaining battalions of the 81st. Infantry Brigade will, on relief, take up the duty of "Brigade in support" under G.O.C. 81st. Infantry Brigade.

The above relief will commence at 5 p.m. under arrangements in detail to be drawn up by G.O.C's 81st. and 82nd. Infantry Brigades in consultation.

Officers proceeding in advance.
2. Officers of 82nd. Infantry Brigade who proceeded to trenches night of 11th. will meet and lead their battalions and companies to their positions in the front line.

3. No trench will on any account be evacuated until actually occupied by relieving troops.

Articles to be handed over on relief.
4. Entrenching tools, ammunition, braziers, buckets and telephones, will be left in trenches and taken over by brigade in relief.

Rations.
5. One day's rations will be taken into the trenches: Water bottles full.

Ammunition.
6. At least 250 rounds S.A.A. per man will be carried to the trenches.

H L Reed
Lieut. Colonel G.S.
27th. Division.

issued at 3.30 pm

SECRET

Copy No. 13

27th Division Operation Order No. 13.

Reference 1/40,000 Map.

BOESCHEPE.
15th January, 1915.

RELIEF.

1.   On evening of 16th instant the 81st Infantry Brigade will relieve the 80th Infantry Brigade as "Brigade in Front Line" under G.O.C., 81st Infantry Brigade. The battalion of the 80th Infantry Brigade in close support on left flank about PLAZ ELZONVALLE will stand fast and come under orders of G.O.C. 81st Infantry Brigade.

The remaining battalions of the 80th Infantry Brigade will, on relief, take up the duty of "Brigade in Support" under G.O.C. 80th Infantry Brigade.

The above relief will commence at 5 p.m. under arrangements in detail to be drawn up by G.O.C's 80th and 81st Infantry Brigades in consultation.

2.   No trench will on any account be evacuated until actually occupied by relieving troops.

3.   Attention is drawn to Standing Orders regarding "Reliefs" dated 12.1.1915.

H J S Cook
Lieut. Colonel, G.S.,
27th Division.

Issued at 6.30. p.m.
15.1.1915.

Copy No. 11

27th Division Operation Order No. 15.

Reference 1/40,000 Map.

BOESCHEPE.
17th January, 1915.

RELIEF.   1.   On evening of 18th instant the 82nd Infantry Brigade will relieve the 81st Infantry Brigade as "Brigade in Front Line" under G.O.C. 82nd Infantry Brigade. The battalion of the 81st Infantry Brigade in close support on ~~left~~ right flank about VIERSTRAAT will stand fast and come under orders of G.O.C. 82nd Infantry Brigade.

The remaining battalions of the 81st Infantry Brigade will, on relief, take up the duty of "Brigade in Support" under G.O.C. 81st Infantry Brigade.

The above relief will commence at 5 p.m. under arrangements in detail to be drawn up by G.O.C's 81st and 82nd Infantry Brigades in consultation.

2.   No trench will on any account be evacuated until actually occupied by relieving troops.

3.   Attention is drawn to Standing Orders regarding "Reliefs" dated 12.1.1915.

H. L. Reed
Lieut. Colonel, G.S.,
27th Division.

Issued at 7.30 a.m.

SECRET.

Copy No. 11

27th Division Operation Order No.16.

BOESCHEPE.
19th January, 1915.

Reference 1/40,000 Map.

RELIEF.

1. On evening of 20th instant the 81st Infantry Brigade will relieve the 82nd Infantry Brigade as "Brigade in Front Line" under G.O.C., 81st Infantry Brigade. The battalion of the 82nd Infantry Brigade in close support on left flank about PLAS ENZONVALLE will stand fast and come under orders of G.O.C., 81st Infantry Brigade. The remaining battalions of the 82nd Infantry Brigade will, on relief, take up the duty of "Brigade in Support" under G.O.C., 82nd Infantry Brigade.

The above relief will commence at 5 p.m. under arrangements in detail to be drawn up by G.O.C's 81st and 82nd Infantry Brigades in consultation.

2. <u>No trench</u> will on any account be evacuated until actually occupied by relieving troops.

3. Attention is drawn to Standing Orders regarding "Reliefs" dated 12.1.1915.

H. L. Reed
Lieut. Colonel, G.S.,
27th Division.

Issued at 8 a.m.

SECRET.

Copy No. 12

27th Division Operation Order No. 17.

Reference 1/40,000 Map.

BOESCHEPE.
20th January, 1915.

RELIEF. 1. On evening of 22nd instant the 82nd Infantry Brigade will relieve the 81st Infantry Brigade as "Brigade in Front Line" under G.O.C. 82nd Infantry Brigade.

The 81st Infantry Brigade will, on relief, take up the duty of "Brigade in Support" under G.O.C. 81st Infantry Brigade.

The above relief will commence at 5-10 p.m. under arrangements in detail to be drawn up by G.O.C's 81st and 82nd Infantry Brigades. in consultation.

2. No trench will on any account be evacuated until actually occupied by relieving troops.

3. Attention is drawn to Standing Orders regarding "Reliefs" dated 12.1.1915.

H. L. Reed
Lieut. Colonel. G.S.,
27th Division.

Issued at 4. pm.

SECRET

Copy No. 12

27th. Division Operation Order No.18.

Reference 1/40,000 Map.

BOESCHEPE.
22nd. January, 1915.

RELIEF. 1. On evening of 23rd. instant the 80th. Infantry Brigade will relieve the 81st. Infantry Brigade as "Brigade in Support" billeted about DICKEBUSCH under orders of the G.O.C. 80th. Inf. Bde.

The 81st. Infantry Brigade on being relieved will proceed to billets in the area vacated by 80th. Infantry Brigade, and form the Divisional Reserve.

TRANSPORT 2. 2nd. Line Transport wagons of 80th. Infantry Brigade will move to positions close to those about to be vacated by transport 81st. Infantry Brigade on morning of 23rd. instant via WESTOUTRE - CROSS ROADS M 17 - LA CLYTTE. This transport, (less Supply Wagons) under command of Brigade Transport Officer, will clear WESTOUTRE at 9-30 a.m., and on reaching LA CLYTTE will march at an interval of 200 yards between transport of each battalion.

Supply Wagons will refill at usual time and place according to standing instructions given by D.A.Q.M.G. After refilling they will proceed to DICKEBUSCH by route followed by remainder of transport. An officer will be detailed to take charge of these wagons and lead them to their destination.

Similarly, 2nd. Line Transport of 81st. Infantry Brigade will be moved back on morning of 23rd. via OUDERDOM - ZEVECOTEN. Head to pass cross roads S.E. Corner of H 32 at 12-30 p.m.

3. The 80th. Infantry Brigade will march via WESTOUTRE - CROSS ROADS M 17 - LA CLYTTE to DICKEBUSCH. (The battalion billeted near RENINGHELST may march direct so as to take its place in column as it passes LA CLYTTE). The march will be timed so that head of column passes LA CLYTTE at 5-10 p.m. The battalions will enter DICKEBUSCH in order of relief, EAST to WEST,

thus,

Operation Order No.18 continued.

battalion proceeding to billets EAST end of DICKEBUSCH will load.

4. No battalion of 81st.Infantry Brigade is to move until actually relieved. On relief, battalions of 81st. Infantry Brigade will march independently via CROSS ROADS S.E.corner of H 32 - OUDERDOM - ZEVECOTEN to billets.

H L Reed
Lieut.Colonel
G.S.
27th. Division.

Issued at 10 am.
22.1.15

SECRET

Copy No. 11

27th Division Operation Order No 22

BOESCHEPE.
Reference 1/40,000 Map.   28th January, 1915.

RELIEF. 1. On evening of 29th instant the 81st Infantry Brigade less ½ battalion will relieve the 82nd Infantry Brigade less ½ battalion as "Brigade in Support" billetted about DICKEBUSCH under orders of the G.O.C., 81st Infantry Brigade.

SUPPORT. ½ battalion 81st Infantry Brigade will relieve the ½ battalion 82nd Infantry Brigade detached under command of G.O.C., 80th Infantry Brigade, "Brigade in Front Line".

This half battalion will take its place in close support at the CHATEAU ½ mile North of KRUISSTRAATHOEK or at such other place as G.O.C. 80th Infantry Brigade may direct.

The 82nd Infantry Brigade on being relieved will proceed to billets in the area vacated by 81st Infantry Brigade, and form the Divisional Reserve.

TRANSPORT. 2. 2nd Line Transport wagons of 81st Infantry Brigade will move to positions close to those about to be vacated by transport 82nd Infantry Brigade on morning of 29th instant via WESTOUTRE - CROSS ROADS M.17 - LA CLYTTE. This transport, (less Supply Wagons) under command of Brigade transport Officer, will clear WESTOUTRE at 9-30 a.m., and on reaching LA CLYTTE will march at an interval of 200 yards between transport of each battalion.

Supply Wagons will refill at usual time and place according to Standing Instructions given by D.A.Q.M.G. After refilling they will proceed to

Operation Order No.21. continued.-

to DICKEBUSCH by route followed by remainder of transport. An officer will be detailed to take charge of these wagons and lead them to their destination.

Similarly, 2nd Line Transport of 82nd Infantry Brigade will be moved back on morning of 29th. via OUDERDOM - ZEVECOTEN. Head to pass crossroads S.E. Corner of H.32 at 12-30 p.m.

3. The 81st Infantry Brigade will march via WESTOUTRE - CROSS ROADS M 17 - LA CLYTTE to DICKEBUSCH. (The battalion billetted near RENINGHELST may march direct so as to take its place in Column as it passes LA CLYTTE). The march will be timed so that head of Column passes LA CLYTTE at 5-15 p.m. The battalions will enter DICKEBUSCH in order of relief, EAST to WEST, thus, battalion proceeding to billets EAST end of DICKEBUSCH will lead.

4. No unit of 82nd Infantry Brigade is to move until actually relieved. On relief, battalions of 82nd Infantry Brigade will march independently via CROSS ROADS S.E. Corner of H.32 - OUDERDOM - ZEVECOTEN to billets.

J. 2 Baumgartner Major
for. Lieut. Colonel,
G.S.,
27th Division.

Issued at 12 noon.

BRIGADE OPERATION ORDERS NOS. 11 to 32.

BRIGADE ORDER No. 11   Copy No. 1
By
Brig. Gen. D.A. Macfarlane, D.S.O. Commdg 81st Infy. Bde.

31st Decr. 1914.

Field Officer of the Day for 1st January, 1914 - Capt.
C.W. Maclean, 2nd Cameron Highrs.

1.   Work will be continued to-morrow morning on the S.
Section of the line as to-day.

2.   The Brigade will be inspected by the Field Marshal
Commanding-in-Chief to-morrow afternoon on the ground near the
road running N. and S. at the M of BOESEGHEM.

Battalions will march from where they are working
independently but in the following order so as to be formed up
on the ground above mentioned at 2-30 p.m.
.   2nd Cameron Highrs.
     1st A. & S. Highrs.
     1st Royal Scots.
     2nd Gloucesters.

Adjutants and 2 markers to be on the road near the M
of BOESEGHEM at 2-30 p.m.
2-20

3.   No vehicles or machine guns detachments will be on
parade.
        DRESS) Marching Order with great-coats. No fancy
caps.
                ROUTINE ORDERS.

4.   FIELD GENERAL COURT-MARTIAL.
        The detail of officers as mentioned below will
assemble at 10 a.m. on Saturday the 2nd January, 1915 in the
lines of the 2nd Gloucester Regt. for the purpose of trying by
a field General Court-Martial, the undermentioned accused person
and such other person or persons as may be brought before them.
                PRESIDENT.
        Major G.H. Wingate, 1st Royal Scots.
                MEMBERS.
        A Captain 1st A. & S. Highrs.
        A Subaltern, 2nd Gloucester Regt.
                ACCUSED PERSON.
        No. 5958, Coy. Qr. Mr. Sergt. R.J. Webber, 2nd Battn.
                Gloucester Regiment.
        The accused will be warned and all witnesses duly required
to attend.
        The O.C. 2nd Gloucester Regt. will detail a Sergt. as
Orderly to the Court and will provide the necessary stationery
accommodation &c.
        The proceedings will be forwarded to Headquarters, 81st
Infantry Brigade.

                                        Captain,
                        Bde. Major 81st Infy. Brigade.

H.Q.

Copy No. 2

BRIGADE ORDER No. 12
By
Brig. Genl. D.A. Macfarlane, D.S.O. Commdg. 81st Infy. Bde.

1st January, 1915.

Field officer of the day for 2nd January, 1915,- Capt. A.E.G. Wilson, 1st A. & S. Highlanders.

(1)   Work to-morrow on the same section as to-day.

(2)   Officers Commanding Battalions and the O.C. 2nd Wessex Field Co. R.E. with a N.C.O. and 2 men per battalion with shovels will meet the Brigadier at the cross roads at point 33 N. of the M of BOESEGHEM at 9-15 a.m. to-morrow to mark out the second line.

(3)   The party for the trenches to-morrow will be at Brigade Headquarters at 8-45 a.m.

ROUTINE ORDERS

4. **FIELD GENERAL COURT-MARTIAL**

With reference to Brigade Order No. 4 of the 31st Decr. 1914, the undermentioned soldier will be tried by Field General Court-Martial by the detail of officers therein ordered to assemble:-

No. 9989, Pte. L. Cross, 1st Royal Scots.

The accused will be warned and all witnesses duly required to attend.
The proceedings will be forwarded to Headquarters, 81st Infantry Brigade.

[signature]
Captain,
Bde. Major 81st Infy. Brigade.

NOTICES.

FOUND.- An eye-piece (high) for Mark III telescope. Owner apply to Adjutant, 2nd Cameron Highlanders.

SUPPLIES:- The following scale of prices may be taken as a guide.

Hay.	70-80 frs. per 1000 K.	Jam.	1 fr. 10 c. per jar.
Oats.	20-22 frs. per 100 K.		
Wood.	25 frs. per 1000 K.	Salt.	20 c. per Kilo.
	5-10 frs. per Stere.	Cattle.	1 fr. 70 c. per kilo dead weight.
	25 c. per bdle of 10 K.		
Straw.	30-40 frs. per 1000 K.	Sheep.	2 fr. 25 c. per kilo dead weight.
Vegetables.	15-20 frs. per 100 K.		
	10 c. per lb.	Beet.	15 fr. per 1000 K.
Potatoes.	Long. 20c. per lb. for small quantities.		
	Round.15 c. per lb. for small quantities.		
Bread.	1 fr. 10 c. per 3 K.		
Tea.	6 fr. 50 c. per Kilo.		
Sugar.	80 c. per Kilo.		

Copy No. 2

BRIGADE ORDER No. 13
By
Brig. Genl. R.A. Macfarlane, C.B.E. Commdg. 81st Infy. Brigade.

2nd January, 1915.

Field Officer of the Day for 3rd January, 1915 - Captain H.S. Fergus, 1st Royal Scots.

1. To-morrow and Monday, 3rd and 4th instants, digging will be carried out in the morning only by half battalions and half 2nd Wessex Field Co. R.E.

The ½ battalions and ½ 2nd Wessex Field Co. R.E. not employed in digging on these days will carry out rifle, kit and other inspections, washing &c.

2. Work for tomorrow.

A second line of trenches will be commenced on the northern section of the line as pointed out to O.C.'s to-day.

Pattern of trench to be constructed as shown on the accompanying diagram.

3. 1st A. & S. Highrs. and 2nd Cameron Highrs. in this order with one Brigade tool wagon will march by the N of RICHEBURG to point 59.

The 2nd Gloucesters and 1st Royal Scots in this order with one Brigade tool wagon will march by BOUT DEUX village to the road junction ¼ mile S. of the H in RICHEBURG and be ready to commence work at 9-30 a.m.

The O.C. 2nd Cameron Highrs. and 2nd Gloucesters respectively will be responsible for the Brigade tool wagons on the march and select the place for the distribution of the tools.

4. Instruction will be given in the various types of hand grenade to-morrow by an Engineer Officer from Headquarters. At least one officer per company will attend. Place of assembly- entrance to FORT DESIRE at 9-45 a.m.

ROUTINE ORDERS.

5. AMMUNITION WAGONS.

The Brigade Reserve Ammunition Wagons will assemble at the entrance to FORT DESIRE at 10 a.m. to-morrow and report to Lieut Fowler, 2nd Cameron Highlanders.

6. Canteen.

The Cafe in the SMALL PLACE called BOUT LEBRAIT is placed out of bounds.

H.C.M. Kirkpatrick.
Staff Captain
for Bde. Major 81st Infy. Bde.

Copy No. 2

BRIGADE ORDERS No. 14
By
Brig. Genl. D.A. Macfarlane, C.B.E. Comndg. 81st Infy. Bde.

3rd January, 1915

Field Officer of the Day for 4th inst. - Captain H.B. Spear, 2nd Gloucester Regt.

1. **Work for to-morrow.**

    There will be no digging to-morrow.
    Battalions will be at the disposal of Commanding Officers.

ROUTINE ORDERS.

2. **SUPPLIES (purchase of)**

    Attention is invited to Brigade Order No. 7 of the 25th ultimo, which must be complied with.

H.C.... Staff Captain,
for Bde. Major, 81st Infy. Bde.

Copy No. 2

BRIGADE ORDER No. 15
By
Brig. Genl. R.A. Macfarlane, C.B., Comdg. 81st Infy. Bde.

4th January, 1915.

Field Officer of the Day for the 5th inst.— Capt. A.W.B. Fraser, D.S.O. 2nd Cameron Highrs.

Moon rises to-morrow 8-52 p.m. Sets 10-8 a.m. on 6th inst.

(1). Work to-morrow will be under Officers Commanding Battalions.

(2). BATTALION SAPPERS.
1 Officer and 25 men carefully selected from each Bn. will be trained in sapping under arrangements made by the O.C. 2nd Wessex Fd. Co. R.E. and in future be known as Battalion Sappers.

These parties will assemble outside Fort Session at 10 a.m. to-morrow under the O.C. 2nd Wessex Fd. Co. R.E. or an officer detailed by him.

The O.C. 2nd Wessex Fd. Co. will take every opportunity of continuing this instruction communicating direct with Officers Commanding Battalions.

(3). Officers Comdg. Bns. will arrange to train 6 N.C.O.'s and men per platoon in the use of hand grenades and fire grenades under the officers who attended the instruction on this subject yesterday. These classes will start to-morrow.

(4) Special care is to be taken by Comdg. Officers to ensure that no unauthorized articles of baggage or stores are put on any vehicle when the Brigade leaves Aire.

All surplus articles of clothing are to be sent away to-morrow.

FIELD GENERAL COURT-MARTIAL.

(5). The detail of officers as mentioned below will assemble at 10 a.m. in the lines of the 2nd Cameron Highrs. for the purpose of trying by a Field General Court-Martial, the undermentioned accused persons and such other person or persons as may be brought before them.

PRESIDENT.
Major R. Connor, 2nd Gloucester Regt.
MEMBERS.
A Captain, 2nd Cameron Highlanders.
A Subaltern, 1st Royal Scots.
ACCUSED PERSONS.
Sergt. W. McFarlane, 2nd Cameron Highlanders.
Sergt. J. Kerr,   "   "   "
Pte.   J. Russell   "   "   "
Pte.   J. Gorroll.   "   "   "

The accused will be warned and all witnesses duly required to attend.

The O.C. 2nd Cameron Highlanders will detail a Sergt. as orderly to the court and will provide the necessary stationery, accommodation &c.

The proceedings will be forwarded to Headquarters 81st Infantry Brigade.

Captain,
Bde. Major 81st Infy. Bde.

Copy No. 2

BRIGADE ORDER No. 16
By
Brig. Genl. ... Macfarlane, D.S.O. Comdg. 81st Infy. Bde.

5th Jan. 1916.

Field Officer of the Day for the 6th inst.- Captain O... No.
... Cameron, 1st A. & S. Highrs.

Moon rises to-morrow at 12-12 p.m. Sets at 10-21 a.m. on the
7th inst.

1.   The Brigade will march to-morrow into the billeting
area JACKETS - MELSTUM - STRATHEIS - BOUND.
        Starting point - entrance to FORT GARRION.
        Order of march:-
            Bde. Hd. Qrs.   }
            2nd Cameron Highrs.   }   9 a.m.

            2nd Essex Fd. Co. R.E.   9-5 a.m.
            1st A. & S. Highrs.   9-10 a.m.
            2nd Gloucester Regt.   9-15 a.m.
            1st Royal Scots.   9-25 a.m.
            Echelon "B" 1st Line Transport.   9-30 a.m.
            Train.   9-35 a.m.
            81st Field Ambulance.   10-20 a.m.
        All S.A.A. carts will accompany the Battalions.

(2)   The personnel and horses of the baggage section of the
train will remain at Battalion Hd. Qrs. to-morrow night and will
be rationed by them for the following day.
        Supply wagons after dumping supplies at Battalion Hd.
Qrs. will be billetted with No. 27 Co. A.S.C.
        The 28th Brigade R.F.A. will march independently, the
head of the column to pass the level crossing at HAZEBROUCK
in rear of the train at 12-30 p.m.
        The O.C. 81st Field Ambulance will ascertain that the
28th Brigade R.F.A. have passed before crossing the roadway at
HAZEBROUCK.

                                    J. Howard   Captain,
                                    Bde. Major 81st Infy. Bde.

Copy No. 1

Infy
81st Brigade Order No 17
By
Brig. Genl. D. Macfarlane DSO Comdg
81st Infy Bde

Reference Map 5A Hazebrouck

METEREN
6/1/15

(1) The Brigade and attached troops will march tomorrow to the neighbourhood of DICKEBOSCH where the 81st Infy Bde will then become a supporting line to the 80th Infy Bde

(2) Starting point - Road Junction about ½ mile W. of BAILLEUL

Order of March -

1 Bn 80th Infy Bde at   9 a.m.

Advance Guard
    2 Coys KSLI 80th Infy Bde.

Main Body
    1 Bn. 80th Infy Bde less 2 Coys
    HQrs 81st Infy Bde   9. a.m.
    1 A & B Hughes   9-15 a.m.
    2/Camerons   9-20 a.m.
    2/Wessex Fd C RE   9-31 a.m.
    20th R.F.A. Bde & Amn Col   9-35 a.m.
    2/Glosters Regt   10.0 a.m.
    1/Royal Scots   10.8 a.m.
    Echelon "B" 1st line Tpt   10-15 a.m.
    Train   10-20 a.m.
    81st Fd Ambulance   10-50 a.m.

(3) The Brigade S.A.A. Reserve will march at the head of Echelon B

Two Ambulance wagons from 81st Fd Ambulance will follow Echelon B 1st line Transport

4) 62 Machine Gun Officer & 1 Guide of the Relieving Battalion of each Route, Will Meet Lieut. R.H. Bone at Meet the Staff Captain at the Starting point at 9 am

5) Moon rises at 10·53 pm on the 7th inst and sets at 10·34 am on the 8th inst.

T Howard Captain
Bde Major 81st Inf Bde

Copy no 1 HQ
        2 1/R Scots
        4 2/Gordons
        5 2/Camerons
        6 1/A & S. H
        7 8th FA Bde
        8 97 Co Train
        9 9 West Fd C
       10 81st Fd Amb

Brigade Order No. 18   8th Jan. 1915.

Field Officer of the day for 9th Jan. 1915 - Capt. H. Campbell, 2nd Cameron Highlanders.

Moon rises Midnight 8th/9th. Sets 10-45 a.m. on the 9th.

Moon rises 12-58 a.m. 9th/10th. Sets 11-1 a.m. on the 10th.

(sd) L. Holland, Captain,
B.M. 81st Infy. Brigade.

Copy No. 2

BRIGADE ORDER No. 191
By
Brig. Genl. D.A. Macfarlane, D.S.O. Commdg. 81st Infy. Bde.

9th Jan. 1915.
1/A. & S.H.

1. Field Officer of the Day for 10th inst Capt N.D.K.McEwan

2. All men who will be in the trenches will be issued with an extra 100 rounds of ammunition to-morrow morning in 2 bandoliers, from Regimental and Brigade Ammunition Reserves.

1A. The Brigade will relieve the 80th Infantry Brigade in trenches to-morrow under orders which will be issued to Officers Commdg. Battalions to-morrow morning.

3. Officers Commanding Battalions and Adjutants will be at Brigade Headquarters at 9-30 a.m. to-morrow.

4. Moon rises at 2-25 a.m. and sets 11-20 a.m. on the 11th inst.

5. The 2nd Gloucester Regt. will find the Bde. Hd. Qrs. Guard to-morrow of 1 N.C.O. and 3 men.

6. The Detail of Officers as mentioned below will assemble at 10 a.m. on the 10th inst. in the lines of the 1st Royal Scots for the purpose of trying by a Field General Court-Martial, the undermentioned accused person and such other person or persons as may be brought before them:-

PRESIDENT.
Major L.O. Graeme, 2nd Cameron Highrs.
MEMBERS.
A Captain, 1st Royal Scots.
A Subaltern, 2nd Gloucester Regt.

ACCUSED PERSON.

No. 9996, Sergt. A. Simpson, 1st Royal Scots.

The accused will be warned and all witnesses duly required to attend.
The O.C..1st Royal Scots will detail a Sergt. as orderly to the Court and will provide the necessary stationery, accommodation &c.
The proceedings will be forwarded to Headquarters 81st Infantry Brigade.

Captain,
Bde. Major 81st Infy. Brigade.

Copy No. 1

81st Inf. Brigade Order No. 20.

Ref Map 1/40,000

10th Jan'y 1915

Relief. 1. Relief of the 80th Inf. Bde tonight will be carried out on following time table.
2nd Camerons relieve 4th K.R.R.C. leaving DICKEBUSCH between 4.30 p.m. and 5.30 p.m.
2 Gloucester R relieve K.S.L.I. leaving DICKEBUSCH between 5.40 p.m. and 6.30 p.m.
1 R Scots relieve 3rd KRRC. leaving between 6.35 p.m. and 7 p.m.
1 A & S Hrs relieve the 4th Rifle Bde. in Support near ELZONWALLE leaving the Cross roads Square H 29 (b) between 8.30 p.m. and 9 p.m.

Ammunition 2.(a) 220 rounds S.A.A. will be carried on the man, and about 50 boxes per Batt'n will be taken over in the trenches.

Rations. (b) One days rations will be taken into the trenches. Waterbottles full.

Tools etc. (c) Tools, Braziers, Buckets, telephones will be taken over from Batt'ns in the trenches.

3. The A & S High'rs before leaving the Cross roads mentioned in ① will ascertain that all vehicles of the 2 Gloucesters, and 2 Camerons are clear of that point on their return to DICKEBUSCH.

Reports. 4. The Batt'n in support at ELZONWALLE will establish a report centre near the 1st K of KRUISSTRAATHOEK from 7 p.m. till just before dawn, to bring reports from the ~~right~~ centre and left sections of trenches. Reports will be sent to reach Brigade H.Q. at 4.30 am. and 7.30 p.m. daily. Urgent reports at any hour.
Tonight duplicate reports by orderly and telephone will be sent by Batt'ns, when relief is complete.

5. Transport will be left in Regimental Tpt. Lines — 1st A & S High'rs in the lines of the 2 Camerons.

Issued at 3 p.m.

J. Holland Captain
B.M. 81st Inf'y Bde.

Copy No. 1

BRIGADE ORDER NO. 21
By
Brig. Genl. D.A. Macfarlane, D.S.O. Commdg. 81st Infy. Bde.

during the night 12/13th

12th Jan. 1915.

1. The 1st Rl. Scots, 2nd Gloucester Regt. and 2nd Cameron Highlanders will be relieved in the trenches ~~to-morrow~~ (tonight) by battalions of the 82nd Infantry Bde. which will leave DICKEBUSCH as follows:-

   Battalions relieving Rl. Scots and 2nd Gloucesters :-
   4-30 p.m.
   Battalion relieving 2nd Camerons :- 5-30 p.m.

2. Everything which the men cannot carry themselves, including machine guns, will be brought by fatigue parties to the dumping places as soon as it is dark enough to leave the trenches.
   Officers Commanding Battalions will report what transport they will require either
   (a) By orderly before dawn,
   or (b) If (a) is not possible by telephone,
   or (c) If (b) is not possible by orderly as soon as it is dark to-morrow evening.

3. One guide per platoon will be at Battalion Headquarters at 6 p.m. to guide relieving companies into the trenches.

4. All entrenching tools, braziers, buckets, telephones, and ammunition in boxes will be handed over to relieving battalions.

5. No trench will on any account be evacuated until actually occupied by relieving troops.

6. The battalions after being relieved will occupy the same billets in DICKEBUSCH as before and become the Brigade in Support.

7. The 1st A. & S. Highlanders will remain in their present position and come under the orders of the O.C. 82nd Infantry Brigade until they are relieved on the night of the 13th/14th instant.

8. OC Bns will report *their arrival* at DICKEBUSCH / at Bde HQ.

Daily casualty report to reach Bde HQ by 6 pm.

Bde. Major 81st Infantry Brigade.

H.Q.

Copy No. 1   amended

BRIGADE ORDERS No. 22
By
Brig. Genl. D.A. Macfarlane, D.S.O. Commdg. 81st Infy. Bde.

12th Jan. 1915.

1. The Brigade will be relieved in support to-morrow evening the 13th inst. by the 82nd Infy. Bde. and will march to the Reserve Billeting Area about WESTOUTRE - distance about 5½ miles. Route- OUDERDOM-ZEVECOTEN-RENINGHELST-Billets.

TRANSPORT. 2. Supply Section of train will join the Divnl. Train at HEKSKEN. Baggage Section will proceed to Battn Hd. Qrs. of Billets direct to-morrow morning under O.C. No; 97 Co. A.S.C.
   The cross roads at S.E. corner of H. 32 are to be clear by 10 a.m.
      Order of march for baggage:-
         Bde. Headquarters.
         2nd Gloucester Regt.
         1st Rl. Scots.
         2nd Cameron Highrs.
         1st A. & S. Highrs.
   The Brigade Reserve tool wagons will remain at DICKEBUSCH.

3. The leading battalion of the 80th Bde. will pass LA CLYTTE at 5 p.m. 13th inst. This Battn. will relieve the 1st A. & S. Highrs who will, after being relieved, march independently.
   Remaining Battns. of the 80th Bde. will relieve the Cameron Highrs., Gloucester Regt. and 1st Rl. Scots in order of march of their Battalions.

4. O's C. Battalions will arrange to place their Battalions on the N.W. side of the LA CLYTTE - DICKEBUSCH Road ready to march off independently as soon as their battalion has been relieved.
   The main road of DICKEBUSCH is to be cleared of both men and transport by 5-20 p.m.

5. One mounted officer per Battn. will meet a Staff Officer, 27th Division at the CONVENT, WESTOUTRE at 10 a.m. on the 13th. They will be shown billets for their battalions and positions for their transport. They will meet the baggage wagons and direct them to the transport lines.
   Battalion billeting parties will report to O.C. No. 97 Co. A.S.C. at MILLE CAPELLEKEN at 7-30 a.m. and be taken in the empty supply wagons to HEKSKEN whence they will march to WESTOUTRE to join the Battalion Billeting Officer.

6. Arrangements for taking back men unfit to march will be published to-morrow.

7. As complete lists as possible will be furnished to-morrow of the number of boxes of ammunition, maching gun ammunition boxes, tools, braziers, &c. that were taken over from Battns. of the 80th Bde. and handed over to Battns. of the 82nd Bde.

8. Any casualties not included in the 6 p.m. report to-night will be reported as soon as possible after arrival in DICKEBUSCH.

J. Hammond Captain,
Bde. Major 81st Infy. Bde.

Copy No: 1

81st INFANTRY BDE

Operation ORDER No. 23

Ref. 1/40,000 map.   14th Jan. 1915.

1. The Brigade will march to DICKEBUSCHE tomorrow and will become BDE in support in relief of the 80th INF BDE.
   Starting point Road Junction 200 yds S.E. of the Second E of WESTOUTRE — Route — Cross Roads M.17C — LACLYTE
   ORDER of march.
   1/A. & S. Highrs.   4. p.m.
   2/Gloucester Regt.   4.18 p.m.
   2/Camerons   4.25 p.m.
   R. Scots.   4.38. p.m.

2. Baggage and Blanket waggons under transport officer 97th Coy A.S.C. will move to positions vacated by those of 82nd INFY. BDE. They will pass the starting point at 9.25 a.m. in order of march.
   On reaching LACLYTE they will march by Battalions at 200 yds interval.
   A mounted officer and two other ranks on Bicycles will proceed to DICKEBUSCHE in time to ascertain the exact position of their transport line and meet their waggons S.W. of DICKEBUSCHE at 10.45 a.m.—
   Royal Scots at MILLE KRUISSE at 10.30 a.m.

3. Battalion billetting parties will proceed meet the Staff Captain outside Bde H.Q. DICKEBUSCHE at 3. p.m. Representatives to meet Battalions at HALLEBASTE CORNER at 5.30 p.m.

4. Instructions regarding Battalion to relieve a Battalion of the 82nd BDE in close support will be issued tomorrow morning.

5. Moon rises 8.22 a.m. night 15th-16th and sets 3.57 p.m. 16th.

Issued at 8.30 p.m.

L. Howard Captain.
Bde Major.
81st INFY. BDE.

Copy No 2

81st Inf Bde Order No 44

16th Jan 1915

Reference map 1/40,000

1. The Regiment will relieve the 80th Inf Bde in the trenches tonight as follows:-

Coys Dickebusch at

2nd Gloucester .... 4:30 pm
1st R.I. & 5th Hussars .... 5:30 pm
1st R.B. Lot .... 6:55 pm

(2) 2/ Gloucester relieve KRRC and part RBrres in Centre Section

1st RB less ... relieve 1st KRRC in right Section

1st R.I. & 1st Hussars relieve PPCLI and part of KRRC in Left Section

(3) Each Bn in the trenches will take 10 Boxes ammunition to Batt HQ of the Section they relieve and arrange to have such ammunition to be taken to the trenches from Bn HQ as is necessary after taking over from the Bn 80th Inf Bde.

(4) Each Bn will take 25 shovels to make good those lost in trenches and report if more are required. Lists of stores taken over will be rendered tomorrow including ammunition.

(5) Report Centres will be established by Batt in close support as follows
   1) 2nd Gloucester at BRASSERIE
   2) 1st KRR at TRAATHOEK ...
   all responsible as far as Report ... where messages will be ...

(6) Orderlies will start from Report Centre ...

(7) ... relieve for Artillery ...

S Howard Captain
Bde 81st Inf Bde

Issued at 1.30 pm

Copy No 1

81st Brigade order No 25

Ref map 1/40000.   17th Jan 1915

Relief 1. The three battalions in trenches will be relieved by the 82nd Inf Bde tomorrow night as follows:—
   1st A & S Hrs by R Irish Regt who leave DICKEBUSCH at 4.30 pm
   2nd Gloucester R. by D. C. L. I.   "   " at 5.15 pm
   1st R Scots by R. Scots Fus.   "   " at 4.30 pm

2. 1 Officer per Coy and a guide per platoon will be sent as follows:—
   1st R Scots   } to VIERSTRAAT and BRASSERIE
   2nd Gloucesters } to VOORMEZEELE
   1st A & S Hrs   }

3. The relieving Regts will leave Transport for machine guns, and [?] at dumping places.

4. Picks and shovels will be brought back to Bn. HQ. and handed over on receipt.
   Lists of other stores handed over in trenches will be given to relieving coys, and the numbers reported to this office.
   Very pistols will be handed over on receipt, also bayonet periscopes.

5. The Cameron Highlanders will remain at VIERSTRAAT.

6. Battalions will occupy the same billets they left.

Issued at 11.25 pm.   L Holland Colelin
                            Bd 81st Inf Bde

N.B. Two suspicious persons dressed in khaki, with one in Glengarry and one with a muffler were reported near the cross roads ½ mile NW of VIERSTRAAT tonight.
Sentries should be warned to arrest any persons asking questions.

Copy No. 2

81st INFY. BDE. ORDER No. 26.

Reference Map- 1/40,000.

1. The Brigade will relieve the 82nd Brigade in the front line to-morrow the 20th inst. as follows:-

	Relieve	Section	Leave DICKEBUSCH.
1 Co. A. & S. H.	1 Co. Cam. Highrs.	BRASSERIE	4-30 p.m.
1/R1. Scots.	(R.I. Fusrs. (1 Co. Cam. Highrs.	Right Section VIERSTRAAT.	4-40 p.m. to 5-15 p.m.
2/Gloucesters.	D.C.L.I.	Centre Section	4-45 p.m.
2/Cameron Hrs.	R.I. Regt.	Left Section	(2 Coys. (5-30 p.m.

The 2 Companies 2nd Cameron Highrs. after being relieved at VIERSTRAAT will draw their supplies at ELZONWALLE on the way to VOORMEZEELE.

The remainder A. & S. Highrs. will relieve the Loinster Regiment at ELZONWALLE leaving DICKEBUSCH at 4-30 a.m. 21st inst.

2. Headquarters of Battalion occupying the Right Section and 1 Coy. as Battalion Reserve will now be posted at VIERSTRAAT.

3. A Report Centre will be established at the Cross Roads KRUIS KRUISSTRAATHOEK by the 1st A. & S. Highrs.

4. Supplies for 2 Companies, 1st Cameron Highrs. now in support will follow the 2nd Gloucester Regt. and dump at ELZON-WALLE.

Battalions will leave transport for the machine guns and stores of the battalions they relieve.

S. Holland Captain,
Bde. Major 81st Infy. Brigade

Copy No. 2

81st INFANTRY BDE. ORDER NO. 27.

21st Jan. 1915.

1. The Brigade will be relieved in the front line to-morrow night, 22nd inst. as follows:-

			Leaving DICKEBUSCH at
D.C.L.I.	relieve	2nd Gloucesters	4-30 p.m.
R.I. Fusrs.	"	1st R. Scots.	4-35 p.m.
Leinster Regt.	"	1/A. & S.H.	5-30 p.m.
R.I. Regt.	"	2/Cameron Hgrs.	6-30 p.m.

1 officer per company and 1 guide per platoon will be at Battn. Hd. Qrs. in time to meet the relieving Battns. in the trenches and at KRUISSTRAATHOEK for the Battalion at ELZONWALLE.

2. Transport will be left by the 82nd Infantry Bde. for corresponding battalions of this brigade, arrangements being made by the transport officers concerned.

3. The 1st Royal Scots and 2nd Gloucesters will occupy their old billets.
    The billets of the 2nd Camerons and 1st A. & S. H. will be arranged to-morrow morning with the Quartermasters.

4. Duplicate lists of ammunition, tools and stores handed over will be sent to Brigade Hd. Qrs. by 11 a.m. 23rd inst.

5. A report will be sent to Brigade Hd. Qrs. on the large pattern "Very" pistols, which will be handed over to relieving battalions.

[signature] Captain,
Bde. Major 81st Infy. Bde.

Copy No. 2

81st INFANTRY BDE. ORDER
No. 28.

22nd Jan. 1915.

1. The Brigade will be relieved by the 80th Infantry Bde. to-morrow and march to the Reserve area where it will remain for six days.

2. Battalions will be billeted to-morrow as follows:-
   1st Rl. Scots on the WESTOUTRE - BOESCHEPE Road
   2nd Gloucesters - WESTOUTRE (South end) (new billets)
   2nd Camerons - WESTOUTRE (North End).
   1st A. & S. Highrs. - REYNGOTEN.

3. A Battalion Billeting Officer (mounted) to meet a Staff Officer, 27th Division at Bde. Hd. Qrs. WESTOUTRE at 10 a.m. to-morrow.
   Billeting parties will meet their billeting Officers in the Battn. Billeting Area at 1 p.m.

4. Baggage wagons under the Transport. Officer, 27th Co. A.S.C. to leave DICKEBUSCH at 12-10 p.m.: Royal Scots wagons to go in front and clear HALLEBAST corner at 12-20 p.m.

5. 1st Line Transport will march independently by Battalions:-
   1/Royal Scots leaving at   2-45 p.m.
   2/Gloucesters   "   "   3 p.m.
   2/Camerons.   "   "   3-15 p.m.
   1/A. &S.H.   "   "   3-30 p.m.

   Battalions will march independently as follows - Route:-
   OUDERDOM) RENINGHELST - WESTOUTRE.
   1st Rl. Scots to clear HALLEBAST corner at 5-15 p.m.
   2/Gloucesters leave DICKEBUSCH at 5-15 p.m.
   2/Camerons   "   "   5-20 p.m.
   1/A. & S. Highrs. "   "   5-25 p.m.
   All Battalions except the 1st Royal Scots will march by the road past the Gloucesters lines.

6. Battalions will arrange for transport for men unable to march with Battalions of the 82nd Infantry Brigade who relieve them to-night.
   A report will be sent to Bde. Hd. Qrs. not later than 10 a.m. to-morrow, saying if further transport is required or not.
   Wagons with men unable to march will leave DICKEBUSCH at 2 p.m. under the Transport Officer on duty, Royal Scots joining at HALLEBAST corner.

7. Battalions will at once indent on the R.E. Park, DICKEBUSCH for such tools as they may require to complete establishment.

J. Hommun Captain,
Bde. Major 81st Infy. Bde.

Copy No. 2

81st INFY. BDE. ORDER No. 29.

28th Jan. 1915.

Reference - 1/40,000 map.

1. The Brigade will relieve the 82nd Infantry Bde. as Brigade in support, to-morrow the 29th inst.

   Starting point - Road Junction immediately S. of the centre of Square H.9.

   Order of March:-

   1st A. & S. Highrs. will march independently to LA CLYTTE corner so as to pass that point at 5.15 p.m. at the head of the brigade.

   2nd Cameron Highrs.   4-20 p.m.

   2nd Gloucesters.   4-25 p.m.

   1st R. Scots,   4-30 p.m.

2. ½ Battn. 1st A. & S. Highrs. will proceed to the Chateau ½ mile N. of KRUISSTRAATHOEK and come under the orders of the G.O.C. 8/th Infantry Brigade.
   The O.C. ½ Battn. will report to G.O.C. 80th Inf. Bde. at 5 p.m., riding on in advance.

3. Baggage wagons will pass the starting point at 9-30 a.m. in order of march under the Transport Officer, 97th Co. A.S.C. assisted by the Battn. Transport Officer on duty.
   On reaching LA CLYTTE the baggage wagons will march by battalions at 200 yards interval.
   Supply wagons, after refilling, will follow the baggage wagons under an officer detailed by O.C. 97 Co. A.S.C.

4. Battalions will be billeted as far as possible in the same areas they left.
   A representative from each battalion will proceed to DICKEBUSCH in advance of the baggage wagons in time to ascertain the exact position of the transport lines and lead their wagons to it.
   Billeting parties (less Royal Scots) will report to the Camp Commandant, xxxxxxxxxx DICKEBUSCH at 3 p.m.

5. Battalions must arrange to complete their tools from the R.E. Depot, DICKEBUSCH to-morrow.

Captain,
B.M. 81st Infy. Brigade.

Copy No. 2

81st INFY. BDE. ORDER No. 30.

28th Jan. 1915.

1.   The Brigade will relieve the 80th Infantry Brigade in the Right Section (old Right and Centre Sections) of the front line to-morrow night under the following arrangements:-

		Leaving DICKEBUSCH at.
1st R1. Scots	relieve 3rd K.R.R.C. on the right.	4-45 p.m.
2nd Gloucesters.	relieve 4th Rifle Bde. and K.S.L.I. on the left.	5 p.m.

An interval of 10 minutes will be left between each company.

The 1st Argyll & Sutherland Highrs. will be in close support at KLE ENWALLE, 1 company at the BRASSERIE.

The 2 Companies now in DICKEBUSCH will leave DICKEBUSCH at 6 p.m.

The 2nd Cameron Highrs. will remain in DICKEBUSCH tomorrow night in Brigade Reserve.

2.   Commanding Officers will come to Brigade Headquarters at 10 a.m. to-morrow when instructions will be issued as to the position of the front line and the reliefs.

Transport Officers will come to Brigade Hd. Qrs. at 12 noon.

3.   When German aeroplanes are sighted, a whistle is blown three times by mounted orderlies who are on the look out. All men must then go into houses and clear the roads, and not look up at the aeroplanes from the street.

T. Holland Captain,
Bde. Major 81st Infy. Bde.

Copy No. 2

81st Infy Bde Order
No 31

Reference Map 1/40000

30th Jan. 1915

1. Tomorrow evening the 31st inst the following reliefs will be carried out.
2/Cameron Highrs will relieve 1st Rl Scots in the trenches leaving DICKEBUSCH at 5=5 pm
1/A & S. Highrs will relieve the 2/Glosters under arrangements made by the OC that Battalion.
The 1/Rl Scots will proceed to ELZENWALLE (1 Coy at the BRASSERIE)
The 2/Glosters will be billeted in DICKEBUSCH

(2) The 1/A & S Highrs in relieving 2/Glosters will march by the BRASSERIE and around VOORMEZEELE.

(3) The actual relief of the trenches in moonlight will be carried out by as small parties as possible and the relieving unit will not open fire unless absolutely necessary till the outgoing unit has had time to get quite clear of the road to DICKEBUSCH.

(4) Support and reserve trenches will not be relieved till the relief of the fire trenches is complete.

(5) Under Divisional Instructions Reports negative if necessary will be sent by Battalions in the trenches every two hours day and night.

Moon rises 30th inst. 3.53 pm.
Sets 7.38 am 31st inst.
Moon rises 31st inst 5.14 pm
Sets 7.59 am 1st Feb.

[signature] Capt.
B.M. 81st Infy Bde.

Issued at 4.45 pm.

Copy No. 2

61st INFY. BDE. ORDER No. 52.

31st Jan. 1915.

1. The order sent by message regarding strengthening the obstacle in front of the line of defence is republished.

Officers Commanding Battalions in the trenches will ensure that something is done every night to strengthen the wire entanglement in front of the trenches.

Some men from each company or trench will be employed on this work every night. If moonlight prevents work in front of the trenches, more wire will be brought up and prepared for more favourable opportunities.

2. Officers Commdg. Battalions concerned will consult and report on the best positions for listening patrols. It is hoped these may be dug and completed with wire during the present tour of duty in the trenches.

As a rough guide it is considered that 4 should be dug in front of each battalion in the trenches as at present distributed, but the Brigadier-General would be glad of the views of Commanding Officers and Company Officers who know the trenches and the ground in front of them, before the actual work is commenced.

Moon rises - 6-37 p.m. 1st Feby. Sets 8-12 a.m. 2nd February.

J Howard
Captain,
Bde. Major 61st Infy. Bde.

81st Inf Bde

INSTRUCTIONS REGARDING TAKING OVER TRENCHES AND THEIR RELIEF.

20th Jan. 1915.

1. REPORTS. *During Relief.*

(i) A report will invariably be sent in that a relief is complete.

(ii) Any opportunity should be taken during a relief to report progress, e.g. Bn. Hd. Qrs. should always report their arrival, by telephone.

Daily Reports.

Officers Commdg. Battns. will send reports so as to reach Bde. Hd. Qrs. at 6-30 a.m. and 5-30 p.m. The report which should be brief should be sent in whether reports from all companies have been received or not. Supplementary reports can be sent in afterwards, if necessary.

2. Casualty Reports.

These will be sent in with (but in a separate message from) the evening reports or as soon after as possible, and in any case not later than 8 p.m. The report will include all casualties since the previous casualty report, whether referred to in other messages or not.

Missing.

Names of men reported missing will be sent in with these reports, except in the case of men missing from the trenches, in which case names will be submitted as soon as possible with a report of the circumstances. Officers Commdg. Companies are held personally responsible that no men are left sick or disabled in the trenches or in billets.

3. Report Centre at KRUISSTRAATHOEK.

This will be found by the Battalion in Support at ELZEN-WALLE.

Composition:- 1 Officer, 20 N.C.O.'s and men.
4 Battalion Orderlies sent back from the centre and left battalions.
Orderlies from the Divl. Cyclist Coy. may be attached.

Orderlies will leave the Report Centre for Brigade Hd. Qrs. at 6 p.m. and 6 a.m. Daily reports which cannot be got through by telephone must be sent in time to be delivered by these orderlies.

Any other messages which require immediate delivery must be marked urgent.

The O.C. Right Section will make his own arrangements for sending messages.

The following orderlies will be sent to Bde. Hd. Qrs. to take messages forward to the Report Centre or the Hd. Qrs. Right Section respectively:-

From the Report Centre (belonging to the Battn. in support) - 4.

From the Battalion in the Right Section - 2.

4.

4. Reports on Trenches.

A report on the trenches occupied will always be sent in by 6 p.m. the day after leaving the trenches.

If a particular trench is referred to a rough sketch should be sent.

The following headings should be reported on.

(a). General state of the trenches since last occupied fire trenches and communications, support or reserve trenches being reported on separately.

(b).(i). Work done in detail for each trench or company. (This is important to hand on to the relieving Brigade)

(ii). New work recommended.

(c). The position of new machine gun emplacements and progress of those begun.

(d). Information of the enemy.
(i) Enemy's trenches, obstacles &c. specially noting exact position of and description of new trenches or saps.
(ii) Any movements of enemy noted, or habits which it may be useful to pass on to relieving units.

5. Ammunition, Stores.

A list of ammunition, tools &c. taken over or found in the trenches will be sent to Bde. Hd. Qrs. the day after going in and a list of stores handed over to the relieving regiment the day after leaving the trenches.

A place should be prepared close behind every trench where tools &c. can be placed for handing over. Otherwise it may be necessary to have these brought in to Bn. Hd. Qrs. each time.

6. Fatigue work for Battns. in Trenches.

R.E. Stores and rations.

All R.E. stores for Battns. in trenches will be carried by fatigue parties from battalions in close support from dumping place to Battalion Hd. Qrs. or such other dumping ground near the trenches as the O.C. Battalions in the trenches will arrange. Such places should be near a road and under cover from enemy's trenches in case stores dumped there cannot all be taken up to the trenches the same night.

The supporting battalion will also carry up rations for men in the trenches to the same place as mentioned above unless O's C. Battalions in trenches arrange with the battalion in support to carry up their own.

Captain,
Bde. Major 81st Infy. Bde.

INSTRUCTIONS FOR COMMENCING NEW TRENCHES NEAR ST. ELOI.

O.C. 1/A. & S. Highrs.

" " 2nd Cameron Highrs.
----

1. Owing to some of the trenches near ST. ELOI having become untenable owing to flooding it has been decided to construct new trenches.
   This work will be begun by the 1st A. & S. H. to-night 21st/22nd inst.
   The following working parties which should as far as possible be taken from companies in support or reserve will be found by 1st A. & S. Highrs.

2. Work to be done.
   (1) New trench X immediately in rear of the old trench East of the ST. ELOI - WARNETON road (left Coy.).
   This trench will be sited by an R.E. Officer and the work will be supervised by Lieutenant Pitt, R.E. who will report to O.C. fatigue party at KRUISSTRAATHOEK cross roads at 9-30 p.m.
   Men required for this trench:-
   (a). 60 men in 3 reliefs of 20 each for digging. Tools - 1 shovel for each man and 5 spare.
   (b). 30 men in 3 reliefs of 10 each for filling sand-bags with rubble at St. ELOI, and carrying to the trench if required.
   An R.E. N.C.O. will superintend who will report to O.C. fatigue party at KRUISSTRAATHOEK cross roads at 9-30 p.m.
   (c). 30 men in 3 reliefs of 10 each to collect timber in St. ELOI for flooring new trench.
   An R.E. N.C.O. will ~~supervise~~ superintend who will report to O.C. fatigue party at KRUISSTRAATHOEK at 9-30 p.m.

   (ii) For constructing new trench Y on the ST. ELOI - MESSINES Road near ruined house.
   Working party, 30 men in 3 reliefs.
   This trench will be sited by an R.E. Officer and supervised by Captain Harvey, R.E. who will report to O.C. fatigue party, A. & S. Highlanders at Bn. Hd. Qrs. VOORMEZEELE at 10 p.m.

3. In addition to the above the work on a sap commenced in the present trench E. of the St. ELOI - WARNETON Road by the 2nd Cameron Highlanders, will be continued by the 1st A. & S. Highrs under an N.C.O. ~~2nd~~ 1st Wessex Field Company who will report to the O.C. 1st A. & S. Highlanders at VOORMEZEELE at 10 p.m.
   A guide will be provided.

4. Bomb Throwers. A party of bomb throwers will report to O.C. 1st A. & S. Highrs. at ELZONWALLE at 5-30 p.m.
   O.C. 1st A. & S. Highlanders is responsible that bombs and detonators now at VOORMEZEELE on charge of the 2nd Cameron Highlanders, are handed over to the bomb throwers and taken into the trenches.
   The bomb throwers will remain in the trenches by day on the 22nd, and return with the 1st A. & S. Highrs. when relieved.

5. Tools for above work will be taken from ELZONWALLE and returned to M. Hd. VOORMEZEELE

                                                    Thoram Captain,
21st Jan. 1915.   Bde. Major 81st Infy. Brigade.

An immediate acknowledgement
is required.

"A" Form. Army Form C. 2121
MESSAGES AND SIGNALS. No. of Message _____

Prefix ____ Code ____ m.	Words	Charge	This message is on a/c of:	Recd. at ____ m.
Office of Origin and Service Instructions.	Sent			Date _____
	At ____ m.		_____ Service.	From _____
	To ____		(Signature of "Franking Officer.")	By _____
	By ____			

TO { 27th Div.

| Sender's Number | Day of Month | In reply to Number | AAA |
| 13M317 | 10th | AE 237 | |

Casualty report for 9th inst
nil add. Casualty report
up to 9 pm 10th inst
nil.

W.D

From 81st Infy Bde
Place
Time 9.30 pm

"A" Form.
Army Form C. 2121
MESSAGES AND SIGNALS. No. of Message _____

Prefix ___ Code ___ m	Words	Charge	This message is on a/c of:	Recd. at ___ m
Office of Origin and Service Instructions.	Sent			Date ___
	At ___ m		___ Service.	From ___
	To ___			By ___
	By ___		(Signature of "Franking Officer.")	

TO { 27 Div.

| Sender's Number | Day of Month | In reply to Number | AAA |
| BM.312 | 10th | G.R.110 | |

82nd Infy Bde Battalion should be placed in Support at VIERSTRAAT with 2 Coys in DICKEBUSCH aaa Am arranging to send representative tonight to see arrangements of the Battn of 80th Bde now at VIERSTRAAT

W D

From 81st Inf Bde
Place
Time 4 pm   Shan

"A" Form.
MESSAGES AND SIGNALS.   No. of Message
Army Form C. 2121

Prefix	Code	m.	Words	Charge	This message is on a/c of :	Rec'd. at	m.
Office of Origin and Service Instructions.			Sent			Date	
			At	m.	Service.	From	
			To			By	
			By		(Signature of "Franking Officer.")		

TO { 27th Div.

Sender's Number: BM 307   Day of Month: 10th   In reply to Number: AAA

Can you please say if
it is approved that many
men going into trenches should
leave their packs aaa. Am
convinced transport can be
arranged on leave the
trenches. BM

From: 81st Infy Bde
Place:
Time: 11.55 am.

The above may be forwarded as now corrected.   (Z)
Censor.   Signature of Addresser or person authorised to telegraph in his name.

* This line should be erased if not required.

"A" Form.　　　　　　　　　　　　　　　　Army Form C. 2121
MESSAGES AND SIGNALS.　　No. of Message _____

Prefix ____ Code ____ m.	Words	Charge	This message is on a/c of :	Recd. at _____ m.
Office of Origin and Service Instructions.	Sent			Date _____
	At _____ m.		_____ Service.	From _____
	To _____			By _____
	By _____	(Signature of "Franking Officer.")	

TO { A.A. Battns.

| Sender's Number | Day of Month | In reply to Number | AAA |
| BM309 | 10th | | |

GOC 27th Div. has NOT approved of men leaving their packs behind on going into the trenches aaa 6 Machine gun belt boxes will be taken into the trenches for each machine gun aaa 7th Akershofen.

W D

From 81st Infy Bde
Place
Time 2 pm.

"A" Form. Army Form C. 2121.
MESSAGES AND SIGNALS. No. of Message _____

Prefix ___ Code ___ m.	Words.	Charge.	This message is on a/c of:	Recd. at ___ m.
Office of Origin and Service Instructions.				Date ___
	Sent		_____ Service.	From ___
	At ___ m.			
	To ___			
	By ___	(Signature of "Franking Officer.")	By ___

TO {

| Sender's Number | Day of Month | In reply to Number | AAA |

The	96th	AAA	The	Commandant
and	a	"peloton"	(eighty men)	are
in	houses	in	the	same
~~rer~~	as	my	Battalion tonight	AAA.
I	attach	General	VIDAL'S	sketches
of	his	Infantry	and	the
~~French~~	Artillery	positions.	AAA	From
the	above	it	will	be
seen	that	we	by	day
and	night	are	well	within
the French side of the ~~~~	boundary	between	the
27th British	and	31st	French	Divisions
AAA.	Please	acknowledge.		

From OC Argylls
Place
Time 7.30 p.m.

The above may be forwarded as now corrected. (Z)

Censor.   Signature of Addressor or person authorised to telegraph in his name

* This line should be erased if not required.

(24473). M.R.Co.,Ltd. Wt.W4843/541. 50,000. 9/14. Forms C2121/10.

"A" Form. Army Form C. 2121.
MESSAGES AND SIGNALS. No. of Message _____

Prefix ___ Code ___ m.	Words.	Charge.	This message is on a/c of:	Recd. at ___ m.
Office of Origin and Service Instructions.	Sent			Date ___
	At 7.35 m.		Service.	From ___
	To B.M.			
	By CO		(Signature of "Franking Officer.")	By ___

TO { Brigade Major
     81st Brigade

Sender's Number	Day of Month	In reply to Number	AAA
* 53	8th January	B.M. 277	

My	officer's	patrol	under	2nd Lieut
Greenfield	has	established	touch	with
the	French	Troops	on	my
left	AAA	He	interviewed	personally
General	VIDAL	Commanding	31st	Division
of	the	XVIth	Army	Corps
whose	position	tonight	will	be
at	REMINGHELST	AAA	The	31st
Division	comprises	the	61st	and
62nd	Infantry	Brigades	AAA	the
62nd	Brigade	is	the	one
on	our	immediate	left	and
is	commanded	by	General	XARDEL
whose	Head	Quarters	are	at
CHATEAU	DE	LANKHOF	square	I 26 D.
AAA	The	Regiment	~~Batln~~	on	the
right	of	this	Brigade	is

From ___
Place ___
Time ___

The above may be forwarded as now corrected. (Z)

Censor. Signature of Addressor or person authorised ___ his name
* This line should be erased if not required.
(24473). M.R.Co.,Ltd. Wt.W4843/541. 50,000. 9/14. Forms C2121/10.

Division General Vidal. 31st Division.
16th Army Corps.

61st and 62nd Div.
(General Vidal.)
Near Trois Rois.

96th Regt " 61st D⁰ ⎰ 81st Regt — 3 b⁶
              ⎨ 96   " — 3 "
              ⎩ 2nd Bat of Chasseurs

         62 D⁰ ⎰ 122 — 3 b⁶
                ⎨ 142 — 3 "
                ⎩ 342 (4 b⁶)
         3e B⁰⁰ d'Afrique (3 C⁹)

G⁰ Vidal ⎰ P.C. Seminar
           ⎨ H.Q. ⎱ Reminghelst
                  ⎰ Poperinghe

G⁰¹ Xavier ⎰ P.C. Chateau de Lavrilof
C = 61 D¹ˢ ⎱ S of 3 Rois.

G⁰¹ K (of Senlis)

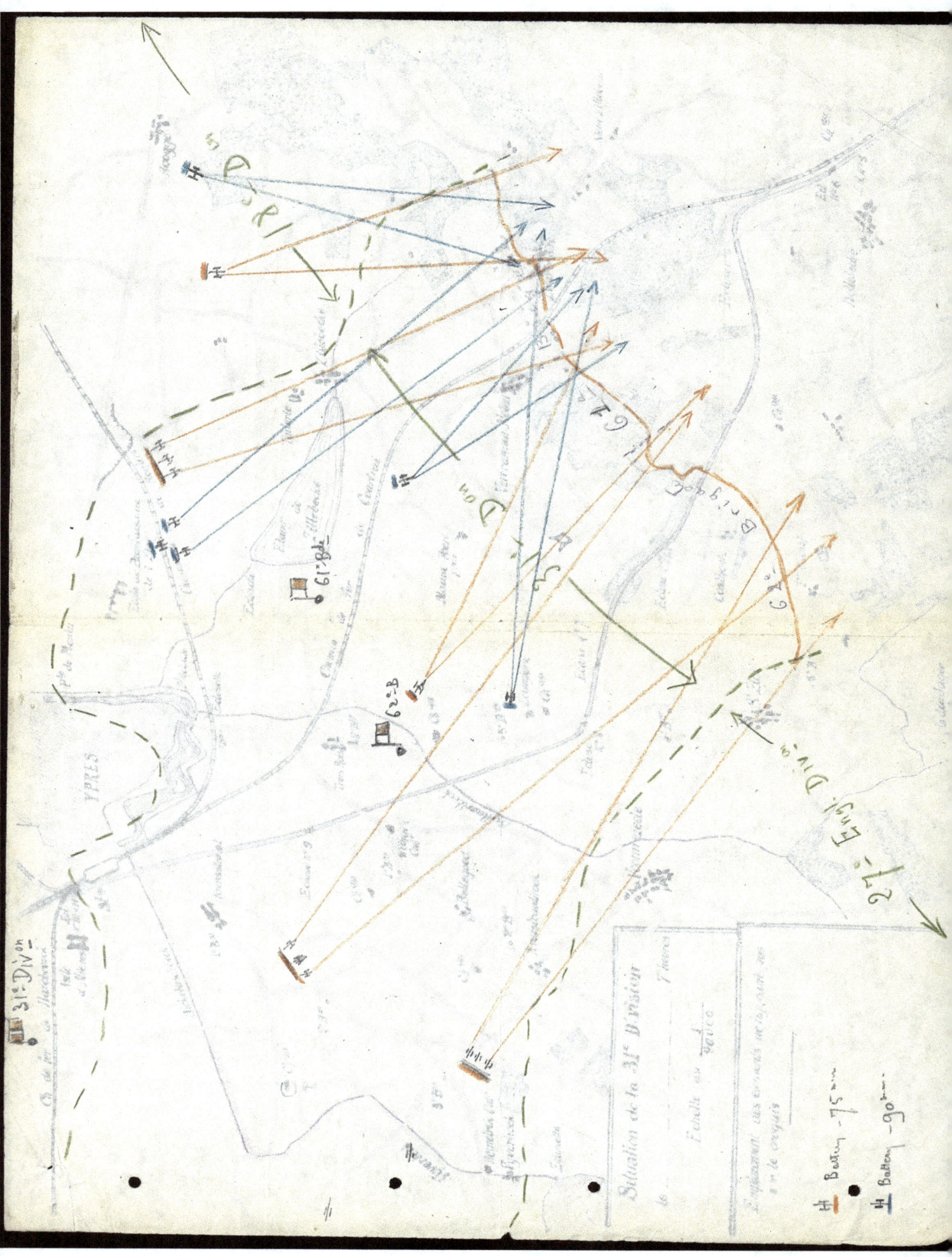

A/4 I.

REPORT ON SAPPING OPERATIONS:-

being carried out by enemy opposite the left of our line (where it joins up with French) near ST. ELOI.
(Reference Shetch Map sent by 81st Brigade on 18.1.1915)

---

1. Sap (d) runs to within (approximate) 30 yards of the trench occupied by the 2nd platoon from our left. Depth of sap five to six feet. The enemy appear to have ceased work on this sap during the last two days. Selected men have been listening at night close to head of this sap but no signs of work have been heard during the night of 19-20th instant or seen during to-day. No barbed wire entanglement exists between the sap and our trenches.
   Object of this sap would appear to be to enfilade with machine gun fire, section of trench occupied by 2nd platoon from our left.

2. Sap (e) at present runs within about 10 yards of the point of trench of our left platoon where it joins up with the French. Work has been carried on apparently by the enemy on this sap during the last two days. Depth of sap five to six feet. A mixture of earth and water has been seen being thorwn out by day from head of sap forming parapet shown on accompanying sketch. This sap can be enfiladed to a certain extent from a portion of our adjacent trench and the fire of six men from this position to-day was sufficient to cause work to cease in the sap.
   Object of sap apparently to:-
   (a) Enfilade French trench on our left. It does not enfilade our own trench.
   (b) Fire on reliefs as they enter trench from communicating trench which is just opposite head of sap.

   A barbed wire entanglement partially destroyed by artillery fire exists between head of sap and our trench.

3. Counter Sapping. A counter sap has been commenced on night of 19th-20th instant against sap (d) but so far this work has only consisted of damming the trench with some sandbags to prevent inundation of counter saps by night and baling operations by day. No counter sap has as yet been commenced against Sap (e).

4. Remarks on saps and out own trenches.
Enemy's saps - It would appear that the enemy are running up a number of saps against our trenches in vicinity of ST.ELOI and in my opinion their intention is when all the necessary saps are completed to simultaneously bring enfilade machine gun fire against this portion of the trenches thus rendering them untenable. The nature of the terrain which is very boggy renders it practically impossible for the Germans to attempt to rush the position, as men who attempt to move over the ground sinks up to the knees in the mire or more.
Our trenches. (a) Owing to constant undercutting of front face of trenches by our men these trenches have in many instances become 15' to 20' broad, the rear face remaining in its original position.
   (b) Most of our trenches in this portion of the line consist of trenches about 50 yards long and are devoid of traverses.
   (c) A large portion of the parapets are not bullet-proof. Owing to the peculiar wet clayey soil a thickness of not less than 6' is necessary.

5. <u>Suggestions</u>.

As in many instances the rear parapet is larger than the front parapet it would be comparatively easy to utilise this parapet as cover to the front and construct fresh trenches with numerous traverses in rear of the present trenches. The rear parapet at present is useless owing to the great width of many of the trenches (already mentioned - para: 4 a.) Constant traverses would prevent the enemy from carrying out their apparent intention of making the trenches untenable by means of enfilade machine gun from the head of each sap.

Higher parapets and shallower trenches would diminish the chances of flooding.

Owing to the rear parapets being higher than the front parapets little dead ground would exist, if any, should the suggestion of making fresh trenches in the immediate rear of the present ones be adopted.

These trenches in rear would be concealed from view by the present rear parapets and could be made unknown to the enemy.

20-21. 1. 1915.   (Sd) H.E. Rudkin, Captain,
                          2nd Bn. Royal Irish Regiment.

REPORT ON SAPPING OPERATIONS:-

being carried out by enemy opposite the left of our line (where
it joins up with French) west 21. L101.
(Reference sketch map sent by 51st Brigade on 19.1.1915)

1. Sap (a) runs to within (approximate) 50 yards of the
trench occupied by the 2nd platoon from our left. Depth of sap
and lie to six feet. The enemy appear to have ceased work
on this sap during the last two days. Selected men have
been listening at night close to head of this sap but no sound
of work have been heard during the night or 13-20th instant
or seen during to-day. No barbed wire entanglement exists
between the sap and our trenches.

Object of this sap would appear to be to enfilade with
machine gun fire, section of trench occupied by 2nd platoon
from our left.

2. Sap (e) at present runs within about 10 yards of the
point of trench of our left platoon where it joins up with
the French. Work has been carried on apparently by the
enemy on this sap during the last two days. Depth of sap
five to six feet. A mixture of earth and water has been
seen being thrown out by day from head of sap forming parapet
shown on accompanying sketch. This sap can be enfiladed
to a certain extent from a position of our adjacent trench
and the fire of six men from this position to-day was
sufficient to cause work to cease in the sap.

Object of sap apparently to:-
(a) Enfilade French trench on our left. If does
not enfilade our own trench.
(b) Fire on reverse as they enter French <strikethrough>enter</strikethrough> from
head communicating trench which is just opposite head
of sap.

A barbed wire entanglement partially destroyed by
artillery rifle exists between head of sap and our trench.

3. Counter sapping. A counter sap has been commenced
on right or last-2oth instant against sap (b) but so far
this work has only consisted of damaging the trench with some
sandbags to prevent inundation of counter saps by rifle and
machine gun fire.   No counter sap has as yet been
putting operations by day.   Counter sap (e) has been
commenced against sap (e).

4. Remarks on saps and our own trenches.
Enemy's saps - It would appear that the enemy are running
up a number of saps against our trenches in vicinity of sq.1014
and in my opinion their intention is when all the necessary
saps are completed to simultaneously ^ spring enfilade machine
gun fire against this position of the trenches thus rendering
their untenable.   The nature of the terrain which is very
boggy renders it practically impossible for the defence of
attempting to rush the position, as men who attempt to move
over the ground sink up to the knees in the mire or more.
Owing to constant unsettling of front face
of trenches. (a) Owing to constant unsettling of front face
of trenches by our men these trenches have in many instances
become 12' to 20' broad, the rear face remaining in its
original position.
(b) Most of our trenches in this portion of the line
consist of trenches about 30 yards long and are devoid of
traverses.
(c) A large portion of the parapets are not bullet-proof.
Owing to the peculiar wet clayey soil a thickness of not
less than 6' is necessary.

5. **Suggestions.**
As in many instances the rear parapet is larger than the front parapet it would be comparatively easy to utilise this parapet as cover to the front and construct fres trenches with numerous traverses in rear of the present trenches. The rear parapet at present is useless owing to the great width of many of the trenches (already mentioned - para: 4 a.) Constant traverses would prevent the enemy from carrying out their apparent intention of making the trenches untenable by means of enfilade machine gun from the head of each sap.

Higher parapets and shallower trenches would diminish the chances of flooding.

Owing to the rear parapets being higher than the front parapetslittle dead ground would exist, if any, should the suggestion of making fresh trenches in the immediate rear of the present ones be adopted.

These trenches in rear would be concealed from view by the present rear parapets and could be made unknown to the enemy.

20-21. 1. 1915.   (Sd) H.E. Rudkin, Captain,
                           2nd Bn. Royal Irish Regiment.

REPORT ON GERMAN SAP HEADS Near St ELOI, NIGHT OF 17th/18th. January 1915.

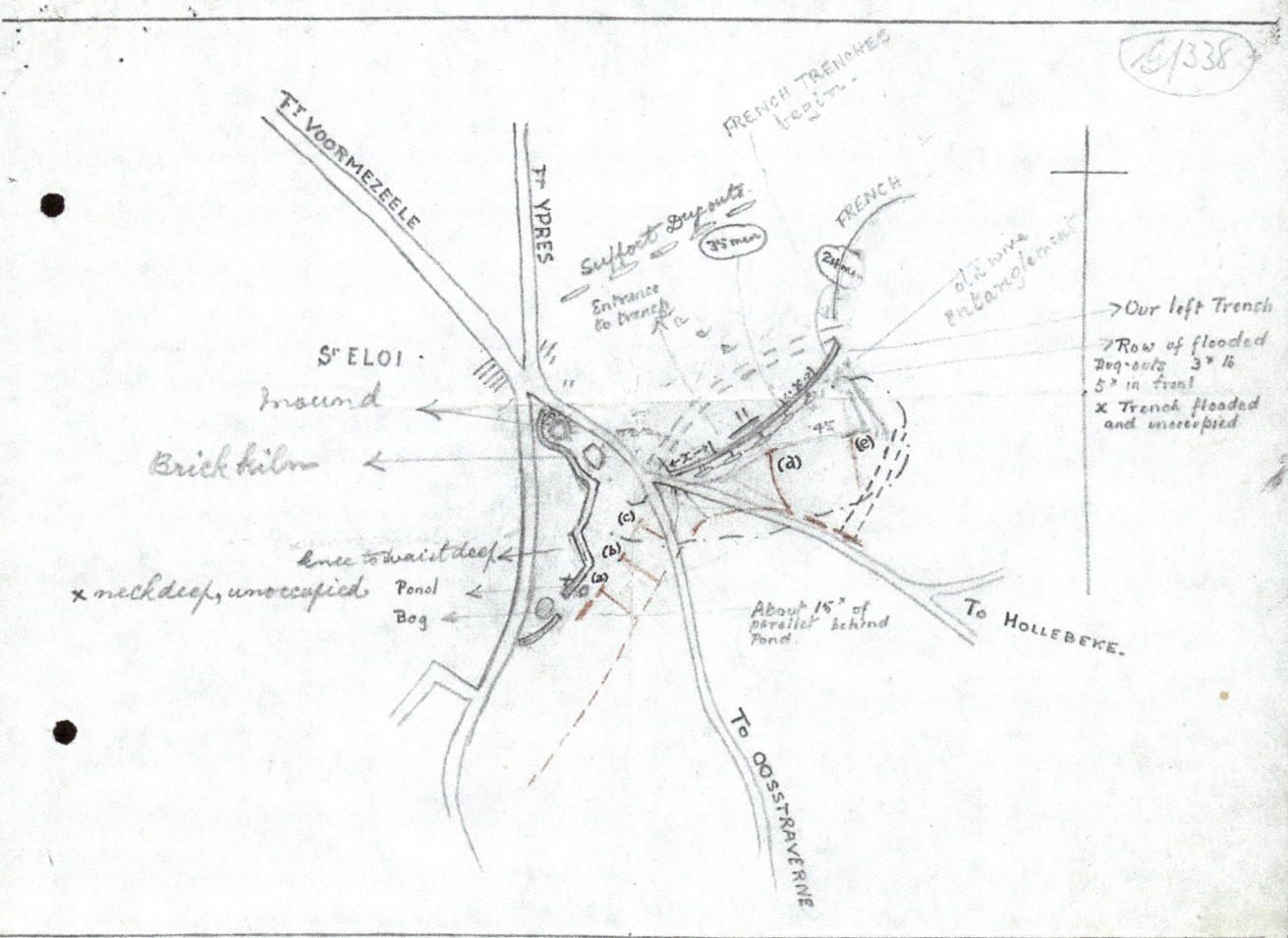

——————— Position of German Trenches, but these cannot be accurately fixed.

———→ Saps.

SAPS.- (a) First reported by O.C.2nd.Camerons. Worked only occasionally by day 17th. and not at all by night. Distance about 30 yards.

(b) Reported by K.R.R. and Leinsters, not advanced
(c) during 17th. as far as yet ascertained.

(d) Reported by 2nd.Lt.Forbes Leith 1st.A & S Hrs. Worked continuously on 17th. by day and advanced some 15' to 18'.
Sap roller used and work covered by men behind excellent loop-holes, to which our men find it difficult to reply.
Distance 20 to 30 yards. Sap apparently 6 feet deep and has struck a rock. Sappers are followed by bailers.

(e) Further off and no sap roller. Earth being thrown on one side only.

———————————

The above notes are from officers of the 1st.A & S Hrs. in the trenches 17th and night 17th/18th. Taken down at VOORMEZEELE about 4 a.m. to 5 a.m. 18th.

18-1-1915.
7-45 a.m.
Sd. L.Holland. Captain.
Bde. Major 81st.Infantry Brigade.

[Sketch map showing St Eloi area with roads to Voormezeele, Hollebeke, and Oostraverne, including a Mound, Pond 150g, entrance to trench, and annotations "35 men", "24 men", "Our left Trench", "Row of flooded dug-outs 3' to 5' in front", "× = French flooded and unoccupied"]

--- — — — line of German trenches but these cannot be accurately fixed.

Saps
(a) First reported by O/C Camerons. Worked only occasionally by day 17th and not all by night. Distance about 30'.

(b)
(c) } Reported by 1st R.B. and Leinsters not worked advanced during 17th as far as yet ascertained.

(d) Worked continuously on 17th by day and advanced some 15' & 18'. Sap roller used and work covered by men behind excellent loopholes, to which our men find it difficult to reply. Distance 20' to 30'. Sappers are followed by [Grenadiers] apparently and has struck rock.

(e) Further off and no sap roller. Earth being thrown on each side only.

From reports of 2/Lt Forbes Leith & 2/Lt Ritchie
1st A & S Highrs
Farm at Voormezeele 8am 18/1/15

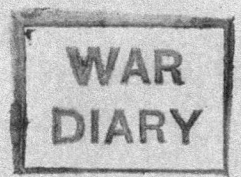

Headquarters,

81st INFANTRY BRIGADE.

(27th Division)

FEBRUARY

1 9 1 5

Attached:

Brigade Operation
Orders Nos. 33 to 41.
Messages.
Reports on Saps.
Proposal for Bde. to
take over R.Section
27th Div.
Sketches of the Mound,
St. Eloi.

Army Form C. 2118.

WAR DIARY
or
INTELLIGENCE SUMMARY
(Erase heading not required.)

Instructions regarding War Diaries and Intelligence Summaries are contained in F.S. Regs., Part II. and the Staff Manual respectively. Title pages will be prepared in manuscript.

Hour, Date, Place 1915	Summary of Events and Information	Remarks and references to Appendices
DICKEBUSCH 1st Feb.	Casualty Report :- Killed. Wounded 1. Arg. & Suth. Hdrs. Nil 10 1. R. Scots Nil Nil 2. Cam'n. Hdrs. 1 1 2. Glouc. R. Nil Nil	8th Feb
DICKEBUSCH 2. Feb.	The following reliefs took place 1. R. Scots relieved 2. Cameron. Hdrs 2. Glouc. R. " 1. Arg. & Suth. Hdrs. 2. Cam'n Hdrs. in close support at ELZENWALLE with 1 Coy. at the BRASSERIE - 1. Arg. & Suth. Hdrs. billeted at DICKEBUSCH. Casualty Report. 1. R. Scots One man wounded remainder Nil.	

Army Form C. 2118.

WAR DIARY
or
INTELLIGENCE SUMMARY

(Erase heading not required.)

Instructions regarding War Diaries and Intelligence Summaries are contained in F.S. Regs., Part II. and the Staff Manual respectively. Title pages will be prepared in manuscript.

Hour, Date, Place	Summary of Events and Information	Remarks and references to Appendices
DICKEBUSCH 3 Feb. 1915	Casualty Report. Killed Wounded. 1 R. Scots 1 2 1 Arg & Suth Hdrs Nil Nil 2. Cam'n Hdrs. Nil Nil 2. Glouc. R. Nil *7	* Includes 2 Officers. Lt L.A.W.B. Lachlan 2/Lt A.V. Blake 3.Essex R. attached 2 Glouc. R.
DICKEBUSCH 4 Feb.	A message was received from H.Q. 27th Div informing the Bde that the Germans had driven back a portion of the 28th Div and were now occupying one of their trenches on our left flank — Under these circumstances the usual relief of the trenches held by the Bde was cancelled the 2/Cam'n Hdrs and 1 Arg & Suth Hdrs remaining in close support — The G.O.C. 81st Inf. Bde left DICKEBUSCH at 9 p.m. and transferred his Hd. Qrs. to the BRASSERIE Early on the morning of the 5th Feb. all being reported quiet the relief took place	

Army Form C. 2118.

WAR DIARY
or
INTELLIGENCE SUMMARY
(Erase heading not required.)

Hour, Date, Place	Summary of Events and Information	Remarks and references to Appendices
DICKEBUSCH 5 Feb. 1915	as under. 2 Cameron Hdrs relieved 1 R. Scots 1 Arg. & Suth. Hdrs " 2. Glouc. R. 2. Glouc. R. remained in close support at ELZONWALLE with one Coy. at the BRASSERIE. The 1. R. Scots received the order to march to DICKEBUSCH at 3 a.m. where they remained in billets. Casualty Report of 4 Feb. Killed Wounded 2 Glouc. R. 2 6 Hd. Qrs and remaining Bns. casualties Nil	81 of Bde

Army Form C. 2118.

WAR DIARY
or
INTELLIGENCE SUMMARY

(Erase heading not required.)

Instructions regarding War Diaries and Intelligence Summaries are contained in F. S. Regs., Part II. and the Staff Manual respectively. Title pages will be prepared in manuscript.

Hour, Date, Place	Summary of Events and Information	Remarks and references to Appendices
1915		
DICKEBUSCH Feb 5	Casualty Report Killed Missing Wounded 2 Cam'n Hdrs. 1 Nil Nil 1 Arg. & Sutt. Hdrs. 2 Nil 1	* ~~illegible~~ RG. * ~~illegible~~ RG.
DICKEBUSCH Feb 6.	Telephone operators warned that any delay in transmitting urgent messages owing to operators being asleep or having temporarily left their instruments renders them liable to trial by Court-martial. 1 R Scots relieved 2 Cam'n Hdrs 2 Glouc " 1 Arg & Sutt Hdrs.	81st Bde

WAR DIARY
or
INTELLIGENCE SUMMARY

(Erase heading not required.)

Army Form C. 2118.

Hour, Date, Place 1915	Summary of Events and Information	Remarks and references to Appendices
DICKEBUSCH Feb 7	Casualty Report. Killed Wounded 2 Glouc R 1 6 2 Cam'n Hdrs 1 1 1 Argylls Nil Nil 1 R Scots 2 Nil	
DICKEBUSCH Feb 8	2 Cam'n Highlanders relieved the 1st R. Scots in the trenches — 1 Arg & Suth Hdrs. relieved the 2 Glouc. R. in the trenches —	Sp Bde
DICKEBUSCH Feb 9	Hostile Aeroplanes dropped bombs into a field close to the Gloucester Transport lines but did no damage —	
DICKEBUSCH Feb 10	The Bde was relieved in the front line by the 80th Infy Bde as follows: The K.S.L.I. relieved 1/ Arg & Suth Hdrs 4th K.R.R.C. " 2/ Cameron Hdrs 3rd K.R.R.C. " 1 R. Scots at ELSENWALLE and VIERSTRAAT	

Army Form C. 2118.

WAR DIARY
or
INTELLIGENCE SUMMARY
(Erase heading not required.)

Instructions regarding War Diaries and Intelligence Summaries are contained in F. S. Regs, Part II. and the Staff Manual respectively. Title pages will be prepared in manuscript.

Hour, Date, Place	Summary of Events and Information	Remarks and references to Appendices
DICKEBUSCH Feb 10 1915	The Bde moved back into the Reserve area and occupied the following billets. 2. Glouc. R — WESTOUTRE 1. R. Scots — RENINGHELST Camerons } Huts at DICKEBUSCH moving Argylls } into Huts at ZEVECOTEN on the morning of the 11th.	
WESTOUTRE and RENINGHELST February 11th to 14th	The Bde remained in Reserve [the men were bathed and received a clean issue of under garments — much needed improvement of Roads and approaches to hut quarters was carried out. Also a number of wire entanglements and fascines were constructed —]	

1247 W 3299 200,000 (E) 8/14 J.B.C. & A. Forms/C. 2118/11.

WAR DIARY
or
INTELLIGENCE SUMMARY

(Erase heading not required.)

Army Form C. 2118.

Hour, Date, Place	Summary of Events and Information	Remarks and references to Appendices
WESTOUTRE 14 Feb. 1915	At 6 pm. the Bde received orders to stand by ready to move at a moments notice — The 2 Glouc R. marched to RENINGHELST where the remainder of the Bde were billeted — Hd. Qrs. moved at once to RENINGHELST — Reporting to Divl. Hd Qrs. At 7.20 pm the following message was issued — "Begins 1.R. Scots and 2 Glouc R. unless ordered to move beyond DICKEBUSCH will occupy hut shelters for the night aaa 2 Cam'n Hdrs and 1 Arg & Suth Hdrs will clear the entrance to the hut shelters and Half without entering DICKEBUSCH aaa. O.C. Bns will report to Brigadier at Hd. Qrs. DICKEBUSCH riding on ahead of their Bns." Ends — 1 R. Scots and 2 Glouc. R occupied Huts 2 Cam'n Hdrs moved up to VOORMEZEELE occupying dugouts in close support. 1 Arg & Suth Hdrs moved to the outskirts of DICKEBUSCH and occupied the Baths sending digging party to improve 2 line of Defence near KRUISSTRAATHOEK.	G.P. Poste

WAR DIARY
or
INTELLIGENCE SUMMARY

(Erase heading not required.)

Army Form C. 2118.

Hour, Date, Place	Summary of Events and Information	Remarks and references to Appendices
DICKEBUSCH 15 Feb. 1915	During the morning the Argylls and Camerons returned to billets at DICKEBUSCH. The following reliefs took place— On Night 15th/16th Argylls & Camerons relieved the 82nd Infy Bde in the trenches— 2 Glouc R in Close Support {2 Coys at KRUISSTRAATHOCK {2 " DICKEBUSCH 1 R. Scots were billeted in DICKEBUSCH. Casualty Report. Killed Wounded 2 Glouc R. Nil Nil 2 Cam'n Hdrs. 1*offr 6 1 Arg. & Suth. Hdrs. Nil 4 1 R. Scots Nil Nil	[signature] * Major Baird killed by Shrapnel passing through the village of VOORMEZEELE during the relief— Buried morning 17th at DICKEBUSCH near the church — His brother Major D. Baird H.Q. Indian Cav. Corps. was present

Army Form C. 2118.

WAR DIARY
or
INTELLIGENCE SUMMARY

(Erase heading not required.)

Hour, Date, Place	Summary of Events and Information	Remarks and references to Appendices
DICKEBUSCH 16 Feb. 1915	2 Glouc. R and 1 R. Scots went into the Trenches. 2 Cam Hdrs in close support {2 Coys KRUISSTRAATHOCK {2 Coys DICKEBUSCH in billets 1 Arg. & Suth. Hdrs. at DICKEBUSCH in billets. Casualty Report: Killed Wounded 2 Glouc. R 1 6 2 Cam'n Hdrs 2 4 1 Arg & Suth Hdrs 4 8 1 R. Scots Nil 1	

Army Form C. 2118.

WAR DIARY
or
INTELLIGENCE SUMMARY
(Erase heading not required.)

Hour, Date, Place	Summary of Events and Information	Remarks and references to Appendices
DICKEBUSCH 17 Feb 1915	Germans were reported to be concentrating. The 82nd Bde was moved up from WESTOUTRE to DICKEBUSCH — The 2 Coys of Cam'n Hdrs at DICKEBUSCH moved up to KRUISSTRAATHOEK. No attack however was made. On the morning of the 18th the 2 Coys of Cam'n Hdrs returned to DICKEBUSCH and later in the day the 82nd Bde returned to WESTOUTRE. Casualty Report Killed Wounded 2/Glos R 1 17 2/Cam'n Hdrs Nil Nil RG. 1/A&S'th Hdrs Nil Nil Y R Scots 2 (3*) 1+2	Includes Capt. A.F. Lumsden Y.R. Scots

Army Form C. 2118.

Instructions regarding War Diaries and Intelligence Summaries are contained in F.S. Regs., Part II. and the Staff Manual respectively. Title pages will be prepared in manuscript.

WAR DIARY
or
INTELLIGENCE SUMMARY
(Erase heading not required.)

Hour, Date, Place	Summary of Events and Information	Remarks and references to Appendices
DICKEBUSCH 18 Feb	The following reliefs took place :— 2 Glouc R. were relieved by 1 Arg. & Suth Hdrs. 1 R. Scots " " 2 Canin Hdrs. 2 Glouc. R. returned to Billets at DICKEBUSCH 1 Coy — " in close support at VOORMEZEELE 1 " " " " KRUISSTRAATHOEK Remainder in billets at DICKEBUSCH Casualty Report as under. Killed Wounded 2/Glouc.R. 1 8 2 Canin Hdrs. 1 6 1 Arg & Suth. Hdrs. Nil 2 1 R. Scots 3 6	McRae
DICKEBUSCH 19 Feb.	Considerable losses took place in Trench 21 - Due to the fact that this trench is enfiladed by the Germans owing to its position Reverse Fire was brought to bear on this Trench from left Rear — Traverses were constructed in rear of this trench on the Night 19th/20th.	Lieut. A. STIRLING 1/Arg. & Suth Hdrs was killed in Trench 21 on the 19th.

WAR DIARY
or
INTELLIGENCE SUMMARY

Army Form C. 2118.

Hour, Date, Place	Summary of Events and Information	Remarks and references to Appendices
DICKEBUSCH 20 Feb. 1915	The following reliefs took place – 2 Glouc. R. relieved 1 Argy. & Suth. Hdrs. 1 R. Scots " 2 Camn. Hdrs. 1 Argy. & Suth Hdrs. went into Close Support { 2 Coys DICKEBUSCH / 2 Coys KRUISSTRAATHOEK 2 Camn. Hdrs. went into Billets in DICKEBUSCH	S/Kerr
DICKEBUSCH 21 Feb.	On the night 20th/21st no casualties occurred in trench 21. The 80th Infy Bde were relieved by the 82nd Infy Bde – The 80th going into Reserve at WESTOUTRE.	

WAR DIARY
or
INTELLIGENCE SUMMARY

(Erase heading not required.)

Army Form C. 2118.

Hour, Date, Place	Summary of Events and Information	Remarks and references to Appendices
DICKEBUSCH Feb 22 1915	2 Coma Hdrs relieved the R. Scots in the Trenches — The R. Scots in so doing relieved into billets in DICKEBUSCH. The Argylls relieved the Gloucesters (who went into Close Support having 2 Coys at the CHATEAU at KRUISSTRAATHOEK and 2 Coys with Bn Hd.Qrs. in billets at DICKEBUSCH	
DICKEBUSCH Feb 23.	Capt. P.W.N. FRASER. D.S.O. Lieut. W.D. NICHOLSON were killed and Lieut. D.G. DAVIDSON wounded of the 2/Coma Hdrs. These Officers were shot by German snipers who were afterwards located and silenced by rapid fire being opened on them — Behind N°16 Trench.	

Army Form C. 2118.

WAR DIARY
or
INTELLIGENCE SUMMARY

(Erase heading not required.)

Hour, Date, Place	Summary of Events and Information	Remarks and references to Appendices
DICKEBUSCH Feb 24 1915	The following reliefs took place. Gloucesters relieved Argylls in Trenches. R. Scots " Camerons " " Camerons were billeted in DICKEBUSCH Argylls had 2 coys with Bn Hd Qrs in DICKEBUSCH and 2 coys in close support at the CHATEAU KRUISSTRAATHOEK.	

Army Form C. 2118.

WAR DIARY
or
INTELLIGENCE SUMMARY

(Erase heading not required.)

Instructions regarding War Diaries and Intelligence Summaries are contained in F. S. Regs., Part II. and the Staff Manual respectively. Title pages will be prepared in manuscript.

Hour, Date, Place	Summary of Events and Information	Remarks and references to Appendices
DICKEBUSCH Feb 1915		

WAR DIARY
or
INTELLIGENCE SUMMARY

(Erase heading not required.)

Army Form C. 2118.

Hour, Date, Place	Summary of Events and Information	Remarks and references to Appendices
DICKEBUSCH Feb 25 1915	R.E. Park ran out of sandbags which were urgently needed — 10000 sandbags arrived by motor lorry next day — The 2 Bns in the firing line often required 5,000 sandbags sent up to them per Night — Handbombs were also difficult to obtain — Rifle grenades in some parts of the line being of no use owing to the *close proximity of the enemy —	*(In some cases 20+) Spoelau
DICKEBUSCH Feb 26	The Relief tookplace as under:— Camerons relieved the R. Scots in the Trenches. Argylls " " " Gloucesters " " The R. Scots went into close support — [Owing to the Chateau at KRUISSTRAATHOEK being heavily shelled during the day accommodation was limited and that Bn was disposed as follows 2 Coys and 2 platoons at DICKEBUSCH, 1 Coy at Chateau KRUISSTRAATHOEK 1 Coy less 2 platoons VOORMEZEELE	

1247 W 3299 200,000 (E) 8/14 J.B.C.&A. Forms/C. 2118/11.

WAR DIARY
or
INTELLIGENCE SUMMARY

Army Form C. 2118.

Place	Hour, Date, 1915	Summary of Events and Information	Remarks and references to Appendices
DICKEBUSCH	Feb 26	The Gloucesters moved into Billets in DICKEBUSCH	
DICKEBUSCH	Feb 27	The Bde was relieved by the 80th Bde. On relief the Gloucesters marched to WESTOUTRE. The R.Scots in DICKEBUSCH marched to billets in RENINGHELST. Remaining Bns in front line were relieved as follows — P.P.C.L.I. relieved Argylls in Trenches 4th Rifle Bde. " Camerons " The R.Scots in CHATEAU were relieved by part of the 4th Rifle Bde. The Bns from the Trenches marched straight to huts at ZEVCOTEN and not to huts at DICKEBUSCH as had previously been the case. Only 4 men in the Argylls required assistance. This should a great improvement of the men's feet. Due to improvement of Trenches also there men had only been one night instead of two in the Trenches	SPRBe

WAR DIARY
or
INTELLIGENCE SUMMARY

(Erase heading not required.)

Army Form C. 2118.

Place	Hour, Date	Summary of Events and Information	Remarks and references to Appendices
WESTOUTRE	Feb 28 1915	Bns in Reserve Area arrangements made for bathing Bns. Construction of knife rests (wire entanglements) and the training of Bomb throwers up to 32 men per Bn. Casualties for the month of February are as follows. 2/Gloucesters. Offrs. 3 wounded O.R. 12 Killed 74 Wounded 2/Camerons. Offrs. 4 Killed 1 Wounded O.R. 14 Killed 37 Wounded 1/Argylls. Offrs. 2 Killed O.R. 17 Killed 54 Wounded 1/R.Scots Offrs. 3 wounded O.R. 32 Killed 45 Wounded TOTAL Offrs. 6 Killed 7 Wounded O.R. 75 Killed 210 Wounded	

BRIGADE OPERATION ORDERS NOS. 33 to 41.

Copy No. 1

81st INFY. BDE. ORDER No. 33.

1st Feby. 1915.

1. The 2nd Cameron Highlanders and 1st Argyll & Sutherland Highlanders will be relieved in the front line to-morrow night by the 1st Royal Scots and 2nd Gloucester Regt. respectively.

2. The 1st Royal Scots will be clear of the BRASSERIE by 5-45 p.m. and will otherwise arrange the relief with O.C. 2nd Cameron Highlanders.

The 2nd Gloucester Regt. will march by the Cross Roads 500 yds. W. of the BRASSERIE and the head of the leading company is not to reach the BRASSERIE before 5-50 p.m.

3. The 2nd Cameron Highlanders will proceed to ELZENWALLE with one company at the BRASSERIE, and be in close support.

The 1st Argyll & Sutherland Highrs. will be billeted in DICKEBUSCH.

Moon rises 7-59 p.m. 2nd Feb. Sets 8-29 a.m. 3rd Feby.
"   "   9-22 p.m. 3rd "   "   8-42 a.m. 4th   "

J. Howard, Captain,
Bde. Major 81st Inf. Bde.

Copy No. 1

81st INFY BDE. ORDER No. 34.

3rd Feb. 1915.

1. The 80th Infy. Bde. will take over the new bit of line E. of ST. ELOI to-night.

2. The 2nd Cameron Highlanders and 1st A. & S. Highrs. will relieve the 1st Royal Scots and 2nd Gloucester Regt. respectively in the front line to-morrow evening.

The 2nd Camerons will be clear of the BRASSERIE by 5-50 p.m. and otherwise will arrange the relief with O.C. 1st Royal Scots.

The 1st A. & S. Highrs. will march by the Cross Roads 500 yards W. of the BRASSERIE, the leading company to reach these Cross Roads at 6 p.m.

3. The 2nd Gloucester Regt. will proceed to ELZONWALLE with 1 Company at the BRASSERIE and be in close support. The 1st Royal Scots will be billeted in DICKEBUSCH.

4. Transport has been arranged with the Transport Officers.

5. With regard to the orders already issued that men are to take cover when German Aeroplanes are sighted, Officers Commanding Battns. acting independently will make their own arrangements to ensure that the signal is given and must take steps to have the order enforced.

6. On no account are any trees to be cut down in the wood where shelters have been built in rear of DICKEBUSCH.

7. The Medical Officer of the Battalion in close support will be in charge of the Regimental Aid Post at the BRASSERIE.

_____ Captain,

Bde. Major 81st Infy. Bde.

AMENDMENT TO BRIGADE ORDER NO. 34 of
3rd Feb. 1915.

Brigade Order No. 34 of to-day will be amended as follows to avoid congestion at the BRASSERIE.

The 1st Argyll & Sutherland Highrs. will leave DICKEBUSCH between 5 p.m. and 5-45 p.m.

The 2nd Camerons will not pass the BRASSERIE Cross Roads till 6-50 p.m. and will ascertain that the 1st Argyll & Sutherland Highrs. have cleared the Cross Roads before the leave the BRASSERIE.

The O.C. 1st A. & S. Highrs. will arrange for an officer to report to an Officer 2nd Cameron Highrs. at the BRASSERIE when that point is clear.

                                               Captain,
                                      Bde. Major 81st Infy. Bde.

Copy No. 1

81st INFY. BDE. ORDER No. 35

5th Feb. 1915.

1.   It is notified for information that the 82nd Infantry Brigade will take over the 3 left trenches of B. Section now held by the 1st A. & S. Highlanders _tomorrow night 6th/7th_ and these are now allotted to the left section.

To-morrow evening the 28th Division retake _part of_ over the trenches taken over from them East of ST. ELOI.

On the night 7th/8th the 3rd Division will take over 500 yards of our trenches on the right of A Section.

2.   Several cases have occurred of delays in transmitting urgent messages through telephone operators being asleep or having temporarily left their instruments. All concerned should be warned that this renders them liable to trial by Court-martial.

3.   Water carts, on returning from supplying battalions in front line or in close support will be filled before returning to their transport lines.

Moon rises Midnight 5th/6th.   Sets 9-8 a.m. 6th.
  "   "   12-12 a.m. 6th/7th   " 9-25 a.m. 7th.

The relief will be carried out tomorrow in accordance with the published programme & the hours of commencing will be notified later.

J. Howard, Captain,
Bde. Major 81st Inf. Bde.

Copy No 1

81st INFY. BDE. ORDER No. 36.

5th Feb. 1915.

RELIEF.

1. The 1st Royal Scots will leave DICKEBUSCH at 5-15 p.m to-morrow to relieve the 2nd Cameron Highlanders. The relief of the 1st Argyll & Sutherland Highlanders by 2nd Gloucester Regt. will be arranged between the Officers Commanding the Battalions concerned.

2. The rations for the 2nd Gloucester Regt. will arrive at BLAONWALLE at 5-45 p.m.

3. Unless further orders are issued the 1st Royal Scots and 2nd Gloucester Regt. will take over the line as held at present by the 2nd Cameron Highrs. and 1st A. & S. Highrs.

On the night of the 7th/8th Feb. the 3rd Division will take over trenches A. 1, 2 and 3 and the support trenches immediately behind them from the 1st Rl. Scots, and the 1st Rl. Scots will be prepared to take over trenches B. 1, 2 and 3 and part of the support trench immediately behind them but definite orders will be issued later.

[signature] Captain,
Bde. Major 81st Infy. Bde.

Copy No. 1

81st INFY. BDE. ORDER No. 38.

7th Feb. 1915.

1.   The 2/Cameron Highlanders will leave DICKEBUSCH at 5-15 p.m. to-morrow to relieve the 1st Rl. Scots in trenches.

The relief of the 2nd Gloucester Regt by the 1st A. & S. Highlanders will be arranged between the Officers Commdg. the battalions concerned.

2.   The rations for the 1st A. & S. Highlanders will leave DICKEBUSCH at 5 p.m.

3.   Attention is drawn to the 1/10,000 map, "VOORMEZEELE" issued to-night showing the new numbering of the trenches which will be adhered to in all reports.

The trench reports issued with these orders will be made out as accurately as possible. Those of the 1st 2nd Cameron Highlanders and 1st A. & S. Highlanders will be sent in before dawn on the 10th inst. and will form a record of stores, ammunition &c. to be handed over to the 80th Infy. Brigade on the evening of the 10th.

    Moon rises 7th/8th 1-41 a.m. Sets 9-49 a.m. on 8th.
    "   "   8th/9th 3-9 a.m.   " 10-11 a.m. on 9th.

                                            Captain,
                               Bde. Major 81st Infy. Bde.

Copy No. 1

81st INFY. BDE. ORDER No. 37.

1. The arrangements for handing over trenches A. 1, 2 and 3 to the 4th Middlesex Regt., 8th Brigade to-morrow night will be made by the O.C. 1st Rl. Scots and 4th Middlesex Regt.

Boxes S.A.A., braziers, tools and bailers in the trenches will be handed over on receipt and a copy forwarded to Brigade Headquarters. Grenades, "Very" pistols, pumps and machine gun ammunition will be withdrawn for use as required.

Nothing at Battalion Headquarters will be handed over.

2. The arrangements for handing over trenches B. 1, 2 and 3 to the 1st Rl. Scots to-morrow evening will be made between the O.C. 1st Rl. Scots and 2nd Gloucester Regt. but the two reliefs will not be carried out simultaneously. O.C. 2nd Gloucesters will inform O.C. 1st Rl. Scots to-night what S.A.A. and stores are in the trenches to be handed over.

3. Battn. H.Q. 1st Rl. Scots and regiments which may relieve them will be established at the BRASSERIE from to-morrow evening inclusive, a report to be furnished to this office and to Artillery at VIERSTRAAT when the change is made.

4. Battn. H.Q. 2nd Gloucester Regt. and Regiments which relieve them will be established at the FARM 500 yards W. of FARM DU CONFLUANT, N. 6 b. 5.4 after the relief of the 1/A. & S.H. is complete to-night, a report being furnished to this office when the new Hd. Qrs. is established.

This farm will be known as NEW FARM.

5. With reference to instructions previously issued, in case orders are issued to take up the 2nd line of defence the point of junction of two battalions holding our portion of the line would now be about 300 yards N.E. of the Cross Roads 500 yards W. of the BRASSERIE, i.e. Square N.5 b. 7.6.

Captain,
Bde. Major 81st Infy. Bde.

Copy No. 1

81st INFY. BDE. ORDER No. 39.

9th Feb. 1915.

1.   The Brigade will be relieved in front line to-morrow by the 80th Infantry Brigade.
       The K.S.L.I. will relieve the 1st A. & S. Highlanders and will reach the Cross Roads 500 yards N.W. of VIERSTRAAT at 5-45 p.m.
       The 4th K.R.R.C. will relieve the 2nd Cameron Highlanders following the K.S.L.I.
       The 3rd K.R.R.C. will relieve the 1st Rl. Scots at ELZENWALLE and the ~~BRASSERIE~~ VIERSTRAAT
       This battalion leaves LA CLYTTE Cross Roads at 5-20 p.m.

2.   The transport of the corresponding battalions of the 80th Infantry Brigade will bring back machine guns, tools &c of corresponding regiments, the amount of transport required being arranged between the transport officers.

3.   Billets to-morrow night:-
       2nd Gloucester Regt.   WESTOUTRE.
       1st Royal Scots.   RENINGHELST.
       2nd Cameron Highlanders.)
       1st A. & S. Highrs.   ) Huts at ~~SEVECOTEN~~ DICKEBUSCH.

4.   The road between the Cross Roads 500 yards N.W. of VIERSTRAAT - DICKEBUSCH are to be kept clear of transport for Royal Artillery relief to-morrow night between 8 and 8-30 p.m. and from DICKEBUSCH to HALLEBLAST Corner between 8-15 and 8-45 p.m.

5.   Particular care is requested in handing over ammunition and stores to the relieving brigade especially as regards S.A.A. tools and "Very Pistols".
       A separate report is to be rendered as to the number of hand and rifle grenades and bombs with detonators.

6.   Commanding officers are to ensure that proper cover is provided for the telephones in the trenches. A roofed in shelter is desirable but in any case the instruments must be kept in a dry box.

                                                               Captain,
                                        Bde. Major 81st Infy. Brigade.

Copy No. 1

81st INFY. BDE. ORDER No. 40.

14th February, 1915.

1. The Brigade will relieve the 82nd Infy. Brigade in the front line in the Left Section on the evening of the 16th inst.

2. The 1st Rl. Scots and 2nd Gloucesters will march to-morrow to the Hut Shelters, DICKEBUSCH, via ZEVECOTEN Road Junction, Square G. 29 d. - Cross Roads Junction of Squares G.36 d. and H. 31 c. and Road Junction H. 31 b.
   The 1st Royal Scots will leave Road Junction at Z of ZEVECOTEN at 4 p.m.
   The 2nd Gloucesters will pass the Road Junction at the 2nd E of WESTOUTRE at 3-30 p.m. All transport will accompany these Battalions.

3. The 2nd Cameron Highrs. and 1st A. & S. Highrs. will march under Lt. Col. Campbell, 2nd Cameron Hrs. to DICKEBUSCH on Tuesday the 16th inst via Cross Roads M.17 - LA CLYTTE to DICKEBUSCH, the head of the Column to pass La CLYTTE at 5-30 p.m.

4. On the 16th inst. baggage wagons of all battalions will move to positions close to those at present occupied by the 82nd Infantry Brigade, the 1st Rl. Scots and 2nd Glosters moving direct to Hut Shelters. The remainder under the Transport Officer No. 97 Co. A.S.C. will clear WESTOUTRE by 9-30 a.m. and march by Cross Roads M. 17 - LA CLYTTE after passing which point they will march at an interval of 200 yards between the transport of each Battn.

5. Officers of the 1st Royal Scots and 2nd Gloucesters will proceed to DICKEBUSCH to-morrow and go into the trenches which their battalions will take over the following night.

6. Billeting parties of the 1st Rl. Scots and 2nd Glosters will proceed to the HUT SHELTERS at 2 p.m. to-morrow 15th inst. and those of the 2nd Camerons and 1st A. & S. Highrs. will report to a representative Bde. H.Q. at DICKEBUSCH at 12 noon on the 16th inst.

J Kreema
Captain,
Bde. Major 81st Infy. Bde.

Copy No.

81st INFY. BDE. ORDER No. 41

26th Feb. 1915.

1. The Brigade will be relieved to-morrow by the 80th Infantry Brigade and march to the Reserve Area.

P.P.C.L.I. will relieve the 1st A. & S. Highrs. leaving DICKEBUSCH at 5-45 p.m.

The 4th Rifle Brigade will relieve the 2nd Cameron Highlanders leaving DICKEBUSCH at 7-15 p.m.

The 1st Royal Scots will be relieved at the CHATEAU by part of the 4th Rifle Brigade.

2. Battalions will occupy the same billets or huts in the Reserve Area as last time.

The 1st Rl. Scots in DICKEBUSCH and 2nd Gloucester Regt. will form up, Gloucesters leading, on the HALLEBAST - OUDERDOM Road, the tail of the Royal Scots clear of HALLEBAST CORNER at 6-10 p.m. ready to march off when the 80th Brigade reach HALLEBAST Cross Roads.

1st Line Transport of both Regiments will be in front of the 2nd Gloucester Regt.

The remainder of the Brigade will march independently on relief.

All baggage wagons, except those required by battalions in the trenches, will march under the Transport Officer, 2nd Gloucester Regiment, at 12-30 p.m.

(3) Route to be followed by battalions and transport - HALLEBAST CORNER - Road Junction H. 31 b. - Cross Rd. at Junction of Squares H.31 c. and G. 36 d. - Road Junction G. 29 d.

Captain,
Bde. Major 81st Infy. Bde.

"C" Form (Duplicate).
MESSAGES AND SIGNALS.
Army Form C. 2123.
No. of Message

PB 228 56
7 BG
w p Pat

Service Instructions: **7 BY Priority**

Handed in at the _____ Office, at 4-22 m. Received here at 4 9 m.

TO: 81st Inf Bde

Sender's Number.	Day of Month.	In reply to Number.	AAA
X 1	14		

Stand by ready to move aaa Should your Brigade have to move towards Dickebusch units will march via Zevecoten road junction square G 29 D cross roads junction of squares G 36 B and H 31 C and road junction H 31 B aaa units Hallte of Zevecoten and Reninghelst inform me aaa acknowledge

FROM: 29th Divn
PLACE:
TIME: 4-20 pm

"B" Form.   Army Form C 2123

MESSAGES AND SIGNALS.

TO 80 Infantry Bde
    81 Infantry Bde

Sender's Number: G273   Day of Month: Fourteenth   AAA

Following message from fifth corps begins G554 fourteenth aaa Information just received from General DUBOIS commanding French ninth corps that two alsations who came today to french lines being cross — examined separately both state that enemy intends to deliver a general attack on fifteenth or sixteenth ends aaa addressed all Inf Bdes and R A

From: Twentyseventh Division 9. pm
Rec'd 9.30 pm

799R

(1390) Wt. W 9044-1194. 12/14. 40,000 Pads. S. B. Ltd.
"B" Form.   Army Form C 2122

MESSAGES AND SIGNALS.   No. of Message _____

Prefix XB	Code MGS m.	Received At 12.17 m. From Copied By M	Sent At 966 m. To _____ By _____	Office Stamp.
Office of Origin and Service Instructions. D/H Pmdy	Words.			

TO { 81st Infy Bde

| Sender's Number GR 544 | Day of Month fourteenth | In reply to Number | AAA |

One battalion 81st Infantry Brigade ordered to march at once to Voormezeele there to report to you aaa One battalion to move to and halt on road about H29 aaa You can call on me for the Voormezeele battalion to be placed at your disposal should you desire it and think the situation demands it addressed 82 Inf Bde repeated 81 Inf Bde

From 27 Div
Place
Time

* This line should be erased if not required.

"C" Form (Triplicate).   Army Form C. 2123 A.
MESSAGES AND SIGNALS.

Office Stamp: 14.11.15

Handed in at the .... Office at 9.50 ... m. Received here at 10.0 ... m.

TO   81 N Inf Bde
      DH

Sender's Number	Day of Month	In reply to Number	AAA
S127	Fourteen	—	

Your Bde must be ready to move at ~~xxx~~ a moment's notice aaa acknowledge

FROM   27 L Div
PLACE
TIME   9.55 pm

"C" Form (Duplicate).   Army Form C. 2123.
MESSAGES AND SIGNALS.   No. of Message

SR 64 L2

| Service Instructions | Charges to Pay. £ s. d. | Office Stamp. |

Handed in at the _____ Office, at _____ .m. Received here at 5·39 p.m.

TO   G O C   71st Inf Bde

| Sender's Number. | Day of Month. | In reply to Number. | AAA |
| SR 522 | 12th | | |

Move your Brigade by route ordered in my X1 to huts between Dickebusch and immediate vicinity aaa Roads are being closed aaa Issue your own orders to battalions here aaa acknowledge

FROM   24th Divn
PLACE
TIME   5.25 p m

"C" Form (Triplicate).   Army Form C. 2123 A.
MESSAGES AND SIGNALS.
No. of Message..............

| | Charges to Pay £ s. d. | Office Stamp. |

Service Instructions

Handed in at the.......... Office, at..............m. Received here at............m

TO

| Sender's Number | Day of Month, | In reply to Number. | AAA |

Fifth Corps wires
Div will tonight attack
trenches which was occupied yesterday by Germans Present
intention being to attack
nine o'ck aaa This requires
consideration by you having
regard to the fact that you are
relieving on left flank
addressed 81st
Bde

FROM   27
PLACE
TIME

"C" Form (Original).
MESSAGES AND SIGNALS.

Army Form C. 2123 A.

Prefix......Code......Words......	Received	Sent, or sent out	Office Stamp.
£ s. d. Charges to collect	From......	At......m.	
Service Instructions P note	By......	To...... By......	

Handed in at the .... Office, at ......m. Received here at ......m.

TO — 81st Inf Bde

*Sender's Number	Day of Month.	In reply to Number.	AAA
AR 55	15/5		

Although no retirement to second line is contemplated the possibility of having to place supporting troops in this line must be considered and line must be improved at once aaa 80th Inf Bde employ all men for which tools are available to improve line from right flank to where road running SE from Blangeville is crossed by line aaa 81st Bde do contrary from same road using battn now on road in H 29 b aaa Battalion 81st Inf/Bde at Hornoye not available for digging at present addressed CRE Hornoye ???? Inf Bde 81st Inf/Bde + repeated second Inf/Bde acknowledge

FROM	
PLACE	27 Division
TIME	5.20 am

* This line should be erased if not required.
GALE & POLDEN, LTD PRINTERS, ALDERSHOT.
(69,017). Wt. 7981—443. 40,000 Pads. 4/13. W.

(4711) Wt. W 3391-411. 10/12. 15,000 Pads. Wy. & S., Ltd. Sch. 18.
"B" Form.   Army Form C 2122.

MESSAGES AND SIGNALS.   No. of Message_____

Prefix____Code____m.	Received	Sent	Office Stamp
Office of Origin and Service Instructions. Words. 33	At 8.27 m. From BG By Chapman	At___m. To___ By___	

TO 81st Inf. Bde

| Sender's Number. 523 | Day of Month 15th | In reply to Number 04 | AAA |

NO VERY pistols available have have wired base for same on 9th instant and have again specially urgent their supply them tonight
(................. ....)

From	Ordnance
Place	27 Div
Time	8.25 pm

* This line should be erased if not required.

(4711) Wt. W 3391-411. 10/12. 15,000 Pads. Wy. & S., Ltd. Sch. 18.

"B" Form.

Army Form C 2122.

MESSAGES AND SIGNALS.

No. of Message_____

Prefix____ Code____ m.	Received	Sent	Office Stamp.
Office of Origin and Service Instructions. Words.	At 5 50 m.	At____ m.	
	From GK	To____	
	By____	By____	

TO   81st Bde

Sender's Number.	Day of Month	In reply to Number	A A A
1 M 5.15	15		

Col TYSON reports Trench 22
reoccupied was assault commences
on other trenches was addressed
27th Div repeated to 80th 81st
Bdes and GOC RA

From	82nd Bde		
Place			
Time	5 25 am		

* This line should be erased if not required.

"C" Form (Quadruplicate).   Army Form C. 2123 A.

MESSAGES AND SIGNALS.

No. of Message......

Charges to Pay   Office Stamp.
£   s.   d.

Service Instructions.

Handed in at the............Office, at.........m. Received here at.........m

TO   81st Bde.

Sender's Number	Day of Month.	In reply to Number.	AAA
SR 955		AAA	

FROM   82nd Brigade

PLACE   5.45 am

TIME

"C" Form (Quadruplicate). Army Form C. 2123 A.
MESSAGES AND SIGNALS. No. of Message

27

Charges to Pay Office Stamp.
£ s. d.

Service Instructions. Priority

Handed in at the ...... Office, at 6.5 a.m. Received here at 7.50 a.m.

TO 21st Bde

Sender's Number Day of Month. In reply to Number. AAA
BM519 15 —

All trescoles now reoccupied AAA Very grateful to RA for tremendous help

FROM 82nd Bde
PLACE
TIME 7.55am

(1390) Wt. W 9044-1194. 12/14. 40,000 Pads. S. B. Ltd.

"B" Form. Army Form C 2122

MESSAGES AND SIGNALS.

No. of Message

Prefix SM Code m.	Received	Sent	Office Stamp.
Office of Origin and Service Instructions. / Words.	At m.	At m.	ARMY D - 15.11.15 - TELEGRAPHS
	From	To	
	By	By	

TO: G O C 51st Inf Bde

* Sender's Number	Day of Month	In reply to Number	AAA
G K 575	Fifteenth	G B 676	

Send at least [illegible]
men for duty as [illegible]
[illegible] here this evening
[illegible] O C [illegible] to report to
O C 81 Infy Bde

[illegible]

From [illegible] Div

Place

Time

* This line should be erased if not required.

(4711) Wt. W 3391-411. 10/12. 15,000 Pads. WY. & S., LTD. Sch. 13.
"B" Form.
MESSAGES AND SIGNALS.
Army Form C 2122.

No. of Message _____

Prefix SB Code AB m.
Office of Origin and Service Instructions. Words.
MBS
Priority 74

Received At 8.43 p.m.
From YBG
By Chapman

Sent At ____ m.
To ____
By ____

Office Stamp.

TO 81st Inf Bde

Sender's Number: 9282
Day of Month: Fifteenth
In reply to Number:
AAA

Reference previous reports from French sources that prisoners had stated that enemy intended to attack fifteenth or sixteenth aaa Prisoners taken by French ninth corps yesterday also make this statement aaa Strong patrols today about five pm in MENIN Road reported by French Officer said by him to afford further corroboration of prisoners information addressed to 80 81 and 82 Inf Bdes and GOC RA.

Summary 9.30 pm

From: 27 Divn
Place:
Time: 8.15 pm

*This line should be erased if not required.

"B" Form.   Army Form C 2122

MESSAGES AND SIGNALS.

Prefix	Code	Received At	Sent At	Office Stamp
Office of Origin	Words 60	From	To	

TO — B. 2. 51 Bde

Sender's Number	Day of Month	In reply to Number	AAA
CHR 51	15		

At 9.10 owing to heavy firing relief was stopped aaa at 9.25 S.O.S. left off & on St Eloy was sent and 8 gunfire being opened rapidly later enemy's fire diminished aaa situation in trenches quiet to my front and flanks have asked artillery to keep firing

From: C.O. 4th Camerons
Time: 9.35 pm

* This line should be erased if not required.

"C" Form (Duplicate).   Army Form C. 2123.
MESSAGES AND SIGNALS.   No. of Message..........

Charges to Pay. | Office Stamp.
£   s.   d.

Service Instructions.

Handed in at............ Office............ m. Received............ m.

TO _F 29 80 Inf Bde_

Sender's Number | Day of Month | In reply to Number | AAA

Following received from fifth
corps begins AT75 Seventeenth
AAA your reserve brigade should
move to DICKEBUSCH at once
if not already ordered there
AAA report what troops you
have in hand and how situated
AAA trenches have been occupied
by enemy in O three B and
T 9 twentynine AAA general
activity apparent along whole
front Second army has been
asked to order a brigade from
BAILLEUL to DICKEBUSCH AAA
ends acknowledge

ack'd BM 829

FROM PLACE & TIME _Twentyseventh Division 11·20 am_

"C" Form (Quadruplicate). Army Form C. 2123 A.

MESSAGES AND SIGNALS.

Sender's Number	Day of Month.	In reply to Number.	
JR 632	15	BM 817	AAA

It is hoped that this extension of the time is only temporary and and must not be considered by G.H. the 28th Div.

FROM: 27 Div
PLACE:
TIME: 3.45 p.m.

"C" Form (Duplicate).

Army Form C. 2123.

MESSAGES AND SIGNALS.

No. of Message

[illegible] 1037 R6

Charges to Pay. £ s. d.

Office Stamp. 18 II 16 [illegible] TELEGRAPHS

Service Instructions.

Handed in at [illegible] Office [illegible] m. Received [illegible] m.

TO [illegible]

Sender's Number	Day of Month	In reply to Number	AAA
[illegible]	16	[illegible] 627	

Gun having been recently numbered
twenty three and known as
[illegible] by 28 Divn and
[illegible]
do [illegible]
[illegible] by enemy
[illegible]

ackd BM 861 [illegible]

Replied BM 862 [illegible]

FROM
PLACE & TIME [illegible] 3 pm

Wt. W.9668—1672. 50,000 Pads. 1584—1/15. S. B. Ltd.—Forms/C.2123.

"C" Form (Duplicate).
MESSAGES AND SIGNALS.

Army Form C. 2123.

No. of Message

R of 181

Charges to Pay. £ s. d.

Office Stamp.

Service Instructions. Priority

Handed in at _____ Office 6.30 p.m. Received _____ m.

TO 81st Inf Bde

Sender's Number: R 627   Day of Month: 18th   In reply to Number: AAA

Following from fifth Corps 4.30 pm begins No 655 eighteen owing to the depleted state of the battns of the twenty eight Divn I want you to take over from them tonight trench M which is next to twenty two on your map is held by one company aaa the brigade holding the trench now is the eighty fourth brigade and the units the NORTHUMBERLAND FUSILIERS ends aaa Get into communication at once with 8th Inf Bde and arrange detail and time of relief aaa

FROM
PLACE & TIME

"C" Form (Duplicate).
MESSAGES AND SIGNALS.

Army Form C. 2123.

TO: 141 Bde Bn ?

Sender's Number: GK 627

Officers and [NCOs?] sundesmen?
to forward early after dark
and come back to lead
relief aaa try and find
out state trenches now
with a view to improvement
the depression one company
is ___ a wide term. find
out length of trench aaa
800 80 Bde and some
units of this brigade know
this trench and can help
you with advice aaa when
arranged let me know how
dispositions of your troops may
be altered as result of this
extension aaa inform OC RE

pTO

"B" Form.
MESSAGES AND SIGNALS. Army Form C 2122.

Prefix Sm	Code MHP m.	Received	Sent	Office Stamp.
Office of Origin and Service Instructions.	Words.	At 12.47 p.m.	At _____ m.	
EK	40	From EK	To	
		By Powse	By	

TO 81st Bde

Sender's Number: 395 ASH
Day of Month: 19TH
In reply to Number:
AAA

reconnaisance carried out by Capt Porteous last night against paralell in front of trench 21 established in his opinion at the paralell was held strongly on enemys left and apparently not at all on right aaa Capt Porteous thinks an attack might be carried out successfully but he must see ground by daylight from trench 21 before making definite statement

From: O C ASH
Place:
Time: 12.35 PM

"B" Form.
MESSAGES AND SIGNALS. Army Form C 2122.

23.2-15

Prefix: Pm Code: CP
Office of Origin and Service Instructions Words: 48
Received At 3·15 a.m. From SP By W B Pat
Office Stamp: D — 23.11.15 — ARMY TELEGRAPHS

TO: B. M. 81 Bde

Sender's Number: 6AX94 Day of Month: 23rd   AAA

All quiet aaa By sudden burst fire small party of enemy killed Capt Fraser Lieut Nicolson and one man and wounded Lieut Davidson and two men aaa Fog still very thick suggest no use Brigadier coming out

From: Comdg Camerons
Place: 2·50 am
Time:

(300) W. W 9044-1194. 12/14. 40,000 Pads. S. B. Ltd.
"B" Form. Army Form C 2122

MESSAGES AND SIGNALS.

No. of Message _____

Prefix CM	Code 26 m.	Received	Sent	Office Stamp.
Office of Origin and Service Instructions. DA	Words. 25	At 10·25 a.m. From 7?9 By horse	At ___ m. To ___ By ___	28.11.15 TELEGRAPHS

TO { 81st Bde

| * Sender's Number CM 13 | Day of Month 28. | In reply to Number | AAA |

report German trench captured eleven Germans killed five or six wounded one prisoner about 30 yards of parapet demolished aaa Party successfully withdrawn casualties about twenty

From 80th Bde
Place 10·10
Time

* This line should be erased if not required.

Reports on Saps

"C" Form (Duplicate).
MESSAGES AND SIGNALS.   Army Form C. 2123.

Handed in at EK   Office 10 53 m.   Received 11 0 m.

TO 81st Bde.

Sender's Number	Day of Month	In reply to Number	
429 40H	23	BM 905	AAA

No work was heard in German Parallels last night and no bomb throwing by either side

FROM PLACE & TIME   O.C. 1/1H.   10.50 a.m.

MESSAGES AND SIGNALS.

Prefix S.M.	Code F.7 a.m.	Received At 6.38 a.m. From SL By SC	Sent At m. To By	Office Stamp.
Office of Origin and Service Instructions. S.L.	Words 58			

TO: BM 81st Bde

Sender's Number.	Day of Month	In reply to Number	AAA
GHX 111	24th		

Daily	report	all	quiet	enemy
reported	sap	in	front	of
15	bailing	only	sap	has
not	progressed	aaa	Report	later
about	17	and	18	aaa
Good	progress	made	on	new
14	which	will	be	held
with	10	men	today	old
13	and	14	being	unoccupied

From: Comdg Camerons
Place:
Time: 6 am

* This line should be erased if not required.

MESSAGES AND SIGNALS.

Prefix **SM** Code **?W**

Office of Origin and Service Instructions: **EK** Words: **28**

Received At **4·10 P**m. From **12K** By **YC**

TO **81st Infy Bde**

Sender's Number: **437 ASH** Day of Month: **24**

AAA

sounds of work heard in enemys parallell oposite left centre trench 21 during night aaa otherwise quiet

From: **O C A.S.H**
Place / Time: **6·45 PM**

* This line should be erased if not required.

"C" Form (Original).
MESSAGES AND SIGNALS.
Army Form C. 2123.

No. .... Message ....

Prefix...... Code...... Words......	Received	Sent, or sent out	Office Stamp.
£ s. d.	From................	At..............m.	
Charges to collect	By................	To................	
Service Instructions.		By................	

Handed in at................Office............m. Received............m.

TO

*Sender's Number	Day of Month	In reply to Number	**A A A**

[Hand-drawn sketch map labelled "St ELOI" showing roads, a sap, "Sap 18", "Trench", "A", "Ground 14.a", "Proposed Work", with annotations including "white over but field too light for use in moon … this was very bad" and "Sniping from Sap which forms gap in hedge through which officer was shot – behind left side of it. Sniping was stopped for remainder of night by bursts of rapid."]

FROM

PLACE & TIME

* This line should be erased if not required.

Service Instructions.			
Handed in at _____ Office _____ m. Received _____ m.			
TO	Brigade Major 81 Bde		
Sender's Number	Day of Month	In reply to Number	
C.H. 180	24th		AAA

The attached is sketch obtained from Officer i/c 17 yesterday and NCO i/c XXX 18 is enfiladed from AA – 16 is enfiladed from saphead. The Officer i/c 17 reports considers that proposed work in turning back left flank of 16 to meet 17 will be quite effective. He considers it will render gun set untenable. The work was in progress last night and about half has been completed. It is hoped that work can be continued tomorrow. Your letter with report by Capt Robertson R Scots has been passed to Capt Ramsay now in the Manor to see and consider.

John Campbey Lt

FROM PLACE & TIME	6 a.m.

W.2884—583. 30,000 Pads—8/14. S. B. Ltd.—Forms/C.2123.

"B" Form.
MESSAGES AND SIGNALS.

Prefix	Code	Received	Sent	Office Stamp.
Office of Origin and Service Instructions.	Words. 41	At 4.73 p.m. From By W B Pat	At ... m. To By	

TO: B. M. 81 Bde

Sender's Number.	Day of Month	In reply to Number	
C H 109	24th		AAA

Evening report except for heavy shelling ours and enemy to our left all quiet aaa My trench report some work observed enemy's parallel this morning 15 trench reports nothing observed

From: ComdG Camerons
Place:
Time: 6.45 p.m.

* This line should be erased if not required.

Relief	complete	3	Camellia	Coming
our	of	S7	wounded	to to
officer	in	new	is	repose
...p	Sup	trenches	made	towards
...	space	victim	old	13
...	14	it	to	Command
from	New	13	and	a
German	was	shot	in	it
today	—	to	work	was
...to	there	except	daily	

Sender's Number: CH K 123
Day of Month: 24

Report on Trench No. 21

24.2.15

While occupying this trench
I heard the enemy working
practically continuously all day of
the 23rd in the parallel out
from their sap. In the morning
there was a little shovelling, but
on the whole, the work seemed
to take the form of hammering
in wooden posts. The parallel
appears to extend nearly the

whole length of this trench
& to be about 15 yds. distant.
There was no attempt on the
part of the enemy to throw
bombs, while I was in occupation.
The enemy devote great attention
to destroying by rifle fire the
top layer of sand bags on our
parapets, which requires repair
every night. No work is
possible by day.
N.B. Reliefs should be carried out

that the usual entrance to
the trench at its centre is
very dangerous. The entrance on
the extreme left is much safer.

E.W. Grant 2/Lt
A.S.N
24.2.18

"B" Form.
MESSAGES AND SIGNALS.

Prefix SM Code EDh	Received At 5.53 p.m. From SL By WBPt	Sent At ___ p.m. To ___ By ___	No. of Message ___ Office Stamp 25.11.15
Office of Origin and Service Instructions. SL	Words. 73		

TO H Qrs 81st Brigade

Sender's Number. *RS264	Day of Month 25th	In reply to Number	AAA

Periscopic observation from mound detects no sign of saps or parallels in front of 18 and 19 trenches aaa Sap opposite left of 17 being worked this morning Sapper exposed himself and was shot aaa work on sap stopped aaa Convent shelled for some time this morning aaa at least five Shells appeared to hit the building aaa Quiet day otherwise

From	6.6 R Scots
Place	
Time	5.25 pm

* This line should be erased if not required.

"C" Form (Duplicate).
MESSAGES AND SIGNALS.
Army Form C. 2123.

MH 47

TO Bn 8th Bde

Sender's Number: G.313
Day of Month: 26th

OC 21 trench reports having found sap opposite Sap in 21 trench aaa saphead about 10 yards from our lines aaa He asked for bomb throwers to deal with party now working there sent

FROM: 2. Glouc. R.
PLACE & TIME: 8 pm

"C" Form (Duplicate).
MESSAGES AND SIGNALS.

SM GTP 41 EK Kennedy

Service Instructions. EK

Handed in at _____ Office _____ m. Received 4:50 p.m.

TO 81st Bde

Sender's Number	Day of Month	In reply to Number		AAA
480 ASH	26TH			

Royal Scots report from 19 trench that enemy have sapped up to within 20 yds of 19 trench aaa will you please send at least 500 more sandbags to KRUISSTRAATHOEK urgently required for machine gun emplacement

FROM   O C ASH
PLACE & TIME   4·45 PM

"C" Form (Duplicate).
MESSAGES AND SIGNALS.

Army Form C. 2123

Office Stamp: D — 26.11.15.

TO — BM 51st Inf Bde

Sender's Number	Day of Month	In reply to Number	AAA
GR 52	26th		

Following received from OC 2% Bn. enemy can be seen throwing up large quantities of dry earth at a point 262 bearing from me and about 50 or 90 yards to my right rear. This appears to be 50 yards clear of any occupied portion of 2% trench and is probably invisible to them as it is very close outside the parapet dividing & connecting 20 and detached post. This same obstacle prevents me seeing whether earth comes from sap or parallel, but will try to find out after dusk. I should like to hear any other information you may have about this.

FROM OC Gloucester R.
PLACE & TIME 1.30 pm

"C" Form (Duplicate). Army Form C. 2123
MESSAGES AND SIGNALS. No. of Message

2 m m H 56 SL
w B Pat

Service Instructions. S L

Handed in at .... Office .... m. Received 12.48 m.

TO   H Qrs 81st Inf Bde

Sender's Number | Day of Month | In reply to Number | AAA
R S 272 | 26 | |

Enemy very busy at saps
in front of trenches 14
and 15 aaa Saps run
forward from five very conspicuous
trees two of which are
broken in Square C 8 a
aaa Have asked 95th Battery
R F A to assist us

FROM   C C Royal Scots
PLACE & TIME   12.30 p m

"C" Form (Original).
MESSAGES AND SIGNALS.
Army Form C. 2123.

Prefix	Code	Words	Received	Sent, or sent out	Office Stamp.
			From	At 27.11.15	
Charges to collect			By	To	
Service Instructions				By	

Handed in at .... Office ....m. Received 5.37 p.m.

TO — 21st Bde

*Sender's Number	Day of Month	In reply to Number	AAA
461 A54	24th		

No work observed opposite 19
trench during day AAA Captain
Strong reports enemy observed
working at end of old
parallel opposite left of 21 trench
at a point estimated 15 yards
in front of 21 trench and at
least 30 yards beyond left point of
21 which we occupy

FROM
PLACE & TIME

"C" Form (Duplicate).
MESSAGES AND SIGNALS.

Army Form C. 2123.
No. of Message

SM ?? S3   EK Kennedy

Charges to Pay £ s. d.

Office Stamp: ARMY TELEGRAPHS 22.11.15

Service Instructions. E K

Handed in at .... Office .... m. Received 1.30 p.m.

TO 81st SDE

Sender's Number: 459 ASH
Day of Month: 24th
In reply to Number:
AAA

Trench number 19 reports all quiet and no work being done in sap since it was bombed last night

For OPCI
Please return
Thomas ??
KM

FROM PLACE & TIME: OC ASH   1.10 PM

Wt. W.9668—1672. 50,000 Pads. 1584—1/15. S. B. Ltd.—Forms/C.2123.

Reference attached map. The General wished to know
a few particulars re as to a distance apart of certain places.

Trench ends 30ˣ E of the road & is entered only by an unusable
ditch. A good but wet communication trench runs from the
right hand point of trench to the mound & letter the road the left of it.

In rear of 19 & 19a (100ˣ by careful pacing) is a hedge behind
which R.E. are making parapets. This hedge turns forwards
at the/its left corner & meets the hedge which has 2ⁿᵈ
support of 19 & 19a at the left corner of the latter.

The mound is about 50ˣ to rear of 19 (as far as one can judge of
it when entered to the road)

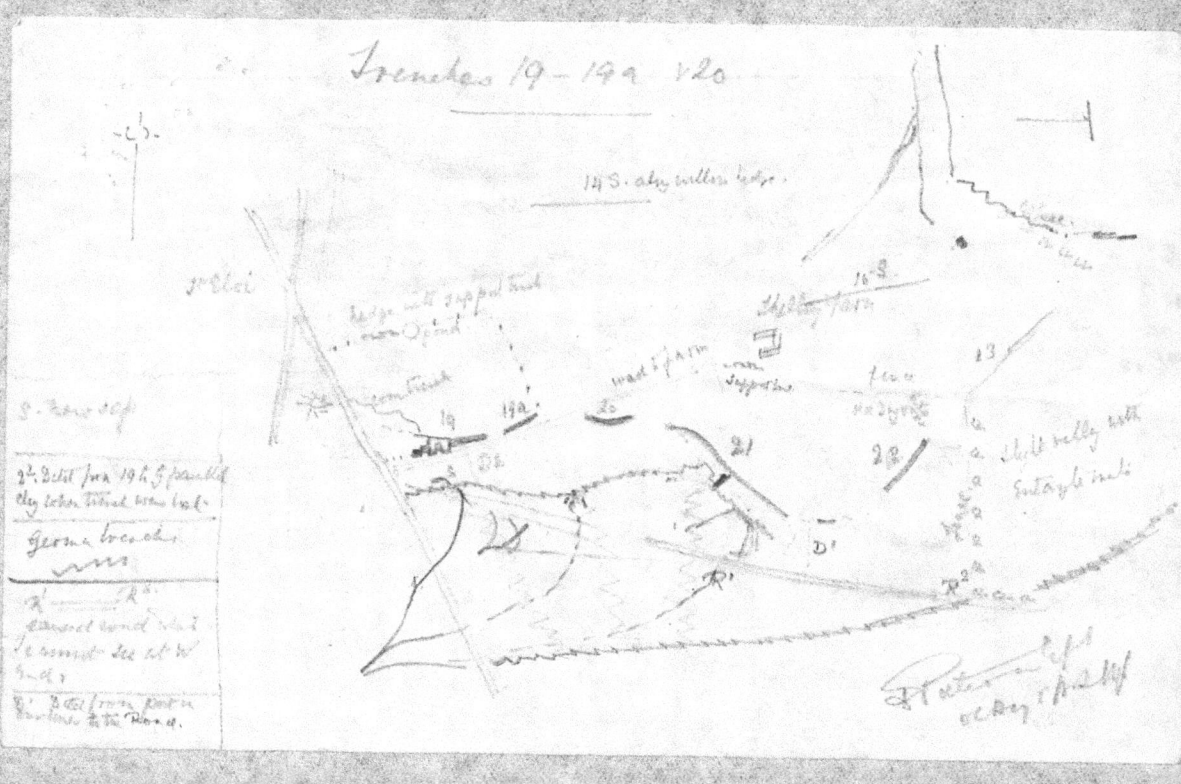

Trenches 19 – 19a & 20

"B" Form. Army Form C 2122.
MESSAGES AND SIGNALS. No. of Message_____

Prefix SM Code CHXA m.	Received	Sent	Office Stamp.
Office of Origin and Service Instructions. Words.	At 4 ___ m.	At ___ m.	FK
FH 88	From FH	To_____	27/2/15
	By_____	By_____	

TO { CMDG ARGYLLS

* Sender's Number | Day of Month | In reply to Number | **AAA**

Capt PORTEOUS reports he has boomed out workers in sap opposite 19 and that work has ceased there AAA He has also built up strong sandbag traverses with iron loopholes low down AAA Capt YOUNG reports he has looked at parallel in front of 21 enemy are working in it ~~front of~~ and are well down enfilade fire would not touch them AAA Bomb throwers have thrown bombs but none have exploded AAA Enemy not coming nearer AAA No further casualties

From CAPT MACEWAN
Place
Time 3.40 AM

* This line should be erased if not required.

"C" Form (Duplicate).
MESSAGES AND SIGNALS. Army Form C. 2123

		Charges to Pay	Office Stamp
Sn 9 am 137 Sh Border R		£ s. d.	ARMY D - 27.11.15 H

Service Instructions. C

Handed in at ____ Office 7-0 a.m. Received 7-20 a.m.

TO RW 85th Bde

Sender's Number	Day of Month	In reply to Number	AAA
CH 199	27th		

Officer in trench 15 reports 6 bombs thrown into nearest Saphead with considerable effect on parapet work ceased then aaa 2 bombs thrown at 15 without effect aaa Patrol reported enemy working in disused trench on night of 15 25 yds away aaa Ordered it to be cleared if practicable or bombed aaa latter not feasible aaa ~~last~~ last report reconnaissance sent out with ~~due to~~ view to former evidently not effected and too light to receive report till dark aaa Post of 4 men dug in from sq to command right flank of 15 aaa Consider situation quite secure aaa suggest shelling enemys trenches this afternoon with lyddite provided aeroplane available to prevent reprisals as our trenches not in condition to stand being shelled aaa

FROM Cmdg Camerons

PLACE & TIME 7 am

"C" Form (Duplicate).
MESSAGES AND SIGNALS.

Army Form C. 2123

R9 99

| Charges to Pay | Office Stamp |
| £ s. d. | |

Service Instructions.

Handed in at **L**   Office **10.45** m. Received m.

TO **Bde Major 81 Bde**

| Sender's Number | Day of Month | In reply to Number | AAA |
| CA 201 | 24th | | |

Suggest aeroplane photo of trenches in OE.C.01 section to clear up situation aaa sap facing old 14 appears to have turned west into small trench 20 yards from old 14 aaa man seen working 6.45 fired on and work ceased aaa old trench north and south between 13 and 12 reconnoitered seems of little importance aaa trench 18 nothing to report aaa Trench 17 reports sap towards right quiescent new sap 20 yards from left aaa 7 rifle grenades fired good result enemys grenades no ~~damage~~ damage

FROM **Comdg Camerons**
PLACE & TIME **10.45 am**

GERMAN SAP IN FRONT OF NO. 17.

From
    2nd Lt. A.L. Collier,
To
    Commanding Officer,
        2nd Cameron Highlanders.

Reference to German Sap in front of Trench 17, the enemy do not appear to me to be working towards 17 but to be joining up two parallels which run towards hedge on left of road. Fire seems to come from German Trench further back.

I think it conceivable that the enemy has dug two T's from main fire trench and is now trying to join the T's together.

(sd) A.L. Collier, 2nd Lieut.

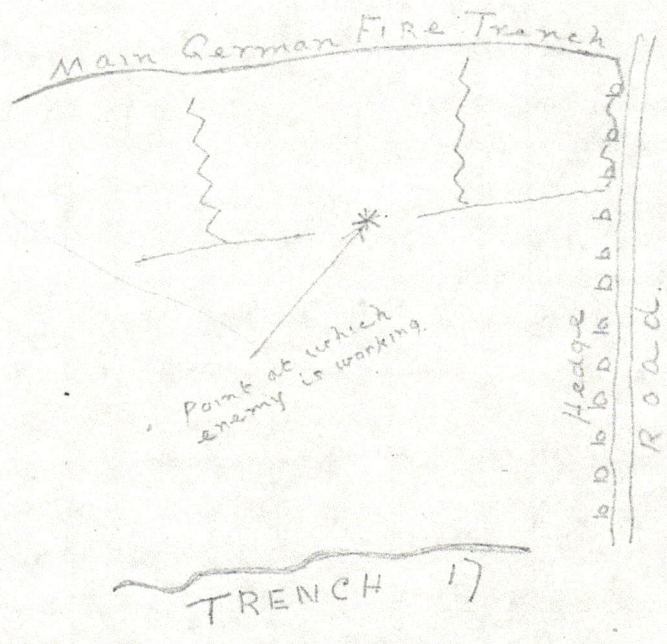

27/2/15

Headquarters,
    27th Division.

        Reference attached report on sapheads, I would suggest that counter-saps be commenced from right end of trench 17, the disuse portion of 16, and from right of 15.

        If light permits an endeavour will be made to reconnoitre and interfere with hostile sap near 15, tonight.

                                        Brig. General,
26th Feb. 1915.   Commanding 81st Infy. Brigade.

Headquarters,
27th Division.

Following information regarding German saps opposite Left Section has been obtained in last few days.

1. Opposite Trenches 13 to 15.

Reports show 5 saps running down towards our trenches as in sketch. Sap-heads start from 5 very conspicuous trees 2 of which are broken.

Sap-heads of the two nearest 15 are reported at 25 yds. and 40 yds. distant from right end of 15. The nearest has been successfully bombed in the last two days.

The above are new since our last occupation of those trenches and have advanced rapidly in last 24 hours. Work on saps opposite 14 and 15 was stopped to-day (26th) by our artillery fire.

2. Opposite Trenches 17 and 18.

Parallels from the original sapheads and probably others started since have been reported running left to right of 17.

The parallels in front of these two trenches are not continuous and from reports so far received do not yet cover the front of 17. No new work reported on the left front of 18.

3. In front of 19 - 21.

These parallels from saps first reported about 17th/18th January are now practically continuous at distances varying from 25 to 50 yards in front of right of 19, 40 to 50 yards in front of 20 to not more than 15 to 25 yards in front of 21.

It seems probable that these parallels were completed before the German attack on the 14th inst.

No work on them was observed during the first few days of our occupation.

For the last 4 or 5 days work has been actively carried on, chiefly baling, pumping and work with stakes and boards.

It is known, however, from the report of Captain Porteous. 1st A. & S. Highrs. on 22nd Feb. that part of the parallel was not revetted or floored and was 2' deep in water and it appears probable the work of the last few days has been getting the trenches fit for occupation.

The latest report (3 p.m. 26th Feb.) is that large quantities of dry (?) earth are being thrown up from about 70 to 80 yards on the right rear of trench 22.

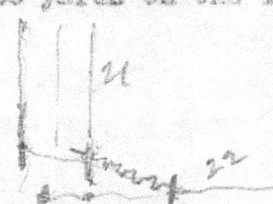

26th Feb. 1915.   Commanding 81st Inf. Bde.   Brig. Genl.

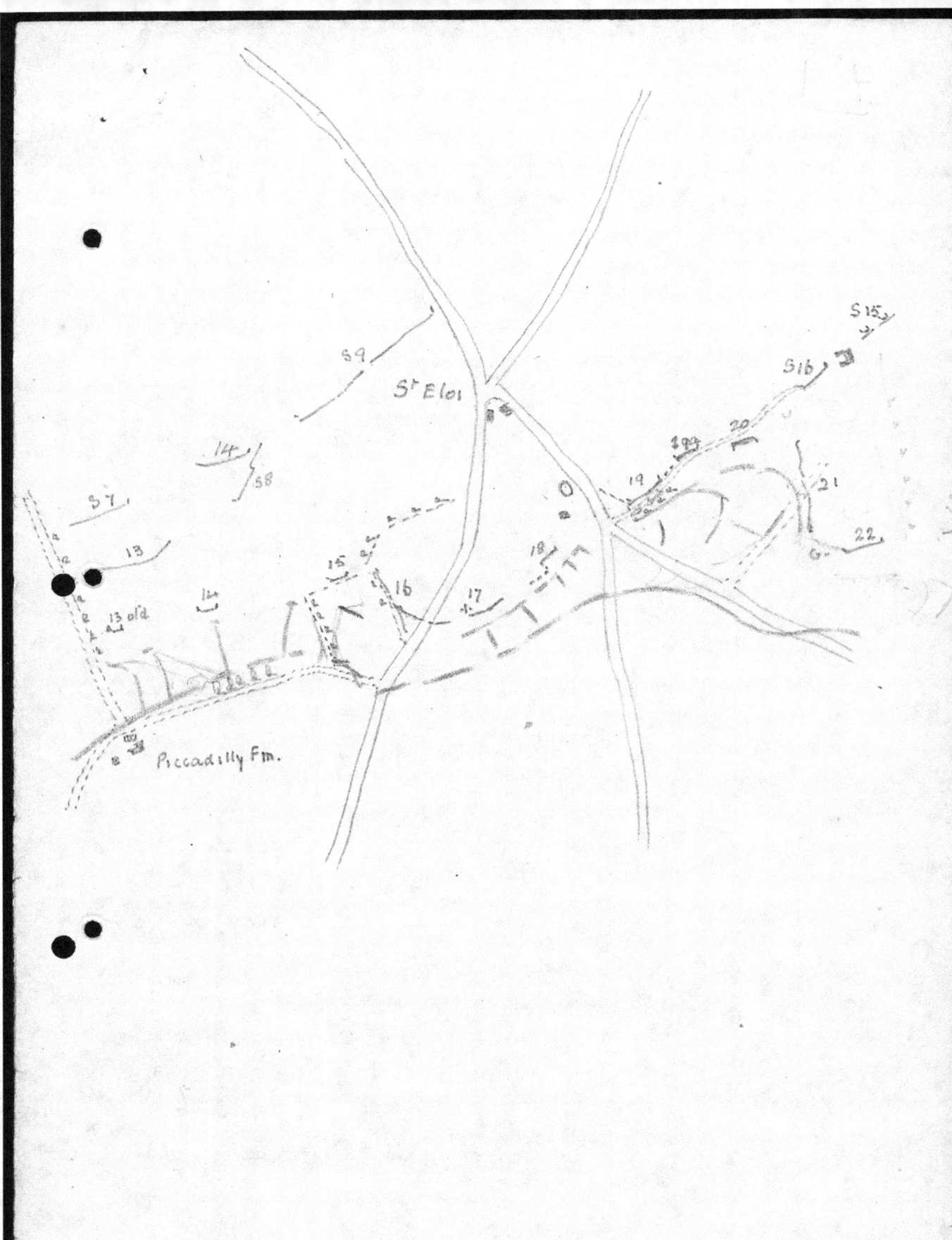

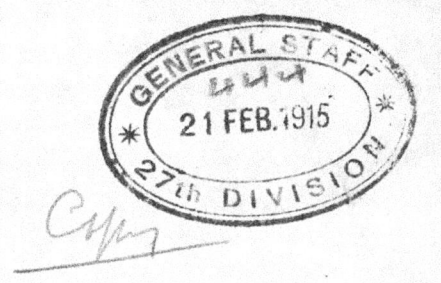

Headquarters,
    27th. Division.

      I forward herewith a report of a reconnaissance carried out by Captain D.M.Porteous, 1st. Argyle and Sutherland Highlanders, on the night of the 18th/19th February, 1915, which contains valuable and interesting information which is of great service.

      This reconnaissance was carried out in a bold and skilful manner by Captain Porteous at considerable personal risk, and I wish to bring his name to the favourable notice of the G.O.C. Division.

20th.February, 1915.   Sd. D.Macfarlane, Br.General.
                              Commanding 81st. Infantry Brigade.

G O C
  81 Inf Bde

1. Please see my G.S. 444 dated 21st Feby 1915 for communication to Captain Porteous.

2. Copy of Captain Porteous' report herewith for perusal & to be passed on to G.O.C. left Section on your relief.

3. The G.O.C. Division suggests for consideration the possibility of a reconnaissance being made of of the other end of the German tunnel opposite 21 — should opportunity occur.

HQrs
27 Divn.
21.2.15.

                          H.L. Reed Lt Col GS

All reference to left or right of saps etc. refer to
our own left or right.
----

1. Report on sap and parallel opposite No.21 Trench.

On the night of 18th/19th. I was asked to make a reconnaissance of the above.

The ground in the vicinity of No.21 Trench was new to me and I spent some time in getting the lie of our own trenches and the general position of the enemy's.

The latter was sniping a good deal and sending up many flares which made it very slow work. Before deciding on the possibility of making a successful attack it is most necessary to see the position by periscope by day, as crawling about by night does not always give you a good general impression of the lie of the ground.

Reference to attached map which does not pretend to more than general accuracy.

(1) Not knowing that A B was a raised road I took it to be a German Trench as my intentions were to find the left of the enemy's sap and parallel and if possible to get behind them on that flank I decided to crawl towards the apparent trench well to the left of the sap.

From the left corner of the left isolated redoubt of No.21 Trench a wet disused ditch or trench runs straight towards the German position. I worked throughout by myself having previously warned the men in No.21 and 22 trenches. I worked up close to the disused trench getting some lateral cover from the bank on the left of it. The raised road as it turned out to be, was about 50 yards from the point I started from and when some 10 yards off I decided that no one was there and got into a good position at the angle of the approach ditch and and the road where a few sand bags were built up and where there was a dip in the ground. The road was quite straight and offers a flat crest some 2 feet above the level of the fields.

3.   In front of it on our side and to my right was a very
open unoccupied flooded ditch. No one was opposite to me
and I could not locate the German Trench beyond, as
frequent flares went up and one would have easily seen over
the straight skyline of the road.

I heard a good deal of talking, and as I thought,
digging to my right front and beyond the road. I could
not observe where the parallel, which was now to my
right rear, was joined to the German Main Trench. I then
crawled back, informed the O.C. No.21 trench of the
nature of the supposed German Trench and crawled out
to a point 10 yards from the left end of the German near
papallel. It was some 20 yards away at most and as I
could hear of no work in it I looked over at a low
point in the parapet. It was unoccupied at that point
and I crawled to the left end which turned in towards our
line for 2 yards. The parallel appeared to run at a
distance of some 20 yards from our No.21, to be heavily
held on our right where the parapet is strongest and
where it is very well protected by barbed wire "knife rests"
On the left there is no wire as yet.

I dropped into the left end of the parallel and
walked along it. It was about 1½ feet deep in water
had some 5 to 5½ feet of cover, was 2 to 3 feet wide and
traversed at intervals. I got to within what appeared
to me about 15 yards from the occupied portion of the
trench and then returned. I could hear people talking and
reloading their rifles. I found a long handled spade
near the left end, which I took back with me and decided
to get back with what information I had and to see the
position by day by periscope, before I went out again.
Unfortunately there was no periscope available. I then
walked along the line of trenches 19 to 23 and tried to
get a rough bearing of the directions they faced in.

Between 21 and 20, I, in company with Lt.Campbell and Storlin walked to within 10 yards of the German Trench which was here about 50 yards from No.20. They were firing hard but appeared unable to see us although we were up to their wire entanglement. They were shooting towards No.19. I could not make out if this piece of trench was a second parallel, a main trench or a continuation of the big parallel I had first reconnoitred. The points that struck me about the German parallel was -

(1) My original position at corner of trench and road might be a useful for a Machine Gun during a night attack but care would be needed not to fire into No.19.

(2) An angular advance from our left covered by the fairly high parapet of the parallel and with bomb throwers working along inside of trench and possibly a Machine Gun in the German side of the trench might be successful. On the first hint of discovery a frontal attack might be pressed home at once as well.

T͞R͞ OLD DUG-OUTS.
g.g. GERMAN TRENCHES OR PARALLELS.

g WIRE IN VALLEY

Road A.B ruined and others straight crest line.
Nearest point to our trench, left corner of 21
from above an old trench goes to road.
Parallel g.g. all 20 x from 21.

Extract from a report by Captain E.J.F. Johnston, 1st Battn.
Royal Scots. d/-25/2/15.

The enemy are very active opposite me and they have carried out a lot of work since I was here 7 days ago. Two new saps have been rapidly constructed. The main position seems to have been strengthened with a second line of loopholes. The enemy's line entirely dominates our trenches. Our New 14 is in the wrong place behind S.7 instead of being in line with New 13 and 15. The enemy have attempted work at intervals during the day on the sap but I have had fire opened whenever they started and stopped work. I imagine they intend working down to the disused French trench. This will make Old 14 untenable and seriously enfilade 15.

Perhaps the opinions of other officers who have been here might be usefully consulted as it is all new since I was here last. The enemy's position can be safely studied from the extreme right of S.9 and a picked shot placed there during the day would, I think, seriously hamper the enemy's work.

My loopholes are so accurately marked by the enemy's fire that firing from them is extremely difficult. I consider this portion of the line requires attention. Our line appears to be dotted about in such a haphazard manner. If the line is to be held as now a trench must be constructed between New 13 and 15 to take the place of Old 14. If you could send someone with rifle grenades here to-night he might usefully bomb the saphead.

In case telephone breaks down would you give me my orders re relief to-morrow, to-night.

Owing to the extreme delicacy of this operation in moonlight as regards the trenches S.7-13, New 14 and Old 14, I would suggest that the parties arrive in following order from Convent. 1st 13 should come up taking advantage of disused trench to lie behind and should keep to the right so as not to come by the obvious straight route. They should go in by small parties round-the-trench so as not to have two whole parties round the trench at the same time. When all in they can relieve listening post at Old 13. S.7 should come next keeping directly in rear so as to have benefit of parapet and can use disused trench in rear of S.7 as a point to rush in from. New 14 and Old 14 should go direct to New 14 in the same way, Old 14 going up from New 14 and keeping behind the parapet all the way. Great care should be taken to avoid noise and even advantage taken of clouds before the moon.

(sd) E.J.F. Johnston, Capt.
Commdg. B. Co. 1st Rl. Scots.

A. New Breastwork
B. New Sap.
C. " "

——— Disused Trenches
——— Hedge.

"G" Form (Duplicate).   Army Form C. 2121.
MESSAGES AND SIGNALS.
No. of Message ....

	Charges to Pay.		Office Stamp.
	£	s. d.	

Service Instructions.

Handed in at _12G_   Office _3.48_ p.m.   Received _4.14_ p.m.

TO   **81st Bde.**

Sender's Number	Day of Month	In reply to Number	AAA
G 267	21		

Fifth Corps report that from information received from the French General Hq it would appear that the enemy's intention on Sunday last was to attack at St Eloi with two full brigades but owing to our attack on Neuve Chappelle they had to detach troops to that point and so attacked at St Eloi with such troops as they had available.

Repeat to Bn

FROM PLACE & TIME   _27th Divn 3.40 pm_

Situation at St Eloi
25th February 1918

1. The German Preparations are now being carried on, on a more extensive scale than before their recent failure.

    Their Sapheads & parallels now cover some 1000ˣ of ground.

    They will not risk another failure with a small body of men.

    Everything tends to a big effort on their part to capture St Eloi — say with 2 Brigades, or a division.

2. Up to the present we have taken no countermeasures.

    The small enterprise by 20 or 30 men can only succeed on especially favourable nights and at best can only delay. That is to say if a big movement is intended, they will not be deterred by the annoyance that can be caused by small enterprises.

    Two offensive means exist against their movements
    ① A big attack cutting off the whole corner from Piccadilly farm to front of 22 trench.
    This has been ruled out.
    It would take 2 or 3 weeks preparation of detail.

2. A big counter sap & mine Campaign
This should include

① Two saps from round
Sap opposite 14.

② 1 Sap against Sap opposite
15

③ Plan between 16 & 17
Say. knocked part of 16
Two Saps from each flank of
17.

④ Mine at 19.

⑤ Most important of all – an
day & night continuation of Sap
from 24 across 21 towards the
Mound – This would soon bring
things to a head in the E of
St Eloi area. Possibly before
the full German preparations are
ready –

<u>Defensive Measure</u>

The only other Course seems to be
to make another line from New 13
– a real defence scheme of Mound
& St Eloi – – 19 . 19a
20 and a new scheme to
connect 20 with 28th Division.

(In any defensive scheme 21 & 22
must be abandoned)

If some scheme of withdrawal is not
prepared the trenches 15 to 21 will

are in great danger before a
very serious attack — and cannot be
adequately strengthened under present
conditions to withstand a
serious assault —

It may it be necessary to consider
a withdrawal further back still
say on line with S9 — ~~St~~
where a really strong line could
be dug ~~when his last moon~~
is ~~on the wane~~. before the
next moon —

S H Lushton
Bde R? M? Bde

25/2/15.

Proposal for Brigade to take over
Right Section of 27th Division.

"A" Form.　　　　　　　　　　　　　　　　Army Form C. 2121.
MESSAGES AND SIGNALS.　　No. of Message _____

Prefix ___ Code ___ m.	Words	Charge	This message is on a/c of :	Recd. at ___ m.
Office of Origin and Service Instructions.	Sent			Date ___
	At ___ m.		Service.	From ___
	To			
	By		(Signature of "Franking Officer.") By	

App III

TO {

| * | Sender's Number | Day of Month | In reply to Number | **A A A** |

① Report on Proposal for 81st Inf
Bde to hold right section 22nd Div
Permanently.

② The right Section 22nd Div.
Policy regarding the holding of the
line

③ The Right Section 22nd Div.
Responsibility of Br. Sector

From				
Place				
Time				

The above may be forwarded as now corrected.　(Z)

Censor.　Signature of Addressor or person authorised to telegraph in his name

*This line should be erased if not required.

81st INFANTRY BRIGADE.

RIGHT SECTION OF DEFENCE.

1. The whole area for which the brigade holding the Right Section is responsible is divided for purposes of defence as follows:-

Front Line.→ Fire trenches, Support Trenches, Battalion Reserves. Officers Commanding Battalions in the trenches are responsible for the defence and maintenance of trenches in this area.

2. The Right Section trenches 1 to 12, S.1 to S.6. R.1 and R.2 and will be divided into 2 Sectors.

Right Sector.- Trenches 1 to 6 inclusive. S.1, S.2, S.3, half of S.4, and R.1.

Left Sector.- Trenches 7 to 12 inclusive, half S.4, S.5, S.6 and R.2

One battalion will usually hold each Sector but the dividing line depends on the strengths of the battalions actually in the trenches.

3. The first principle in the defence of the section is to hold the line of fire trenches in order to avoid costly counter-attacks, Until sufficient support and communication trenches close to the fire trenches are constructed, it is necessary to hold the fire trenches day and night, as strongly as possible.

4. Functions of the support trenches.
The present support trenches can be divided into 2 classes.
(i). Those close to the fire trenches (30 yds. to 50 yds) with communication trenches made or under construction.
These are S.1, S.2, S.4.
The garrisons of these are intended to fill up the fire trenches in case of attack or to fill up casualties, or in case a trench is temporarily lost, to resist further attack, or to counterattack.

(ii) Those which are some distance from the fire trenches and from which communication trenches do not at present exist.
These are S.3, S.5, S.6.
Under certain circumstances the fire trenches could and should be reinforced from these trenches.
Their other function is to break and resist a strong attack which may have broken through the fire trenches. For this purpose fire trenches have been constructed in connection with the dug-outs.
These still require extension and improvement and more obstacles.

5. The Redoubts (R.1 and R.2)
A garrison will always be told off for the redoubts, which will be manned immediately in case of any alarm.
They are provided with all round defence and the garrison will not retire from them without orders from the Brigadier.

6. The Intermediate Line.

This has been reconnoitred and work on it will be taken in hand in the near future.

The trenches at present consist of existing old trenches or trenches under construction which could only be occupied in emergency.

These trenches are shewn in pencil and the numbering is only temporary.

The machine gun policy for this line has already been explained but alternative positions will be considered.

The OLD FARMS position (2 guns) will be occupied by the battalion coming out of the Right Sector; the NEW FARM and MOATED GRANGE positions by that coming out of the Left Sector.

The intermediate line within their own sectors can be used by battalion reserves either to resist an overwhelming attack which may have broken the front line and passed the support trenches and redoubts, or as a jumping-off place for counter-attacks.

7. The battalion in close support is at present billeted in DICKEBUSCH and has one or two companies forward at ELZENWALLE and VIERSTRAAT according to the strengths of the battalions. Further accommodation in farms West of RIDGE WOOD is under consideration.

The battalion in close support will always be the first to support the battalions in the trenches.

Its first duty in case of alarm is to cover the advance of the Brigade Reserve from DICKEBUSCH by holding the intermediate line. The O.C. this battalion will always tell off companies for this duty.

These companies are not at the disposal of Officers Commanding Battalions in trenches and will only be called on by them in cases of extreme urgency.

12th March, 1915.

Captain,
Bde. Major 81st Infy. Bde.

81st INFANTRY BRIGADE.

THE ROLE OF THE DIFFERENT PORTIONS OF THE FRONT LINE AND POLICY WITH REGARD TO IT.

1. The first principle to hold line fire trenches in order to avoid costly counter-attacks.

This means a really strong line of fire trenches, which, until we can construct good cover trenches where men can rest, must be held day and night.

Fire trenches in this sense can only include the actual line of fire trenches and cover trenches in the same line as the fire trenches, and cover or support trenches which are within short distance, say a maximum of 40 yards to 50 yards and from which really good communication trenches exist to the fire trenches.

Under the existing conditions, and with the length of line which we have to hold at present, we cannot hope to hold more than the fire trenches as above defined with 2 Coys. of each battalion in the firing line.

2. Thus, the dug-outs in the BOIS CARRE and East of it (trench S.3), the support trench behind 6 and 7 (S.4), S.6 and the redoubts must come under another class.

3. It has been a matter for consideration whether they should be held at all or not, the alternative being to try and keep 2 complete companies back and prepare a fresh line roughly on the line VIERSTRAAT - VOORMEZEELE (not continuous trench) which could be held in case of a sudden attack in overwhelming numbers.

This policy would work in well with that of the 3rd Division who have prepared a position for such an emergency in front of the VIERSTRAAT - NEUVE EGLISE road and could easily be joined to what may be called a reserve line (at present chiefly dug-outs) now being prepared about 500 yds. S.E. of VOORMEZEELE.

4. The disadvantages of this scheme are :-
(i) That the fire trenches and cover trenches are not at present considered strong enough to be left without closer support.

(ii) To commence another line with soldier labour would deprive the first line of labour and material which will be necessary for a considerable time to make it reasonably secure and comfortable.

(iii) The fact that a long continuous line with other troops on our flanks makes it imperative that we should be able to break a second attack (even if our first line is broken) in such a way as to prevent the troops on our flanks being enfiladed.

(iv) It is much easier and quicker to improve existing trenches and even to convert dug-outs into fire trenches, than to construct an entirely new line.

5. Taking everything into consideration our best policy for the near future would appear to be:-
(a). To continue strengthening our fire trenches till we can put a maximum garrison in them and support trenches which must be constructed within say 30 yds. or 40 yds. with communication trenches, or cover trenches either in disused bits of fire trenches or close behind them (10 yds. to 20 yds.)

(b). To convert or improve S.3, S.4, S.5, S.6, into good fire positions with flanking fire and surrounded with wire, would, in conjunction with the redoubts, prevent an attack which might succeed against the first line, from passing the WYTSCHAETEBECK (a useful obstacle in itself) and reach line

VIERSTRAAT-

VIERSTRAAT - VOORMEZEELE without any further opposition, and incidentally enfilade the trenches of the 3rd Division.

    (c). Try and have the line VIERSTRAAT - VOORMEZEELE dug as soon as possible by civilian labour.

    (There is no prospect of our being able to really take this in hand for many weeks).

6.   Without in any way depriving subordinate commanders of their initiative of their duty of acting in accordance with circumstances, the role of support trenches such as S.3, S.4, S.5, S.6 can be laid down as follows:-

    (i) In case of an attack which is repulsed to fill up the fire trenches so as to be able to resist further attacks.

    (ii) In case of part of the 1st line being driven in by an overpowering attack to prevent any further advance except by fresh troops, which means delay, and to break up this attack before it becomes dangerous to our neighbours on the flanks and to give time and opportunity for the Battn. Reserves to counter-attack and the Brigade Reserves to come up in support.

7.   The Brigadier trusts that nothing has been said to lessen the determination which exists to hold what we have at all costs in case of attack, and to regain as soon as possible what might be temporarily lost by means of counter-attacks.

8th February, 1915.

81st INFANTRY BRIGADE.

WORK ON RIGHT SECTION, NIGHTS 8th/9th TILL RELIEVED ON EVENING, 10th.

This is intended as a guide to work which should be carried on in the next 2 days, in addition to ordinary trench work detailed by O.C. Battalions.

Right Battalion.

1. Completion of redoubt R.1.

2. Convert or dig when necessary fire trenches in communication with S.3 both in and East of BOIS CARRE.
Any trench begun to be completed by 10th.

3. Communication trench from S.1 to 1

4. Sap forward from 1 and 2 about 6 to 8 yards and commence parallel for new fire trench covering the gap.
When this is completed part of 1 and 2 to be made into cover with lying down shelter for garrisons of 1 and 2 and new trench 1 a.

5. Complete communication trenches from S.2 to 3 and 4.

6. Repairing parts of old trench between 3 and 4.

7. Trench mortar emplacement.

8. An efficient barricade across the road between 4 & 5.

Left Battalion. A. & S. Highlanders.

9. Completion of dug-outs for H.Q. and Reserve Coy.
Any work begun must be completed so as not to show new roofing timber or corrugated iron to aeroplanes.

10. Completion of fire trenches in connection with S.4 and continuation of communication trench S.4 to 8.

11. Completion of new fire trench out of 8 towards 9.

12. Completion of redoubt.

Both Battalions.

Wire in front of each trench especially filling up gaps from 8 to 12.

13. Lateral communication between trenches to be considered. Where communication trenches do not exist company officers to devise a plan of communication such as an endless string.
Every trench should be able to send a message to reach one of the trenches in which there is a telephone, and communication must be established between the 3rd Division on our right and the left section on our left.

ACB Kirkpatrick S/Lt Capt.
for Captain,

8th Feb. 1915.   Bde. Major 81st Infy. Brigade.

HEADQUARTERS
No. 222
Date 6/3/15
81st INFANTRY BRIGADE

Headquarters,
    27th Division.

    With reference to my report of 5th March and your G.R. 836 the following modifications are submitted:-

    By slightly reducing the Garrisons of some of the trenches and by improving the accomodation of certain support trenches so that the men can be made more comfortable, it will be possible to arrange that the actual duty in the trenches is made easier for the troops.

    By considering the Battalion in Reserve at DICKEBUSCH to be "at rest" until such time as enough Territorials are absorbed to do duty in the trenches. A proportionate period of "rest" can be arranged.

    The scheme put forward in para. 11 of my above mentioned report will be so carried out that the Platoons and Companies of Territorials gradually introduced into the trenches will be placed under the command of the O.C. Regular Battalions until the Territorial Battalions are fitted to take their complete share of responsibility; and the line will be always held by Regular Battns., together with, later on, a half or, perhaps, one Territorial Battn. in addition.

    It will be arranged that the Permanent Digging Party under the orders of the C.R.E. and the Carrying Party under the orders of G.O.C. 80th Brigade detailed from the Territorial Battalions will be the 1st of their respective Battalions to be put into the trenches, so that there will be no necessity to relieve these parties for at least 2 or 3 weeks.

    (Sd) D.A. Macfarlane.
    Brigadier General.
    Commanding 81st Infantry Brigade.

6/3/15.

REPORT ON PROPOSED SCHEME FOR HOLDING RIGHT SECTION
PERMANENTLY.

Headquarters,

27th Division.

1. With reference to G.R. No. 797 the principle which is essential is that no man, under normal conditions, should be required to be in the trenches (i.e. fire and support trenches) for more than 48 hours consecutively.

2. At present the average number of rifles available for trench duty is 500 per battalion.

3. The numbers required for fire and support trenches in the Right Section as at present constituted is 826.

4. Until the Territorial Battalions are ready to take their place in the trenches it will be necessary to relieve the 2 battalions in trenches every 48 hours.

5. It will take roughly three weeks before the Territorial Battalions are ready to take their full share of responsibility in the trenches and even then the present extent of the R.E. Section would prevent the troops getting the same proportion of rest, viz:- 1 - 2 that they now have.

6. In these circumstances it is evident that the present extent of the Right Section is too great to be held by one Brigade continuously having due regard to wastage, adequate period of rest, and general efficiency of the troops.

7. If No. 1 and S.1. were taken over by the 3rd Division and No. 12 by the Left Section, the numbers required in trenches of Right Section would be reduced by about 100 rifles.
This reduction would enable satisfactory arrangements to be made with the present numbers.

8. As regards the Territorial Battalions it is not safe to count on their present numbers being maintained as they have no adequate reserve of either officers or men.

9. The personnel of the Signal Section would require to be increased. They already are very hard worked, having 24 hours on and 24 hours off and should be increased to enable men to have a period of rest.
A Company of R.E. should be allotted permanently to the Right Section.

10. Until sufficient accommodation can be constructed in the forward line, billets for 2 battalions would be required in DICKEBUSCH.

11.   The scheme proposed is briefly to begin by relieving 2 battalions in trenches every 48 hours and putting 2 platoons of Territorials in the trenches for 24 hours until 4 companies have had the experience.- (10 days).

The next step would be to have 2 regular battalions and 2 Territorial Companies in trenches for 4 days, with 2 fresh platoons every 24 hours.

These would be relieved by the other 2 regular battalions and 2 Territorial Companiess with 2 fresh platoons every 24 hours - for another period of 4 days. At the end of this time all platoons would have been in the trenches and the Terr. Battns. would be ready to take their full share

The conditions necessary for the carrying out of this scheme are-
 (a) Reduction of No. of trenches as indicated in para 7.
 (b) The Terr. Bns. being left entirely at the disposal of G.O.C. Brigade.

Brig. General,

5th March, 1915.   Commanding 81st Infantry Bde.

To all Battalions 4.3.1[5]

Officer Commanding,

————————————————

Attached report has been sent to 27th Division and is forwarded for your information. It is regretted that there was no time to consult Commanding Officers before making the report.

(Sgd) T. Holland. Captain.
Brigade Major, 81st Infantry Brigade.

4/3/15.

(1390) Wt. W 9044-1194. 12/14. 40,000 Pads. S. B. Ltd.
"B" Form.   Army Form C. 2122.

MESSAGES AND SIGNALS.

Prefix Sm	Code L B m.	Received At 11-31 a.m. From 709 By Cordey	Sent At m. To By	Office Stamp.
Office of Origin and Service Instructions. 709	Words. 101			

TO { 91st Infy Bde

| Sender's Number GR 797 | Day of Month 4th | In reply to Number | AAA |

Regarding new proposals for occupation of front line aaa Supposing right section as it stands is allotted to your brigade including your two Territorial Battns which will gradually be absorbed in front line but at first only one or two platoons at a time. aaa Further than you are allotted at Dickebusch billetting accommodation for at least one and half Battns and at huts Zevicotin and M6A accommodation for one and half Battns aaa Submit, in short, scheme for occupation permanently by your brigade of present right section as soon as possible

From	27 Divn	10.45 am	
Place			
Time			

* This line should be erased if not required.

REPORT BY BRIGADIER-GENERAL J.E. GORDON 81st INFANTRY BRIGADE
ON PROPOSAL TO HOLD ONE SECTION OF TRENCHES BY ONE BRIGADE
FINDING ITS OWN RELIEFS AND THE OTHER SECTION BY TWO BRIGADES
WHO RELIEVE EACHOTHER.

——————————————————

1. It is assumed that the Section to be held by 1 brigade continuously must be the Right Section as the situation at St. ELOI is too difficult to be undertaken by 1 brigade continuously.

2. I am strongly in favour of this system which seems to me to have the following advantages:-

(i). The battalions and companies always go back to the same trenches which they get to thoroughly know as well as the position of the enemy's trenches opposite them and his movements.

(ii). I am convinced it is the only way to have a continuity of policy as well as to get the best work out of the men who know that they will benefit by their labours.

(iii) Another important advantage is that Billets in DICKEBUSCH and in the Reserve Area can be permanently allotted to the Brigade and this would have a marked effect on improving the sanitary conditions and everything else connected with billets.

Even in the case of the Section where a Brigade relieves a Brigade the conditions of the billeting will be much improved though they would not benefit to the same extent.

(iv). It would be a great advantage to have an R.E. Company and Officers and the same Royal Artillery permanently working with the same officers and men and in the Left Section co-operation would be facilitated as well.

3. The disadvantages are:-

Firstly the weakening of the Brigade Reserve in the Right Section which will now be held practically by three Bns. This could be minimised by having the battalion in Brigade Reserve of this Section in the huts nearest to DICKEBUSCH and also by having part of the Territorial Battalions always at DICKEBUSCH.

Secondly, the Brigade Staff of this Section would never have a period of rest but I think considering the advantages are so great that this should not be allowed to stand in the way.

4. The length of Line that the Right Section could hold.

What I think should be aimed at in the Right Section is to have 1 battalion always at rest, 1 battalion in DICKEBUSCH and 2 battalions in front of DICKEBUSCH.

Assuming that the 4 battalions have each 500 rifles for the trenches (which is perhaps too high an estimate) the fire and support trenches for this section should not require more than 500 rifles or else the men will be forced to do more than 48 hours in the actual trenches

fire' Support.

This

This scheme would allow another 500 rifles to be divided between VIERSTRAAT, the BRASSERIE and ELZENWALLE which is just about their maximum accommodation. But the present Right Section requires by the estimate given to me to-day by the 82nd Brigade, a maximum of 835 rifles for the fire and support trenches.

The present Left Section can take a maximum of about 650 rifles, say 800 rifles allowing for the 3 extra trenches taken over from the 28th Division. It would seem, therefore that the Left Section should take over 2 or 3 trenches from the present Right Section. It is difficult to suggest a dividing line owing to the tactical situation at present and as the tendency in both sections is to increase the number of rifles which can be put in the fire and support trenches.

The calculation of figures alone would put the dividing line at the left of No. 8.
The calculation of space alone would put it somewhere about the same place.
I would suggest the right of 11 or the right of 12 as the best compromise under the existing conditions.
I would also suggest that one more trench should be given over to the 3rd Division, if possible, which would make the big drain or stream between 1 and 2 trenches the dividing line between the divisions.

3/3/1915.

(Signed) Brig. General,
Commanding 81st Infantry Brigade.

Sketches of the MOUND - St.ELOI.

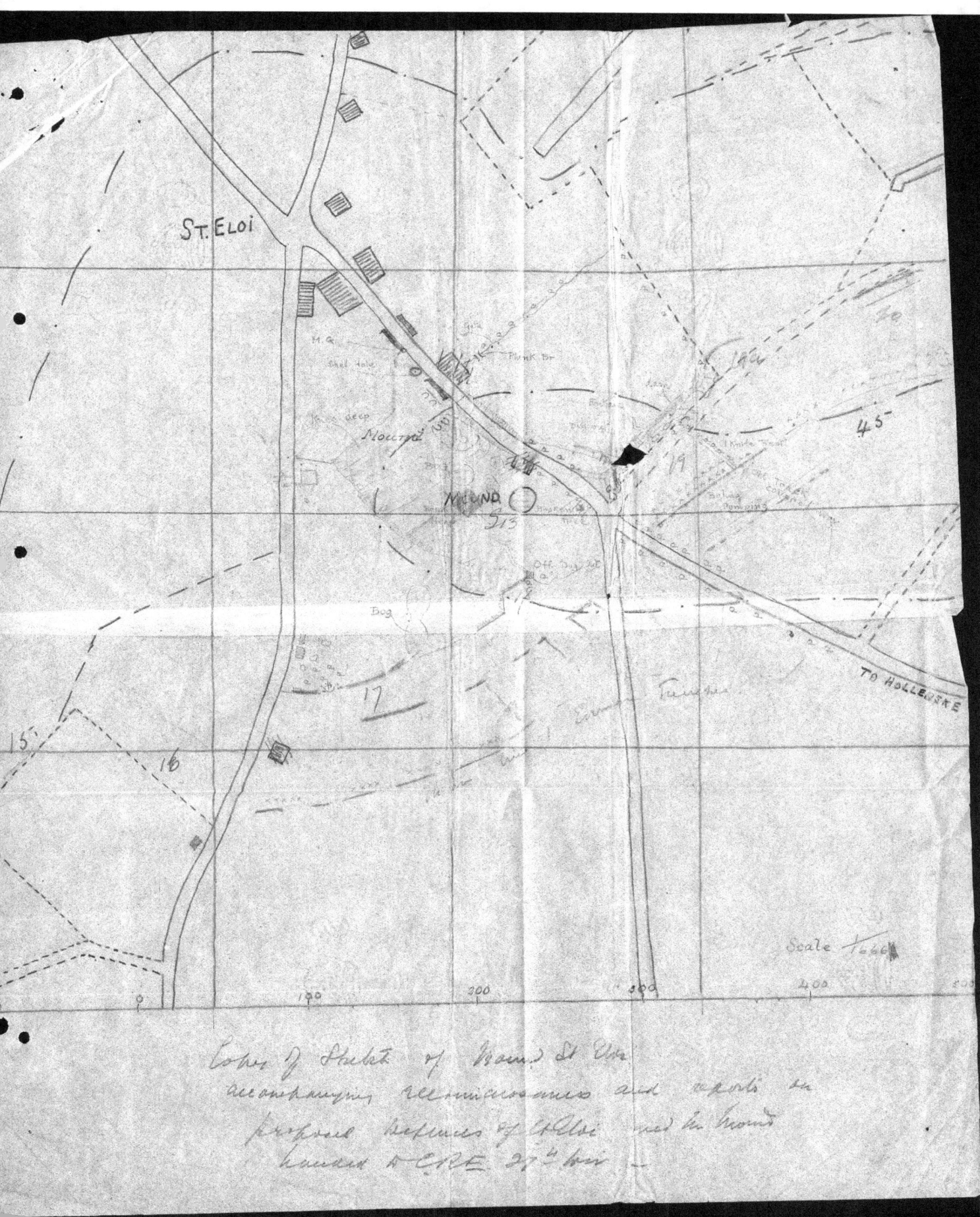

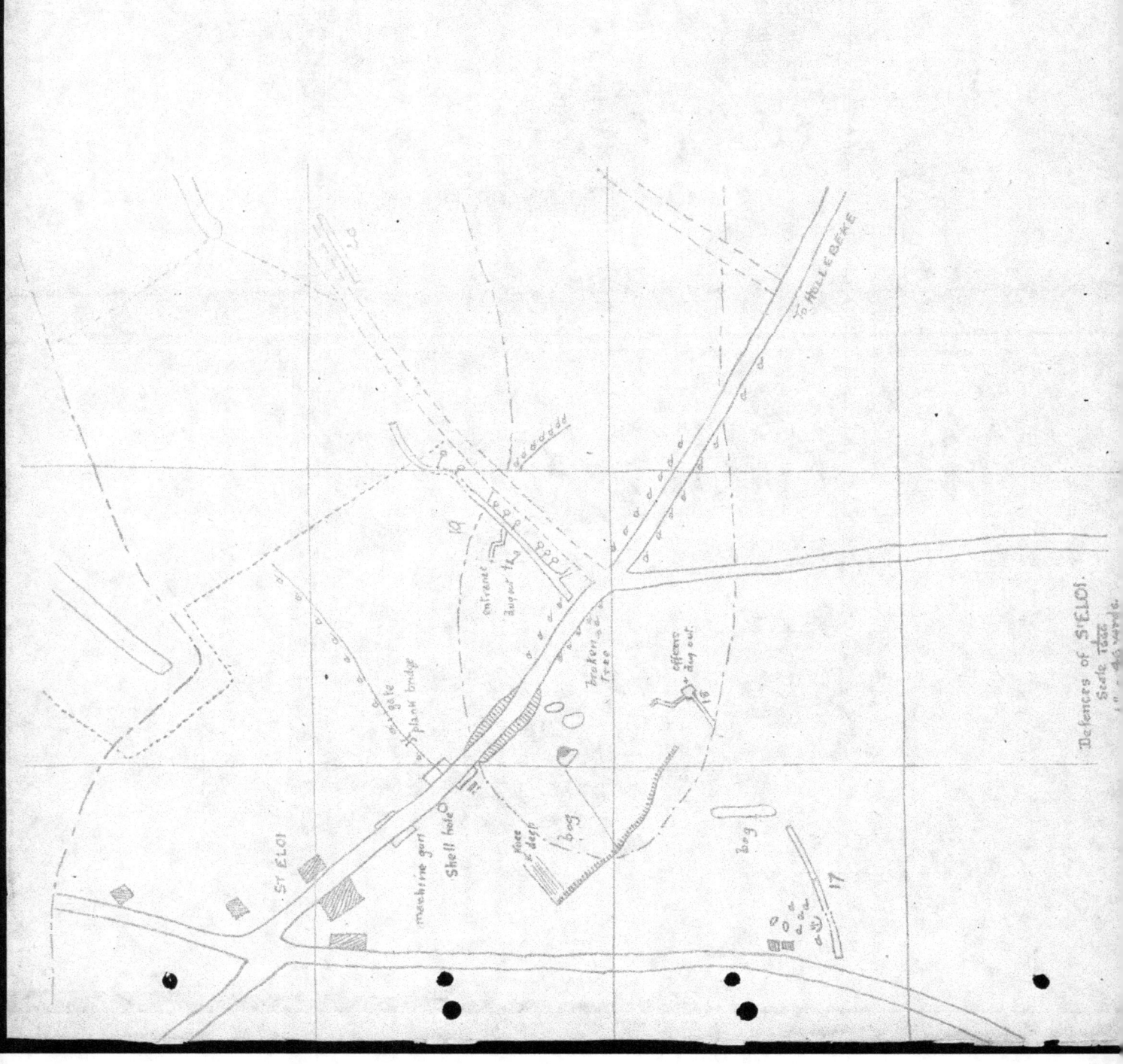

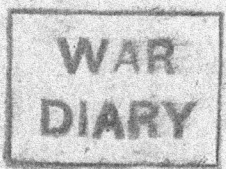

B. H. Q. 81st INFANTRY BRIGADE

M A R C H   1 9 1 5

Attached:-

    Bde. O.Os. 42 to 49.
    MAPS.

Army Form C. 2118.

WAR DIARY
or
INTELLIGENCE SUMMARY
(Erase heading not required.)

Instructions regarding War Diaries and Intelligence Summaries are contained in F. S. Regs., Part II. and the Staff Manual respectively. Title pages will be prepared in manuscript.

Hour, Date, Place	Summary of Events and Information	Remarks and references to Appendices
March 1st to 4th 1915 WESTOUTRE	The Bde remained in the Reserve area — Bomb throwers up to 32 per Bn were specially trained — [All Bns. were halted and received a change of clothing — About four hundred Knife Rests were constructed (Wire entanglements)] One Bn in the Bde was warned each Night to be ready to move at an hours notice —	
WESTOUTRE March 5th	The Bde marched to DICKEBUSCH relieving the 92nd Bde in the front line — [Bns. for the Trenches moved from WESTOUTRE to the huts DICKEBUSCH where they had tea — As soon as it was dark the Bns moved direct to the Trenches.] The Relief was carried out as follows — 2 Glouc. R relieved The Leinsters in the Trenches 1 R Scots " " Irish Fusiliers " 1 Argyll & Suth. Hdrs in close support with 1 Coy at ELZENWALLE remainder in DICKEBUSCH 2 Coms Hdrs in DICKEBUSCH	

WAR DIARY
INTELLIGENCE SUMMARY
(Erase heading not required.)

Army Form C. 2118.

Instructions regarding War Diaries and Intelligence Summaries are contained in F. S. Regs., Part II. and the Staff Manual respectively. Title pages will be prepared in manuscript.

Hour, Date, Place	Summary of Events and Information	Remarks and references to Appendices
DICKEBUSCH 6th MAR. 1915	MT KOKEREELE It was decided to move the 9th Argylls from LA CLYTTE road to the ROSEN HILL HuTs on the RENINGHELST road. [Billeting party was sent on in advance and the Bn. less 2 platoons (at DICKEBUSCH Huts) moved into huts on the 7th.]	
DICKEBUSCH 7th MAR.	Reliefs took place as follows — 1 Argylls relieved the Gloucesters in the Trenches 1 R.Scots relieved the Camerons in the Trenches. The Gloucesters moved into close Support The 1st Argylls were billeted in DICKEBUSCH.	

Army Form C. 2118.

WAR DIARY
or
INTELLIGENCE SUMMARY
(Erase heading not required.)

Instructions regarding War Diaries and Intelligence Summaries are contained in F.S. Regs, Part II. and the Staff Manual respectively. Title pages will be prepared in manuscript.

Hour, Date, Place 1915	Summary of Events and Information	Remarks and references to Appendices
DICKEBUSCH 8th MAR	Owing to the Germans shelling the LA CLYTTE – DICKEBUSCH road near HELLEBLAST corner this portion of the road was closed during the hours of daylight – Wagons in the daytime making a detour via OUDERDOM – ZEVECOTEN – RENINGHELST to WESTOUTRE. The 9th R. Scots sent 4 Platoons into the Trenches – 2 Platoons were attached to the 1 Argylls and 2 to the Camerons	
DICKEBUSCH 9th MAR	The Relief was carried out as follows – The 1 Argylls were relieved by the Gloucesters The Camerons " " 1.R. Scots 4 Platoons were again sent by the 9th R. Scots 2 being attached to the Gloucesters and 2 to the 1 R. Scots these Platoons only remained 24 hrs in the Trenches being relieved on succeeding nights until all companies had completed one tour in the Trenches. The Camerons went into close support, the 1 Argylls being in Reserve at DICKEBUSCH	

1247 W 3299 200,000 (E) 8/14 J.B.C. & A. Forms/C. 2118/11.

WAR DIARY or **INTELLIGENCE SUMMARY**

Army Form C 2118.

(Erase heading not required.)

Instructions regarding War Diaries and Intelligence Summaries are contained in F. S. Regs., Part II. and the Staff Manual respectively. Title pages will be prepared in manuscript.

Hour, Date, Place	Summary of Events and Information	Remarks and references to Appendices
DICKEBUSCH 12th Mar. DICKEBUSCH 10th Mar. 1915	The 3rd Divn. attacked in the neighbt. of WYTSCHAETE-ABEELE it was decided to move up the troops to the huts DICKEBUSCH this move took place on the 12th —	
DICKEBUSCH 11th	The Relief took place as under :— The Gloucesters were relieved by the 1st Argylls The 1 R Scots " " " the Camerons The 1 R Scots moved back into Close Support The Gloucesters were billeted in DICKEBUSCH	

Army Form C. 2118.

WAR DIARY
or
INTELLIGENCE SUMMARY
(Erase heading not required.)

Instructions regarding War Diaries and Intelligence Summaries are contained in F. S. Regs., Part II. and the Staff Manual respectively. Title pages will be prepared in manuscript.

Hour, Date, Place	Summary of Events and Information	Remarks and references to Appendices
DICKEBUSCH 18th March.	Operations were delayed by fog in the morning. Attack supported by rapid rifle fire from all trenches towards HOLLANDSCHESCHUUR FARM. CASUALTIES W.3 +13 Gloucesters killed nil wounded 3 1 Argylls killed nil wounded 1 Camerons killed nil wounded 1 1 R. Scots killed 3 wounded 8. Operations against HOLLANDSCHESCHUUR FARM were continued in the afternoon. + support given by rifle fire from trenches. Casualties	

WAR DIARY
or
INTELLIGENCE SUMMARY

(Erase heading not required.)

Army Form C. 2118.

Instructions regarding War Diaries and Intelligence Summaries are contained in F. S. Regs., Part II. and the Staff Manual respectively. Title pages will be prepared in manuscript.

Hour, Date, Place	Summary of Events and Information	Remarks and references to Appendices
WEREBUSCH 14th March	Artillery operations continued against HOLLAND SCHESSCHUR FARM. During afternoon, about 6 p.m. enemy made strong attack against 82nd Bdr. in trenches at ST. ELOI. This was preceded by a very violent bombardment.	
(1000 Glosters + R Scots in trenches)	81st Bdr. marched out about 4 p.m. to work a subsidiary line of trenches in Sq N 5 b. Work was carried out all night. Brigade headquarters moved to BRASSERIE (N6b).	
"	Casualties:— Cameron wounded 2 K.1 w.14 1 R. Scots wounded 3 Gloucesters killed 1 wounded 8 1 Argylls wounded 1	
15th March	During day Camerons + 1 Royal Argylls remained in subsidiary line. At night following units took place. Camerons relieved 1 Royal Scots Argylls " Gloucesters. Two platoons 9th Royal Scots were attached to Camerons " " " " Argylls	

WAR DIARY or INTELLIGENCE SUMMARY

Army Form C. 2118.

(Erase heading not required.)

Instructions regarding War Diaries and Intelligence Summaries are contained in F. S. Regs., Part II. and the Staff Manual respectively. Title pages will be prepared in manuscript.

Hour, Date, Place	Summary of Events and Information	Remarks and references to Appendices
15th March (continued)	Casualties K2. W9 — 1st R.Scots wounded 2; 9th R.Scots killed 1 wounded 2; Camerons killed 1 wounded 2; 1st Argylls wounded 1; Gloucesters wounded 2.	
DICKEBOSCH 16 March.	Casualties K2. W13 — 1st Argylls killed 2 wounded 4; 9th Argylls wounded 4; 9th R.Scots wounded 2. 4 platoons of R. Argylls were attached to Camerons vice Argylls.	
DICKEBOSCH 17 March.	Casualties during past 24 hours. K2. W5 — 1st Argylls killed 2 wounded 4; Camerons wounded 1.	

WAR DIARY
or
INTELLIGENCE SUMMARY

(Erase heading not required.)

Army Form C. 2118.

Instructions regarding War Diaries and Intelligence Summaries are contained in F. S. Regs., Part II. and the Staff Manual respectively. Title pages will be prepared in manuscript.

Hour, Date, Place	Summary of Events and Information	Remarks and references to Appendices
DICKEBUSCH. 18th March	Officers 8th Bn. 3rd Division visited trenches with a view to their taking them over.	
	One company 9th Argylls attached to Camerons – " " " " – Argylls	
	Casualties	
	1st Argylls wounded 3	
	9th Argylls " 7	
	9 R. Scots " 2 #	# Officers wounded.
	Camerons " 2 #	CAPT. A. RAEBURN (remained with unit)
	Gloucesters " 6	2/Lt J. MURRAY
	W 2 + 18	
DICKEBUSCH. 19 March	3rd Division took over the trenches occupied by 8th Bn. (Right section 27'B'M.) Lucerne 1 & 10ft.(?)	
	Camerons) were relieved by 8th Bn.	Chievres 11.15 Sq including R.E. trenches
	Argylls)	
	1st Royal Scots) relieved 9th Bn. in the right ST ELOI section	Officer killed
	Gloucesters)	Lt. H.M. HARRISON. Glosters
	Casualties Gloucesters killed 1 wounded 1	
	1 R. Scots killed 1 wounded 1	
	9 R. Scots wounded 2	
	K1+2 9 Argylls killed 1 wounded 4	
	W 10 9 Argylls wounded 2	

Army Form C 2118.

WAR DIARY
or
INTELLIGENCE SUMMARY

(Erase heading not required.)

Instructions regarding War Diaries and Intelligence Summaries are contained in F. S. Regs., Part II. and the Staff Manual respectively. Title pages will be prepared in manuscript.

Hour, Date, Place	Summary of Events and Information	Remarks and references to Appendices
DICKEBUSCH 20 March	Casualties K 1 W 12 Gloucesters killed 2 wounded 3 1 R. Scots killed 1 wounded 8 9th R. Scots wounded 1	Officer killed 2Lt R. S. Croft Gloucester
DICKEBUSCH 21st March	Casualties K 1 - W 19 Gloucesters killed 1 wounded 4 1st Royal Scots wounded 10 9th R. Scots wounded 1 9th Argylls wounded 4	
DICKEBUSCH 22nd March	Officers of 85th Inf Bde visited trenches with a view to taking them over. Casualties K 5 W 1+16 Gloucesters wounded 5 1st R. Scots killed 4 wounded 2 (killed a shell in leg) 9th Argylls wounded 7 9th R. Scots killed 1 wounded 2 1st Argylls wounded 1 Lt Chapman and Capt/Johnston (7952) examined Lap trench - 2nd Gloucesters in front of trench 13 about 3.30 am 93rd inst. No Germans in traps. No furnace yet formed. Both returned in safety.	Officer wounded Lt A. G. BELFRAGE 9th Argylls

WAR DIARY
OR
INTELLIGENCE SUMMARY

(Erase heading not required.)

Army Form C 2118.

Hour, Date, Place	Summary of Events and Information	Remarks and references to Appendices
DICKEBUSCH 23rd March	81st Bde relieved by 85th Inf Bde (3rd Divn) for twelve run frontline 11th Sq b - 3rd relief as HAS	
	9th Royal Scots } moved to vicinity of BOESCHEPE	
	9th Argylls	
	1st CAMERONS } moved to CANADA HUTS (H.32c)	
	Gloucesters } moved to ROSENHILL HUTS (M 6 a)	
	1st Royal Scots	
	Casualties { Gloucesters wounded 1	
	K 4. W 7 { 1st Royal Scots killed 4 wounded 6.	
ZEVECOTEN. 24th March	Bde Head Quarters moved to ZEVECOTEN at 5 p.m. (Sq G 35 D)	
	Casualties { Camerons wounded 4 O.R	
	WS { 9th Royal Scots wounded 1 OR	

WAR DIARY
or
INTELLIGENCE SUMMARY
(Erase heading not required.)

Army Form C. 2118.

Hour, Date, Place	Summary of Events and Information	Remarks and references to Appendices
ZEVECOTEN 25th March	CAMERONS & 1st Argylls provided working parties on G.H.Q. 2nd line. Glosters & 1st Royal Scots under orders of 82nd Inf Bde. in reserve. Cameron [9 wounded] 1st Argyll [1 wounded]	
ZEVECOTEN 26th March	9th Royal Scots and 1st Argylls marched to YPRES to provide working parties under C.R.E. 28th Division. They marched in light order + motor lorries were placed at their disposal to carry packs.	
ZEVECOTEN 27th March	A party of officers and N.C.O's were sent to visit the trenches E. of YPRES on the YPRES-MENIN road with a view to taking them over. G.O.C. Bde inspected Camerons and 1st Argylls at CANADA H'Qrs.	Party consisted of Bde H.Q. Brigade Major, Superior Staff, R.E. 75 Officers N.Co's min of 1st Argylls 2/ Camerons 9 Argylls ? 2 Intelligence
ZEVECOTEN 28th March	G.O.C. 5th Corps inspected 1st + 2nd Btls of units in the Bde at 10 a.m.	

Army Form C. 2118.

WAR DIARY
or
INTELLIGENCE SUMMARY
(Erase heading not required.)

Instructions regarding War Diaries and Intelligence Summaries are contained in F. S. Regs., Part II. and the Staff Manual respectively. Title pages will be prepared in manuscript.

Hour, Date, Place	Summary of Events and Information	Remarks and references to Appendices
ZEVECOTEN 29th March	Reinforcements of following strengths arrived + were billeted in billets with unit 2 Seaforths 1 officer 24 men 2 Cameron 1 officer 138 men 1st Argylls 50 men at BOOTSCHAPE G.O.C. Bde inspected 1st Royal Scots at 12 noon The Brigade was placed in reserve under the orders of G.O.C. 3rd Divn in case of emergency The Royal Irish Fusiliers & Cornwall Light Infantry came under the orders of G.O.C. Bde to replace two battalions digging, + to make up Brigade to strength	6 to mind 2/1/15 K. 13. W. 40. 4/1/15 K. 2. W. 15. 6/1/15 K+3. W. 33. 7/4/15 K. 1 W2+10 9/1/15 K. 3. 13 7/1/15 W1+15 K2+22, W3+13 =
ZEVECOTEN 30th March	No working parties from 51st but whole except at YPRES or Manual Wks 2 (Lieut) Battalions in YPRES in Reserve to 3rd Divn.	

1247 W 3299 200,000 (E) 8/14 J.B.C. & A. Forms/C. 2118/11.

Army Form C. 2118.

WAR DIARY
or
INTELLIGENCE SUMMARY

(Erase heading not required.)

Instructions regarding War Diaries and Intelligence Summaries are contained in F. S. Regs, Part II. and the Staff Manual respectively. Title pages will be prepared in manuscript.

Hour, Date, Place	Summary of Events and Information	Remarks and references to Appendices
31st March	11 Divn. Yeomanry pwd making forty seven CRE for 2nd line men. ADMINISTRATION. Div. March. (Lieut I. T. Pratter and 1st R Lunates Gloucesters last with spell cine R hire & 2nd Near attached) in Reserve to 3rd Divn.	

BRIGADE OPERATION ORDERS NOS. 42 to 49.

Copy No.

81st INFANTRY BRIGADE ORDER No. 42.

4th March, 1915.

1. The Brigade will relieve the 82nd Brigade in the front line to-morrow.

    The 1st Rl. Scots and 2nd Gloucester Regt. in the trenches, the 2nd Cameron Highlanders Dickebusch, 1st A. & S. Highlanders in DICKEBUSCH with 1 Company at ELZENWALLE.

2. The 1st Royal Scots and 2nd Gloucesters will leave RENINGHELST and WESTOUTRE respectively at 2-15 p.m. and march via Road Junction, Square G.29 d - Cross Rds. Junction of Squares G. 36 d. and H. 31 c. and Rd. Junction H. 31 b to DICKEBUSCH Huts.

    The cooks wagons of both regiments will leave ZEVECOTEN at 2 p.m. and march by the same route. Remaining transport less supply wagons will follow each battalion.

3. The 1st Royal Scots will leave DICKEBUSCH between 5-30 and 6-30 to relieve the Right Battalion in the trenches. The 2nd Gloucesters will leave DICKEBUSCH between 6-30 and 7-15 p.m. to relieve the left battalion in the trenches.

4. The 1st A. & S. Highlanders and 2nd Cameron Highlanders, under Lt. Col. Campbell will march to DICKEBUSCH via LA CLYTTE so as to pass LA CLYTTE Cross Roads at 6-10 p.m.

    Baggage wagons of these battalions under the transport officer, 1st A. & S. Highlanders, will march via LA CLYTTE to DICKEBUSCH at 10 a.m. After passing LA CLYTTE an interval of 50 yards will be kept between each wagon and 150 yards between the wagons of the 2 battalions.

5. All concerned are reminded that no troops or transport are to approach nearer than 500 yards to N.W. of VIERSTRAAT without ascertaining that that point is clear of 3rd Division troops and transport.

the Cross Roads 500 yards

J. Howard
Captain,
Brigade Major 81st Inf. Bde.

Copy No. 1

81st INFY. BDE. ORDER No. 43.

4th March, 1915.

1.   ½ Coy. 9th A. & S. Highlanders will march to-morrow via WESTOUTRE – HEKSKEN – ZEVECOTEN – Road Junction G.29 d. – Road Junction G.36 d. – Road Junction H. 31 b. to the Hut Shelters behind DICKEBUSCH, when they will come under the orders of the G.O.C. 80th Infantry Brigade.
     The ½ Company will pass the Road Junction at the 2nd E of WESTOUTRE at 10 a.m. where they will be met by an officer detailed by O.C. 2nd Gloucester Regiment who will guide them to the Huts.
     The O.C. the ½ Coy. will report himself to the G.O.C. 80th Infantry Brigade at Brigade Headquarters, DICKEBUSCH on arrival.

2.   The O.C. 97th Co. Train will arrange with the O.C. 9th Argyll & Sutherland Highlanders to meet and guide the transport required by the ½ company to DICKEBUSCH, following the route taken by the Supply Column. This transport should be sent early enough to allow the men's dinners to be cooked at DICKEBUSCH.

3.   1 Company, 9th Royal Scots and 1 Company 9th Argyll & Sutherland Highlanders will proceed to DICKEBUSCH on Saturday the 6th instant, following the route detailed in Order No. 1.
     The 9th Royal Scots leading will pass the Road Junction about 1 mile S.E. of BOESCHEPE at 1-50 p.m. A guide will be detailed by Brigade Headquarters to guide these companies to report to O.C. 9th Royal Scots at WESTOUTRE.
     The transport required by these two companies will be conducted to DICKEBUSCH under arrangements to be made by the O.C. 97th Co. A.S.C. who will consult with the Officers Commanding these Battalions.

[signature] Captain,
Brigade Major 81st Inf. Brigade.

Copy No. 1

81st INFY. BDE. ORDER No. 44.

5th March, 1915.

1. The enemy's line of defence will be heavily bombarded from 12 noon to about 4 p.m. to-morrow in front of trenches 15 to 21 with a view to their destruction.

2. Trenches Nos. 15, 16, and 17, 18 and 19 will be temporarily evacuated just before dawn and re-occupied immediately it is dark enough.
   The garrisons of trenches 19 a and 20 will be withdrawn by communication trenches at 11-45 a.m. and re-occupied as soon as the bombardment ceases.

3. Special vigilance is required to prevent any attempt by the enemy to occupy our "vacated trenches," by rifle and machine gun fire.

4. The garrison of trenches in the Right Section of defence will be strengthened before dawn on the 6th (to-morrow) with a view to preventing any possible effort of the enemy to divert attention from the left section during the bombardment by attempting an attack on this part of our line.
   The usual guns of the 1st and 19th F.A. Brigades will be ready to assist in dealing with such a contingency and the O.C. 1st Royal Scots and 2nd Gloucesters will take steps to place themselves in communication with the R.A. concerned.

5. Special care is to be taken in selecting the lines of fire of machine guns and rifles in case the enemy are forced to retire from their trenches, especially behind PICCADILLY FARM.

6. Telephone communications from Brigade Headquarters to Battalion Headquarters and thence to the trenches are to be tested at 11 a.m. and report sent to Brigade Headquarters.

7. Observations of officers or N.C.O.'s in trenches, of the effect of our artillery fire to be reported with the times carefully noted.

8. Nothing in these orders is to be communicated to anybody not directly concerned, till after 12 noon to-morrow.

Issued at 9 p.m.

J. Howard, Captain,
Brigade Major 81st Infy. Brigade.

Copy No. 1

81st Infantry Brigade Order No. 45.

8th March 1915.

(1) O.C. 9th A.& S. Highrs. will detail four platoons to go into the trenches to-night for twenty four hours. Two from one company to be attached to the Cameron Highlanders and two from another company who will be attached to the 1st A. & S. Highrs.
   These parties will leave their huts so as to pass LA CLYTTE cross roads at 6-10 p.m.
   Guides from the 2nd Camerons and 1st A. & S. Highrs respectively to be at the BRASSERIE at 7 p.m.
   120 rounds of ammunition per man will be carried.
   Rations for twenty four hours will be carried on the man.
   Packs will not be carried.
   On leaving the trenches on the evening of the 9th inst these platoons will return to ROSENHILL HUTS.
   Two other platoons will be prepared to go into the trenches on the 9th inst and on succeeding nights till all the companies have completed one tour of twenty four hours.

                                          Captain.
                      Brigade Major, 81st Infantry Brigade.

Copy No. 1

81st INFY. BDE. ORDER No. 46.

8th March, 1915.

1. The enemy's trenches in front of our trenches 14 to 21 will be bombarded to-morrow from 7 a.m. to 6 p.m., our trenches 15, 16, 17 and 18 being withdrawn before daylight.

2. It is considered possible that the enemy may attempt to divert our fire by making a demonstration in front of the Right Section. Officers Commanding 2nd Cameron Highlanders and 1st Argyll and Sutherland Highlanders must be prepared to prevent this.

3. The trenches will be re-occupied after 6 p.m. and a sharp look-out must be kept to prevent any attempt by the enemy to prevent their re-occupation.

4. All Officers and N.C.O.'s in trenches will be specially warned to observe and report the effect of our artillery fire.

Issued 6-45 p.m.

J. Kounn, Captain,
Brigade Major 81st Infy. Bde.

Copy No. 1

81st Brigade Order No. 46

Reference Maps
1/40000
1/10000
and attached Sketch.

11th March 1915.

1. The 3rd Division will attack tomorrow in the direction of WYTSCHAETE. The 5th Corps will cooperate by employing artillery and rifle fire, especially directed against HOLLAND-ESCHUR FARM.

2. Registration of Artillery targets will take place between 7am and 7.50 am.
   8am - 8.15 am. Artillery fire for wire cutting in front of HOLLANDESCHUR FARM.

3. At 8.15 am - Rapid rifle fire will be directed through all loopholes, or, by snipers or any other means without reckless exposure, on the front L M N O ie, on the Enemy's defences round HOLLANDESCHUR farm by fire and support trenches, which can see this target. All other trenches will fire at targets opposite them. Rifle fire will be as intense as possible from 8.15 am. to 8.20 am. After 8.20 am. it will be intermittent, but every advantage will be taken of any good targets that may be offered.

4. 8.20 am. - 9.15 am. Artillery fire on the front O P N M L.
   8.45 - 9.15. Heavy Batteries 27th and 28th Divs. fire on HOLLANDESCHUR FARM.
   At 9.15 am. fire on O P N M L will cease except by heavy batteries, or in case RA or Infantry observers consider an advantage will be gained in continuing it.

5. One Aeroplane will cooperate with each divisional artillery.

6. Telephone communications to be tested before dawn in time to mend faults and again at 7 am. when a report will be sent to Bde. H.Q.

7. Signal time to be obtained at 7.10 am.

Issued 11.10 p.m.
By order.

J. Howard Captain
B.M. 81st Inf. Bde.

8th Bde   Operation Order No 47.   Copy No 1.

Ref Maps
- 1/40,000 sheet 28
- 1/10,000 VOORMEZEELE

13 March 1915

& tracing issued with Operation Order No 46.

(1) 5th Corps will continue offensive action to-day against the enemy about HOLLANDSCHUR FARM.

(2) 1 p.m. to 1.15 p.m.
   Artillery fire on M.N. & NO

(3) 2.15 p.m. Rapid fire will be opened on the front NO through all loopholes, by snipers & by any other means without reckless exposure, from fire & support trenches, which can engage this front.

Other trenches will engage enemy's trenches opposite them.

Rifle fire will be as intense as possible from 2.15 p.m. to 2.20 p.m. After 2.20 p.m. it will be intermittent but advantage will be taken of any good target.

(4) At 2.20 p.m.
   Artillery fire on OP, ON, NM, NL & ground in rear of LMNO against enemy's supports.

(5) One aeroplane will cooperate with each divisional artillery

(6) Telephone communication to be tested before dawn, at noon & again at 12.30 p.m. when a report will be sent to 8th D. H.Q.

(7) Signal drum to be obtained at 9.5 a.m.

Issued at 2.45 a.m.
by order

                                    [signature]
                                    Bde Major
                                    8th Inf Bde

Copy No. 1

81st INFANTRY BDE. ORDER No. 48.

19th March, 1915.

The following extract from 27th Divisional Operation Order No. 36, dated 18th March, 1915 is published for information:-

x　　x　　x　　x　　x　　x　　x

"It must be clearly understood that by all ranks that the object of the shortening of the 27th Division line is in order that the portion henceforth to be defended is to be rendered absolutely secure. So strong that it will resist any attack, however powerful, which the enemy may make. This will entail larger garrisons in the trenches, fire and support, now held, and continuous work in improving them.

It also entails working parties being told off every night to construct new lines in support of those held. These parties will be told off daily in consultation with C.R.E. New support trenches as constructed will be immediately garrisoned and manned day and night. Every available man that is not actually in the defence line will be made use of each night for working or carrying until ST. ELOI defences are finished.

The new line will be divided as follows for front line, subsidiary line and G.H.Q. line:-

Right Section of Defence.

From the Right Flank Boundary already referred to, to the KRUISSTRAATHOEK - VOORMEZEELE - ST. ELOI - MESSINES Road exclusive.

Left Section of Defence.

From the KRUISSTRAATHOEK - VOORMEZEELE - ST. ELOI - MESSINES Road inclusive, to our boundary with 28th Division. (This boundary runs approximately from CHATEAU KRUISSTRAATHOEK (inclusive to 27th Division) - to point on road track 250 yards S.W. of ECLUSE No. 8 - point of juncture I 32 d. with O. 3 a. to left of trench No. 23.

As regards accommodation, KRUISSTRAATHOEK - VOORMEZEELE ST. ELOI Road is also the dividing line. The whole village of VOORMEZEELE is, however, allotted for this purpose to the 80th Infantry Brigade, except that the G.O.C. of that brigade will afford G.O.C. 82nd Infantry Brigade accommodation for at least half company reserve in that village.

4.　　The Right Section of Defence will be held permanently by the 81st Infantry Brigade. The Left Section of Defence alternately by the 80th and 82nd Infantry Brigades. "

x　　x　　x　　x　　x　　x　　x

The boundary of between the right of the 27th Division and the left of the 3rd Division will be stream between No. 11 and 12 trenches thence along brook to its junction with BALLAARTBEEK then to point on VIERSTRAAT - KRUISSTRAATHOEK Road about where road crosses boundary between H. 36 c. and N. 6 a. thence to point where G.H.Q. line crosses road in H. 35 d.

[signature] Captain,
Bde. MAJOR 81st INF. BDE

19.3.15.

Copy No. 1

81st Inf Bde Order No. 49

Ref. map 1/40000 YPRES.   25th March 1915.

1. The 9th R. Scots and 9th Argyll and Sutherland Highlanders will march tomorrow 26th inst to YPRES under Lt Col Blair 9th R. Scots. Route - WESTOUTRE - RENINGHELST - SUDERDOM - VLAMERTINGHE.

2. 9th R. Scots will reach the 2nd E of WESTOUTRE at 7.50 a.m. and the 9th A&S Hrs at 8.20 a.m.

3. On arrival at WESTOUTRE packs will be taken off and packed by companies at a place which will be pointed out by a Staff Officer 27th Div. 1 NCO and 4 men per Company will be left to load the packs on to motor lorries which will arrive at 11 a.m.

4. The 9th R. Scots will clear the road junction 2nd E of WESTOUTRE at 8.15 a.m. the 9th A&S High'rs at 9 a.m.
The 9th A&S Highrs will clear the VLAMERTINGHE cross roads at 11 a.m.

5. An officer will meet battalions at the GRANDE PLACE, YPRES and show them their billets.

6. Both battalions will work on the GHQ 2nd Line on the nights of the 26th and 27th inst. under supervision of an officer 17th Coy F. Coy R.E.

7. The exact position of H.Q. of each battalion will be notified to the Bde office by wire, immediately on arrival.
Two orderlies from each Batt'n to be sent to the 28th Div. Signal Office (Report Centre) square H11 B on arrival to remain day & night till the battalions rejoin the brigade.

Issued at 8.10 p.m.
by Motor Cyclist.

L. Howard Lushan
BM 81st Inf Bde

Maps

I. No. 1. Section Outpost line 28/2/15
II. Section held by 81st Bde 5-20th March
III. Situation at St Eloi after German attack 14/3/15.
IV. Sketches showing work done by R.E. 17/18/3/15
V. Sketch showing details round trench no 10.
VI. Sketch showing Communications & Dugouts in Bois Carré
VII. Sketch showing trench

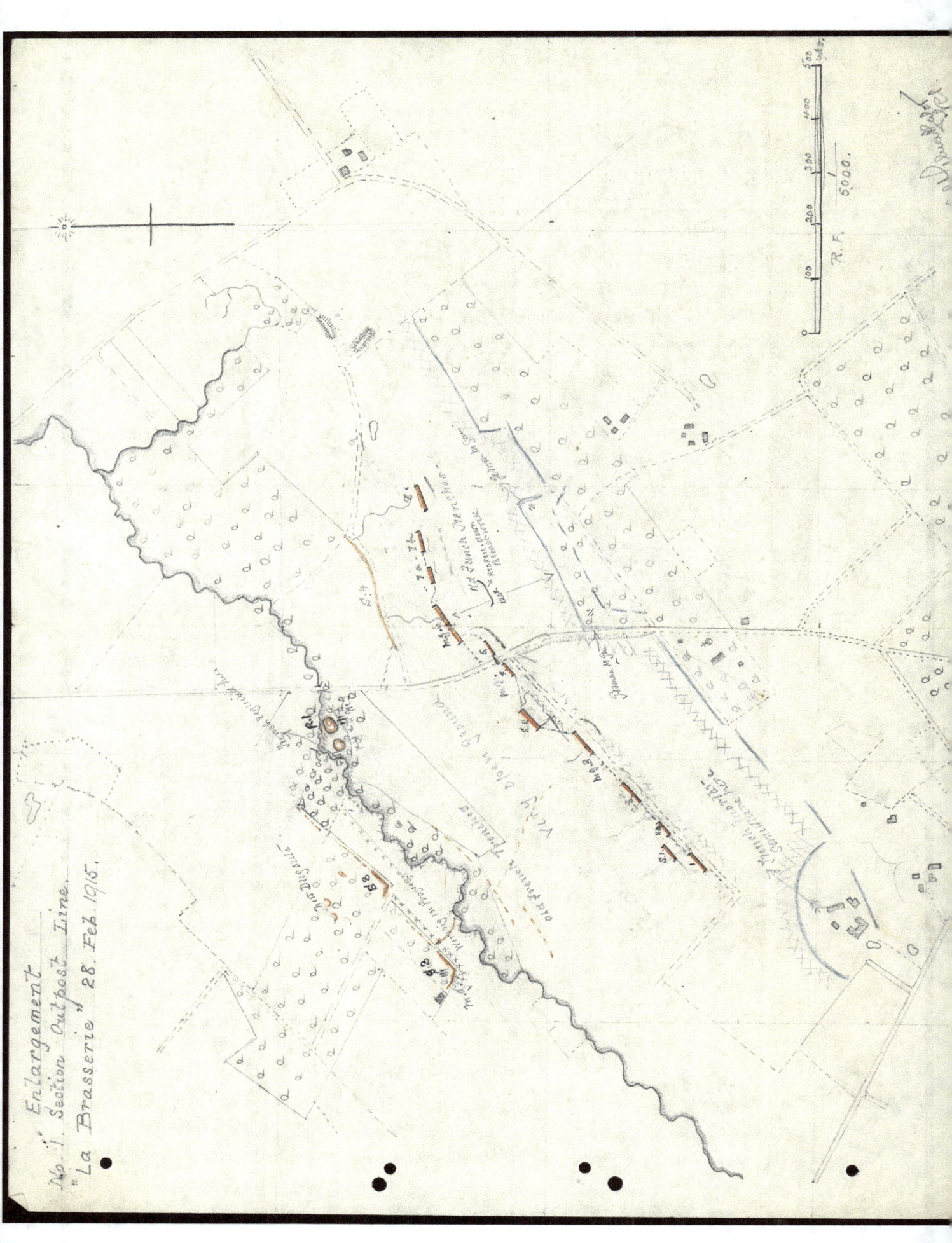

2nd Camerons,
1st A. & S. Highrs.

(In trenches Rt Section)
Remarks all Battln)

B.M. 229.

Attached sketch shows the situation at ST ELOI.

The attack on the 14th was started from the parallels and fire trenches.

The attack was apparently carried out by the 22nd & 23rd Bavarians with Prussian Pioneers (the same troops who attacked a month ago, 14th Feb.)

The trenches from 15 to 22 were all attacked; the mound was attacked from both sides of the road and apparently fell for want of effective rifle fire.

17, 18, mound and 19 were blown up simultaneously

15, 16 and 20 and R.B., K.S.L.I. trenches and part of breastwork were captured.

20 recaptured by Leinsters, 19 and 19a by P.P.C.L.I. R.B. and K.S.L.I. by the Rifle Brigade.

Counter attacks on the mound by the P.P.C.L.I from 19 and R. Bde. and K.S.L.I. from R.B. trench and ST. ELOI failed owing to machine guns posted on mound.

Germans lost heavily in attacking especially from 22 and machine guns in S.7 and S.9.

Our artillery fire prevented their supports from coming up and 2 German prisoners admit heavy losses.

The Germans are reported to have joined 19, 19a and the mound by sandbag ~~loop~~ breastworks and to have made new trench opposite the K.S.L.I. Trench which became untenable and is not now held by us.

Trenches S.7, New 14, S.9 are joined by a 3' high communication trench with two breastworks in the gaps.

R.B.

R.B. Trench is turned back to face the mound. Germans occupy the Mound when it is not being shelled and have been seen trying to crawl forward towards ST ELOI and apparently trying to loophole house behind the breastwork marked

                                            (sd) L. Holland, Captain,
16/3/1915.   Bde. Major 81st Inf. Bde.

Situation after German
Attack 14th March
1111 Shews Trenches blown up
or captured by enemy, or
evacuated by us.

IV

②

C. Made communication trench to A & B.
D. Constructed position for 6 rifles in branch of old French trench.
E. Dug entrance to Sap, leaving old entrance as drain for sap.
F. Barricaded Post for one rifle at entrance to sap.

N.B. A, B & D were occupied by infantry before daybreak.

Sap. This is now progressing very well indeed. It is through the softer sodden ground around the old French trenches & the walls are now standing well. The Miners are now accustomed to the conditions & are working very well. About 60 f/90 feet of tunnel at 4 a.m.

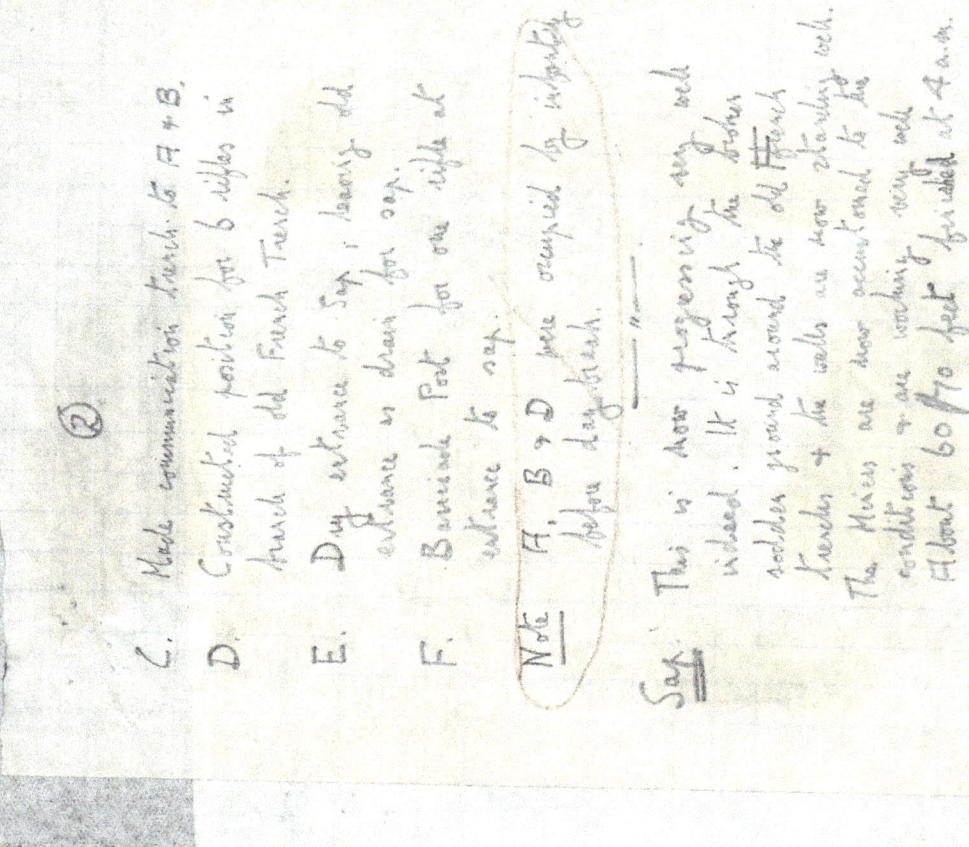

① March 18th 1915.

To C.R.E. 27ᵗʰ Division

Report on work done night of 17/18ᵗʰ inst.

FRENCH TRENCH TO 4
FRENCH TRENCH TO 3
DRAIN FROM SAP

Defences of Sap between S₂ & 3.
(Work done is shown shaded in above sketch)

A. Cleared out old French Trench & constructed position for 4 rifles. Traversed at 4 rifles.
B. Constructed position for 4 rifles. Traversed at left end.

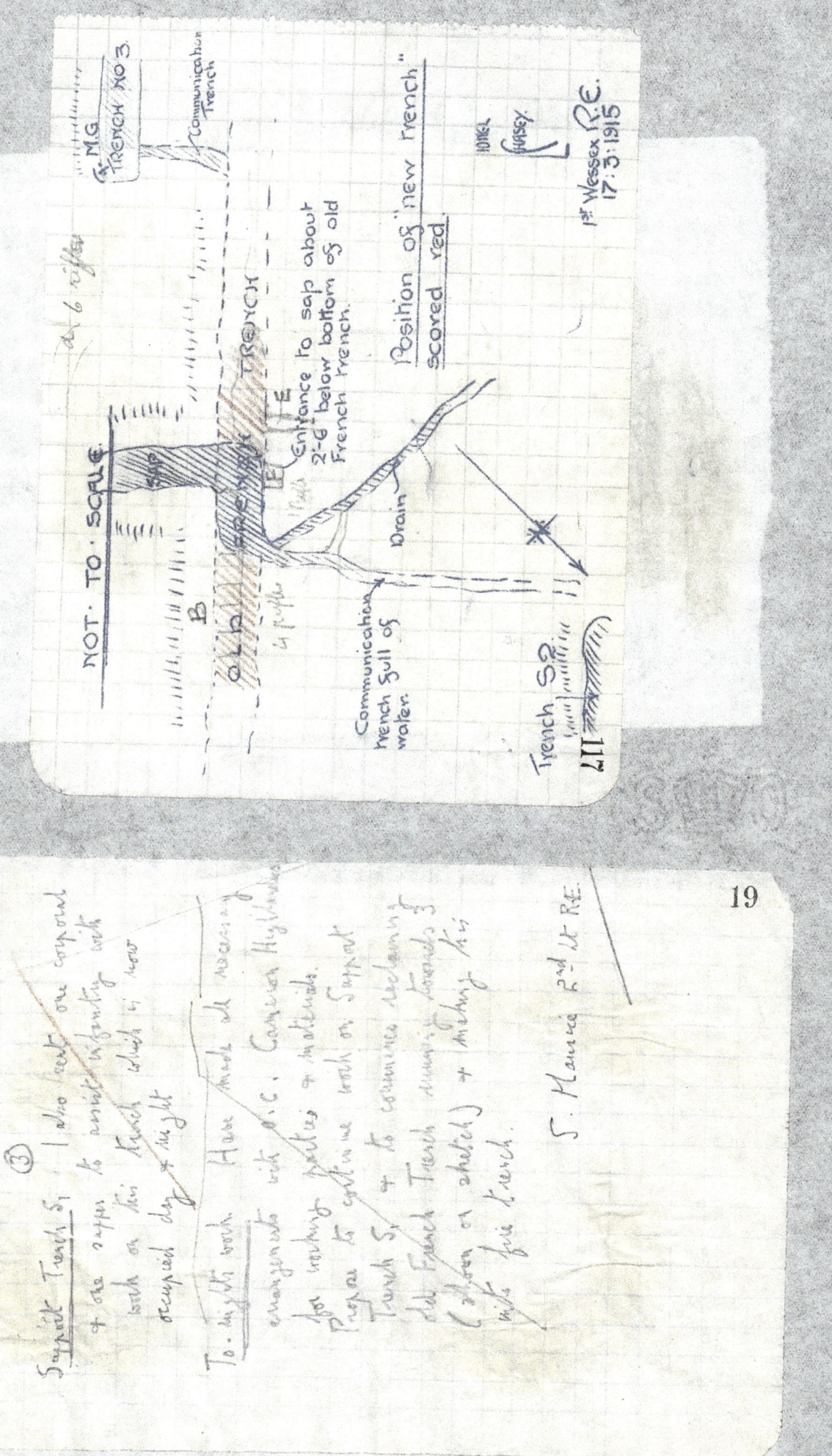

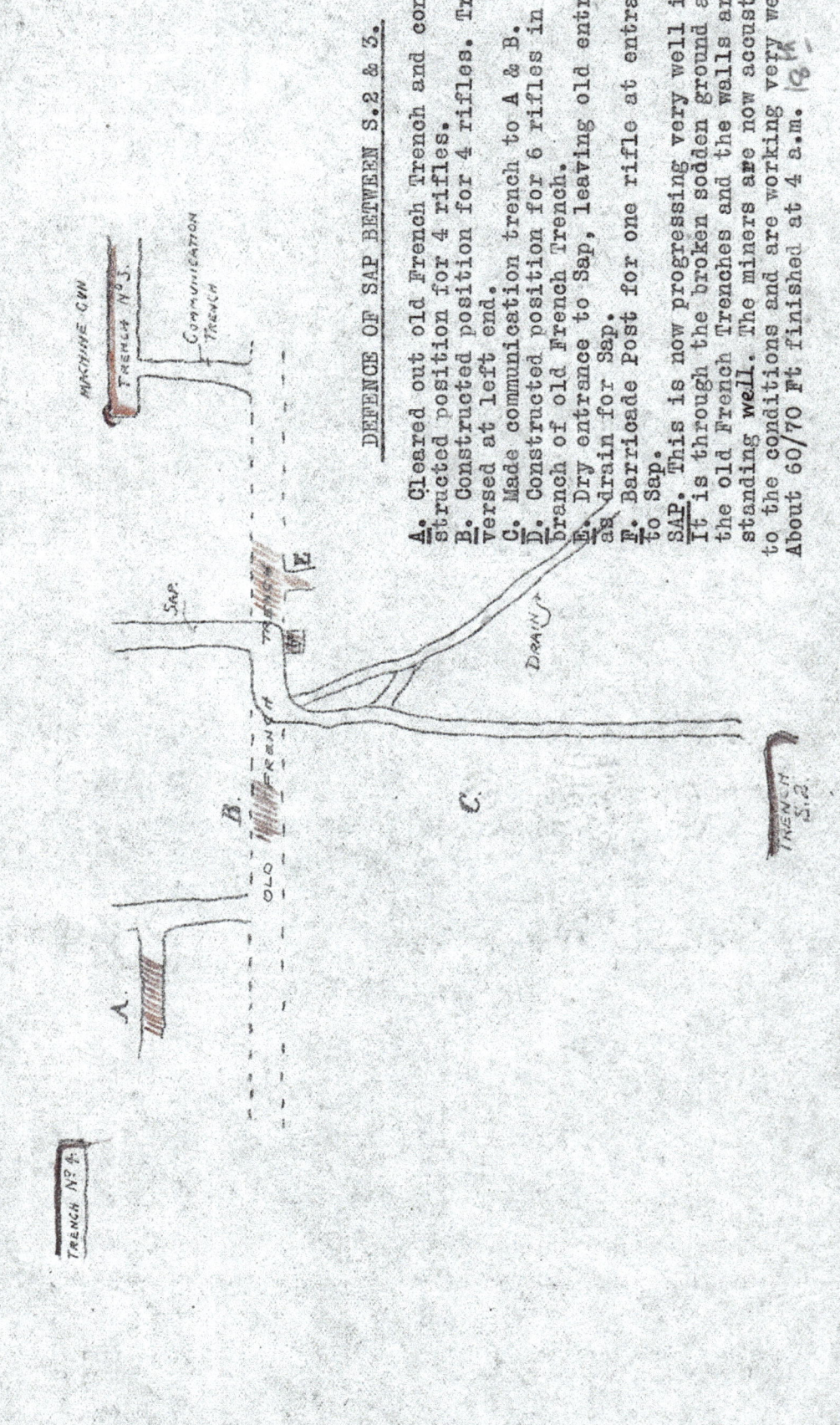

DEFENCE OF SAP BETWEEN S.2 & 3.

A. Cleared out old French Trench and constructed position for 4 rifles.
B. Constructed position for 4 rifles. Traversed at left end.
C. Made communication trench to A & B.
D. Constructed position for 6 rifles in branch of old French Trench.
E. Dry entrance to Sap, leaving old entrance as drain for Sap.
F. Barricade Post for one rifle at entrance to Sap.
SAP. This is now progressing very well indeed It is through the broken sodden ground around the old French Trenches and the walls are now standing well. The miners are now accustomed to the conditions and are working very well. About 60/70 Ft finished at 4 a.m. 16/R

DEFENCE OF SAP BETWEEN S.2 & 3.

A. Cleared out old French Trench and constructed position for 4 rifles.
B. Constructed position for 4 rifles. Traversed at left end.
C. Made communication trench to A & B.
D. Constructed position for 6 rifles in branch of old French Trench.
E. Dry entrance to Sap, leaving old entrance as drain for Sap.
F. Barricade Post for one rifle at entrance to Sap.

SAP. This is now progressing very well indeed It is through the broken sodden ground around the old French Trenches and the walls are now standing well. The miners are now accustomed to the conditions and are working very well. About 60/70 Ft finished at 4 a.m.

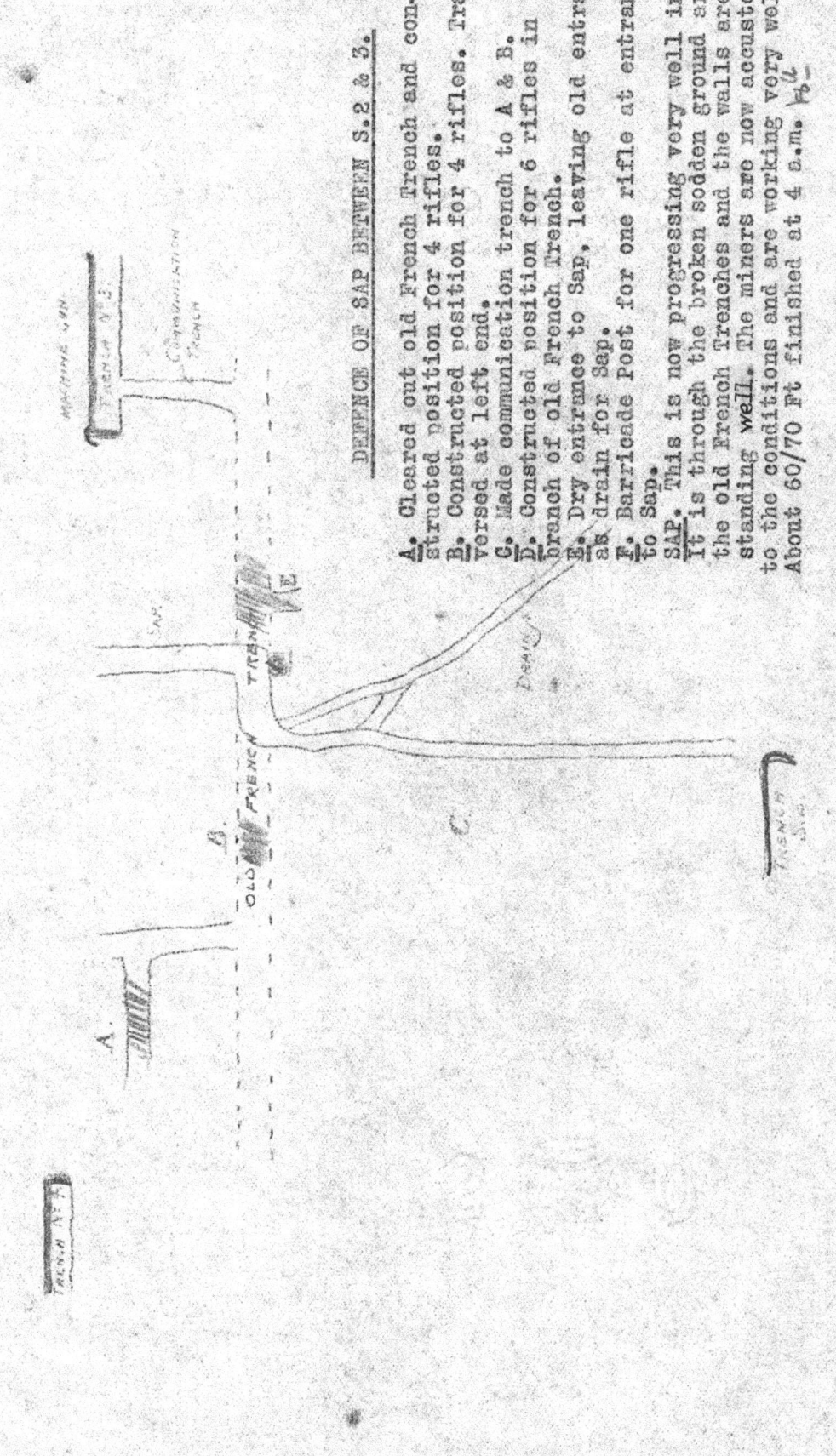

Details round Trench No. 10.

Note.
The distances are paced only and are roughly about one yard.

Scale about 50 Yards to 1 inch.

N.

Ground under cultivation.

Old French Trench & Dug Outs.

Old French Trench.

Wood that has been cleared.

Try Drain draining No. 9 Trench.

Bridge
Machine Gun
No. 10.
Dug Out
Bridge
Sap.

No. 11.

No. 9. Pond.

No. 8.

"A" Form.   Army Form C. 2121.
MESSAGES AND SIGNALS.
No. of message _____

Prefix ____ Code ____ in	Words	Charge	This message is on a/c of	Recd. at ____ m.
Office of Origin and Service Instructions				Date ____
	Sent			From ____
At ____ m.			Service.	
To ____				

Sketch R.I.

51

R – Block occupied by
enemy rifles.
xxxxx – wire through
$\triangle$ – however into Block
10ᵗʰ Hus. 15ᵗʰ formed edge,
$\rightarrow$ – drove out for 20.
M.G. Captured.
$\Rightarrow$ – trench recommended
but kept waste
flattery transmitted

M-3rd K.R. Rif S.

AAA

To Brown Creek

● RUINED FARM

Telephone Lines from Bois Carré.
(No scale)

to Brasserie

to Brasserie

S3

S4

S2

1 2 2A 3 5 6

from sketch
by Capt. Macpherson
3/Coon Hrs

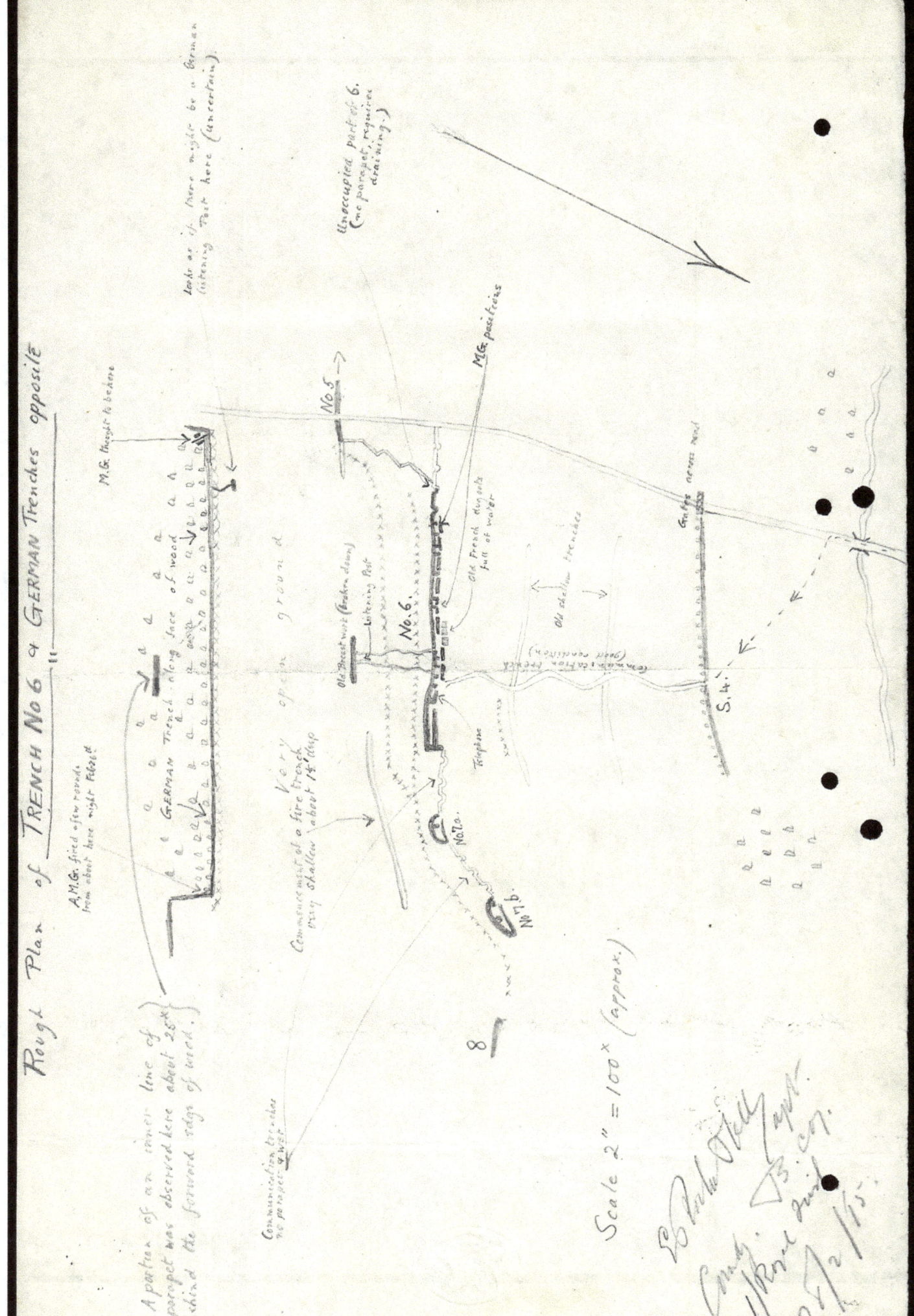

27th Division.

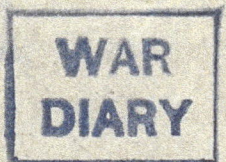

B. H. Q. 81st INFANTRY BRIGADE.

April

1915

Army Form C. 2118.

WAR DIARY
or
INTELLIGENCE SUMMARY

(Erase heading not required.)

Instructions regarding War Diaries and Intelligence Summaries are contained in F.S. Regs., Part II. and the Staff Manual respectively. Title pages will be prepared in manuscript.

Hour, Date, Place	Summary of Events and Information	Remarks and references to Appendices

Confidential

WAR DIARY
of
Hd. Qrs. 81st Infy Bde 27th Divn.

from 1st April 1915 to 30th April 1915
(Volume V)

R Guild Capt
attached Hd. Qrs. 81st Infy Bde.
13. 5. 15

Army Form C. 2118.

WAR DIARY
or
INTELLIGENCE SUMMARY

(Erase heading not required.)

81st Inf Bde.

Hour, Date, Place	Summary of Events and Information	Remarks and references to Appendices
1st April. 1915.	Disposition of Brigade. Bau Hd. BENINGHELST 1st R Scots 2nd Gloucesters } ROSENHILL HUTS near LEVECOTEN 2nd Cameron 1st Gd Hghrs } CANADA HUTS near OUDERDOM. 9th R. Scots (Ter) 9th A.M. Hghrs (Ter) } YPRES near ONE 25yds adjoining on G.H.Q Line of defence. Receiving orders to move on 4th April to take over part of line from 17th French Div. The two Reserve Battalions were inspected by Sir Horace SMITH-DORRIEN Comdg 2nd Army. was LEVECOTEN.	27th Div OO Order 39.
2nd April.	Brigadier General CROKER and Bde Majr visited trench held at HOOGE with a view to taking over new line on the 4th inst. (68th Regt) 1st R Scots and Gloucesters working on G.H.Q Line. Cameron, 1st Argylls with K.S.LI. and P.P.C.L.I attached from 80th Bde form Reserve to 3rd Div.	
3rd April.	Orders to relieve 17th French Div in trenches East of YPRES on 4th inst. 3- 6. 4pm. 4th Camerons to be Reserve Brigade to 3rd Div. at 12 midnight.	27 Div OO Order 42. 81st Bde Order 50.

1247 W 9299 200,000 (E) 8/14 J.B.C. & A. Forms/C. 2118/11. 3/4½ inst.

Army Form C. 2118.

WAR DIARY
or
INTELLIGENCE SUMMARY
(Erase heading not required.)

81st Inf Bde.

Instructions regarding War Diaries and Intelligence Summaries are contained in F. S. Regs., Part II. and the Staff Manual respectively. Title pages will be prepared in manuscript.

Hour, Date, Place	Summary of Events and Information	Remarks and references to Appendices
1915		
4th April	The Bde moved from ZEVECOTEN (vicinity of) and took over Trenches East of YPRES from the French — Dispositions under — 9th R Scots 2 Camn Hdrs } in the Trenches 1 Argylls In close support to Bn 9th R Scots behind Chateau SANS NOM 1 Coy 2nd Glouc R West of ETANG DE BELLEWARDE 1 Coy 2 Glouc. R attached to 1 Argylls near Hd Qrs left Battalion. 2 Coys 2 Glouc R. and H.Q. in billets at YPRES ready to move at a moment's notice. 1 R Scots at POPERINGHE 9 Argylls billets ~~VLAMERTINGHE~~ VLAMERTINGHE Bde Hd Qrs at HOOGE – Staff Capt and Officer at YPRES	Line running from N.W. corner 29 15a through squares of sq 14d to S.W. corner 20 b 4. Ref 1/40,000 sheet 27 BELGIUM JPG
5th April	Relief was completed 5 men slightly wounded	JPG
6th April	French artillery were relieved by British artillery	JPG
7th April	In the Trenches 1 Argylls 2 Camerons 9th Argylls in close support ~~to~~ ~~tr~~ 2 Glouc. R. less 2 Coys and 9th R Scots less 2 Coys.	JPG

1247 W 3299 200,000 (E) 8/14 J.B.C. & A. Forms/C. 2118/11.

Army Form C. 2118.

WAR DIARY
or
INTELLIGENCE SUMMARY
(Erase heading not required.)

Instructions regarding War Diaries and Intelligence Summaries are contained in F. S. Regs., Part II. and the Staff Manual respectively. Title pages will be prepared in manuscript.

Hour, Date, Place	Summary of Events and Information	Remarks and references to Appendices
8th April	The Bde relief took place dispositions as under –	Night 8th/9th.
	In the Trenches. 2 Gloucesters	
	1 R. Scots (from POPERINGHE)	
	9 R Scots	
8th April to night 12th/13th April	In Close Support 2 Cameron Hdrs. (SANCTUARY WOOD) ref Sheet 28 Sq J 13.c.	1/40,000 map BELGIUM
	1 Argylls	
	AT YPRES	
	AT VLAMERTINGHE 9 Argylls	
	16 Casualties from shell fire.	
9th April	Relief completed satisfactorily – Adjutant 9 Argylls ordered away Capt. YOUNG 1 Argylls sent to replace him. Till successor is appointed by G.H.Q.	Capt GRAY
11th April	Explosion of Bomb Store near FREZENBURG all Transport Officers warned of unexploded bombs guides sent to conduct Transport to new dumping ground	

Army Form C. 2118.

WAR DIARY
or
INTELLIGENCE SUMMARY
(Erase heading not required.)

Instructions regarding War Diaries and Intelligence Summaries are contained in F.S. Regs., Part II. and the Staff Manual respectively. Title pages will be prepared in manuscript.

Hour, Date, Place	Summary of Events and Information	Remarks and references to Appendices
12th April	The Bde relief took place dispositions as under — In the Trenches. 1 Argylls relieved 2 Gloucesters 2. Camerons " 1 R. Scots 9 Argylls " 9 R. Scots In Close Support. 1 R. Scots relieved 2 Camerons AT YPRES 2 Gloucesters. AT VLAMERTINGHE 9th R. Scots	F.G.
12th April to night 16/17th inst.	Units warned that Germans had been seen wearing white armlets and not to mistake them for stretcher bearers — These were shown by their attacks on ST ELOI	
13th April	Staff Capt. and Office of H.Q. moved from YPRES to POTIJZE	F.G.
14th April	Anti aircraft section of 2 machine guns attached to Bde in Close support for aeroplane observations	Fired at STIRLING CASTLE about J 15 d 7.7 3½" 1/40,000 map BELGIUM. F.G.
16th April	1 Argylls, 2 Camerons and 9th Argylls trekked to hand over 2 Machine Guns and catapults to relieving Bns.	F.G.

1247 W 3299 200,000 (E) 8/14 J.B.C. & A. Forms/C. 2118/11.

Army Form C. 2118.

WAR DIARY
or
INTELLIGENCE SUMMARY
(Erase heading not required.)

Instructions regarding War Diaries and Intelligence Summaries are contained in F. S. Regs., Part II. and the Staff Manual respectively. Title pages will be prepared in manuscript.

Hour, Date, Place	Summary of Events and Information	Remarks and references to Appendices
16th April	The Bde Relief took place – Bns. in the Trenches relieved as under	
16th April to Night 20th/21st inst.	2 Gloucesters relieved 1 Argylls 1 R. Scots " 2 Camerons 9 R. Scots " 9 Argylls	RG
17th April	One officer and four other ranks per Coy instructed in the Bomb by Major SANKEY R.E. Units in Trenches informed that enemy were attacking 5th Divn Strongly	RG
18th April		RG
19th April	Officers and Other Ranks instructed in use of new Hand grenades by Major SANKEY R.E. – Precautions taken to keep men (in the vicinity of HOOGE) under cover by day except when on duty. 5th Divn reported HILL 60 strongly held by us	RG

Army Form C. 2118.

WAR DIARY
or
INTELLIGENCE SUMMARY

(Erase heading not required.)

Instructions regarding War Diaries and Intelligence Summaries are contained in F.S. Regs, Part II. and the Staff Manual respectively. Title pages will be prepared in manuscript.

Hour, Date, Place	Summary of Events and Information	Remarks and references to Appendices
20th April	1st R Scots were not relieved by 2 Camerons other Bns were relieved as under – 9th Argylls relieved 1th R. Scots 1st Argylls " 2 Gloucesters 1st R Scots remained in Trenches	
	2 Gloucesters moved into close support 2 Camerons " in YPRES 9 R Scots and 5 VLAMERTINGHE	RG
21st April	2 Camerons were placed under the orders of 5th Divn. Camerons sent to near ZILLEBEKE in close support with BEDFORDS	RG
22nd April	2 Gloucesters relieved 1 R Scots Trenches 1 R Scots went into support Germans launched gas attack 2/ Gloucesters unable to relieve 1 R Scots without Keystone Rg message received that Germans have attacked trenches on left of Canadians – No relief to take place	RG
23rd April	No relief took place	RG

1247 W 3290 200,000 (E) 8/14 J.B.C. & A. Forms/C. 2118/11.

Army Form C. 2118.

WAR DIARY
or
INTELLIGENCE SUMMARY

(Erase heading not required.)

Instructions regarding War Diaries and Intelligence Summaries are contained in F.S. Regs, Part II. and the Staff Manual respectively. Title pages will be prepared in manuscript.

Hour, Date, Place	Summary of Events and Information	Remarks and references to Appendices
9.45am 24th April	2 Coys Gloucesters under senior major placed under orders of Brigadier 82nd Infy Bde as Brigade Reserve. Sent Infy Bde. No relief took place - 1 R. Scots, 7 Argylls and 1 Argylls in the Trenches. 2 Camerons still under orders of 5th Divn.	
12.4 P.m.	2 Gloucesters ordered to move to VERLORENHOEK area and placed under orders of Brigadier Genl. SMITH 80th Bde	
2.50 P.m.	Bns. in Trenches ordered to send one coy each to SANCTUARY wood under Major WINGATE 1 R. Scots to replace Glouc R ordered away.	
6.20 P.m.	Gloucesters no longer required by 80th Bde owing to arrival of reinforcements - returned SANCTUARY WOOD	R.G.
9.45 am 25th April	One coy Gloucesters sent to BELLEWARDE LAKE and placed under orders of the 84th Bde	
3.5 P.m. 26th April	Gloucesters ordered to be ready to move at a moments notice - Coy. attached 80th Bde to move with Bn.	

Forms/C. 2118/11.
1247 W 3299 200,000 (E) 8/14 J.B.C. & A.

WAR DIARY or INTELLIGENCE SUMMARY

Army Form C. 2118.

Hour, Date, Place	Summary of Events and Information	Remarks and references to Appendices
3.40 pm. 26th April	Gloucesters order to move at once by railway crossing 1 1/b and POTIZE to take up a position S. of YPRES - POTIZE road with right on POTIZE - ZILLEBEKE road - One Bn of 82nd Bde was on Gloucesters left - The Coy 2 Glouc.R attached 80th Bde did not move - During the night 26/27 2 Gloucesters less 2 Coys returned to SANCTUARY WOOD forming Brigade Reserve One Coy Gloucesters attached 80th Bde - One Coy attached 82nd Bde.	Ref 1/40000 map BELGIUM sheet 28. T.G.
27th April	Divn asked if 2 Gloucesters may relieve 1 R. Scots - No relief took place.	T.G.
28th April	9th R Scots returned to the Bde. and became Bde Reserve to 80th and 82nd Bde. Hd Qrs and 2 Coys 82nd Bde remaining 2 Coys under senior major to 80th Bde. - 2 Coys and 2 Platoons Glouc.R in Bde Reserve remainder in fire trenches of 1 Argylls and 1 R. Scots	T.G.

Army Form C. 2118.

WAR DIARY
or
INTELLIGENCE SUMMARY
(Erase heading not required.)

Hour, Date, Place	Summary of Events and Information	Remarks and references to Appendices
29 April	2nd Cameron Hdqrs. attached 5th Division move to POTIJZE and form Divnl. Reserve.	RG.
30th April	Units warned that Germans are in many cases wearing British uniforms – O.C. Coys made responsible for providing troops with some sort of protection for eyes and mouth against asphyxiating gases	RG.

81st INFANTRY BRIGADE.
Move Table for 4th April, 1915.

UNIT	Leave	At	Arrive YPRES at	Leave YPRES EAST END GRAND PLACE x1 8.b. E.of YPRES at	1st Trench Party to reach cross roads x1 8.b. E.of YPRES at	
Camerons.	Canada Huts	4-15 p.m.	6-45 p.m.	8-25 p.m.	8-30 p.m.	Leave YPRES by Trench Parties.
Glosters.	Rosenhill Huts.	4-30 p.m.	Arrive POTIJZE			Go direct to POTIJZE HUTS. Bicycl Orderly of Coy. to report to O.C. 1st A. & S. H. in YPRES.
1/A. & S. Highrs.	Canada Huts.	4-45 p.m.	7 p.m.	8-55 p.m.	9 p.m.	Leave YPRES by trench parties. 1 Coy. Glosters to report.
			7-15 p.m.			
1/Wess. Fd. Co. R.E. less Bridg- ing Section	KENINGHELST Cross Rds.	4-34 d.				
4/A. & S. Highrs.	YPRES			7-55 p.m.	8 p.m.	March by KENINGHELST to POPER- INGHE BILLETS.
1/Rl. Scots.	ROSEHILL Huts.	4-50 p.m.				
9/A. & S. Highrs.	YPRES.			7-55 p.m.	8 p.m.	1 Co. & 1 Machine Gun & team to report to O.C. Camerons in YPRES.
9/R. Scots H.Q.& 2 Coys.	YPRES.			7-25 p.m.	7-30 p.m.	
9Y Co.A.S.C. (Br. Sec. 1st Wess. Fd. Co. attached.	MEXXKEN		HEKSKEN via POPERINGHE			To new Billets via POPERINGHE.
Sec. 20th F.A. Bde Amm. Col.	BOESCHEPE.	5 p.m.	Via POP-INGHE			To new Billets arranged by C.R.A.

x Trench Guides from French 87th Divn. will be waiting here from 8 p.m. onwards.

G.O.C.
81st Inf Bde.

Reference G.S. 531 of 6th April re 1st Subsidiary Line.

The following alterations are made :-

<u>81st Brigade.</u> <u>Right Flank</u> is extended to Cross roads near the R of RIDE in square J.19.c.

<u>82nd Brigade.</u> <u>Left Flank</u> Cross roads near R of RIDE in square J.19.c.

<u>Right Flank</u> Junction of roads square I.30 A. 5.3.

G.O.C. R.A.
C.R.E.
80th Bde.
81st Bde.
82nd Bde.

14th April, 1915.

Major G.S.,
27th Division.

G.S. 331.

Secret. Have 1 copy
of this done for
each Bde & for 1st Army R.E.

First Subsidiary Line.

1. **Extent.**
   (i) The line extends from the O of GREEN JACKET RIDE Square I.30.B on the right to road junction Square J.9.B B.6
   (ii) This line has been partially constructed by the French and the general direction taken by them is to be followed.
   (iii) The line does not connect on either flank with any line belonging to the neighbouring divisions.

2. **Object of the Line.**
   The object of the construction of this line is to provide some place close behind the trench line from which, in the event of any portion of the trench line being captured, the enemy's further advance can be checked and arrangements for counter-attack made.

3. **Brigade Sections.**
   The line is divided into Sections as follows:-
   Right. 82nd Infantry Brigade.
   O of GREEN JACKET RIDE Square I.30.B to Road Junction 850 yards South of D in Stirling Castle exclusive.
   Centre. 81st Infantry Brigade.
   Road junction 850 yards South of D in Stirling Castle inclusive to S.E. corner of Glencorse Wood. En East
   Left. 80th Infantry Brigade.
   S.E. corner of Glencorse Wood to Road Junction Square J.9.B B.6

4. **Responsibility.**
   The Brigadier General Commanding each Section is responsible for the construction, upkeep and defence.

5. **Artillery.**
   The G.O.C. R.A. is responsible for the selection, construction, and upkeep of gun positions in support of the line.

6th April, 1915.

Major, G.S.,
27th Division.

SECRET

81st Bde

SECOND SUBSIDIARY LINE.

Reference 1/20,000 and 1/10,000 map.

Extent of Line.   1.   The Line extends from Road junction 300 yards South of Z in ZILLEBEKE Square I 23 C, via HOOGE - WESTHOEK to a point on road in square J 2 C - 325 yards North of H in WESTHOEK.

This line connects on the right with the 5th Division and on the left with the 28th Division lines.

Object of the Line.   2.   The object of this line is to have a strong defensive position to take the place of the trench line should retirement from the latter be necessary.

Brigade Sections.   3.   **Right. 82nd Brigade.**

From Road junction 300 yards South of Z in ZILLE-BEKE Square I 23 C, to a point 160 yards N.W. of N.W. corner of ZOUAVE WOOD.

Centre. 81st Brigade.

Point 160 yards N.W. of N.W. corner of ZOUAVE WOOD I 18 C, to South edge of narrow wood in centre of J 7 C.

Left. 80th Brigade.

South edge of narrow wood in centre of J 7 C, to point on road in square J 2 C, 325 yards North of H in WESTHOEK.

Responsibility.   4.   A considerable amount of work has already been done on this line by the French.

The Division will be responsible for its improvement and maintenance, the necessary working parties being found from the Brigade in Reserve, or from Civilian labour.

Artillery.   5.   The G.O.C. R.A. is responsible for the selection construction, and upkeep of gun positions in support of this line.

[signature]

8th April, 1915.

Major G.S.,
27th Division.

SECRET. G.S. 531.

Headquarters,
 81st Infantry Brigade.

The General Staff Officers of the Division, and the G.O.C., have now visited the French Subsidiary Line immediately in rear of the front line at several points.

From what they have seen they are all more or less in agreement that this line, good in places, indifferent in others, is too close up to take the place of a line in which to retire suddenly. At the same time too far back from the front line to act as a support line.

It is a question for consideration whether it would not be better to put all your work into providing a good support line immediately in rear of the trenches, in which supports could be kept close up, and to which men in the trenches could retire if mined, rather than keeping up the present French line above referred to.

The G.O.C. would be glad of your opinion.

7th. April, 1915.

Lieut.Colonel G.S.
27th. Division.

Headquarters,
   27th Division.
   ----

(1).   With reference to your letter No. G.S. 531 of the 7th inst. on the question of the French Subsidiary Line in rear of the front line I am of opinion that this line should not be given up for the following reasons:-

   (i). If a general retreat was ordered to the HOOGE - WESTHOEK line it would act as a most useful stepping stone to carry out the retirement.

   (ii). If we leave the ridge which in my section of defence runs from STIRLING CASTLE - GLENCORSE WOOD, many points between YPRES and that line would come under observation of the enemy.

(2).   I consider that in some portions of the line behind trenches which seem specially dangerous or against which mining operations may be possible support trenches within 20 to 50 yards of our present 1st Line trenches may be necessary and it is intended to construct these where they are found necessary.

(3).   A reconnaissance is being made of the line in question in my section and it is my present intention to improve certain sections to be fit for immediate occupation and perhaps convert others into strong supporting points.

                                    Brig. General,
8/4/1915.   Commanding 81st Infy. Brigade.

Secret

G.O.C.

81st Brigade.

Reference this office No. 531 of 8th instant.

1. The boundaries of the 2nd Subsiduary Line have been altered by the Fifth Corps as follows :-

   a. Between 5th Division and 27th Division.

   A line drawn S.E. from the angle of the road in I.23.A 3.5.

   b. Between 27th Division and 28th Division.

   The road running S.E. and S through J.1 - WESTHOEK to YPRES - MENIN road (inclusive to 27th Division)

2. The 2nd Subsiduary Line is therefore divided into sections as follows :-

   82nd Brigade.

Right Point where line drawn S.E. from the angle of the road in I.23.A 3.5 cuts Subsiduary Line (about 100 yards S. of Southernmost building of DORMY HO.)

Left   Point in fence in I.17.D 175 yards N.W. of the N.W. corner of ZOUAVE WOOD.

   81st Brigade.

Right Left boundary of 82nd Brigade.

Left   North Bank of ETANG DE BELLEWAARDE in square J.7.C 0.5.

   80th Brigade.

Right Left boundary of 81st Brigade.

Left   Point where Subsiduary Line cuts Road in square J.7.C close to WESTHOEK Cross Roads.

J.C.Baumgarten

11th April, 1915.

Major, G.S.
27th Division.

G.O.C. R.A.
80th Bde.
81st Bde.
82nd Bde.
C.R.E.

Ap 22' WW — Report on French Centre Sector
up to 11th April 1915 —

1. General Condition of Trenches.
A good start has been made in making the parapet bullet proof, and lowering it so as to allow the men to use their rifles over it in case of attack. In many places the trenches are still very wet and constant baling and pumping is necessary. The R.E. have been asked to supply more pumps and balers.

2. In places the wire is still very weak and a large number of knife rests have been already placed in position.

3. Other gaps have now been wired, but in places this of course requires strengthening.

4. Construction of new Trenches.
The line of support trenches has been commenced behind the trenches which are most liable to attack viz. 26 to 28, 31, and across the MENIN Road.

5. Much good work has been done by reconnoitring patrols, especially by

the Cameron Highlanders, and
Snipers of this regiment and the Gloucesters
especially have had good shooting
and gained some useful information.

6. Battalion HQrs, night Battalion
of this section has been moved
to BODMIN copse where they are
much better placed behind their
trenches.

7. From reports so far received, it
would appear that the certain parts
of their line are weakly held, and
that they have strong points in the
line where they are very active
during the night.

11/4/15   N.L.L. Cotter. B.Gen!
                           G.O.C. 8yor Inf. Brigade.

Report on ~~Eight~~ Entire Section
of Trenches 27th Div. held by
81st Inf. Brigade —
18th April '15

1. General Condition of the Trenches —
During the past week much work
has been done on the reconstruction
of the parapets, which are now in
a more satisfactory state.
A want of materials has however
delayed some of this work as
also the proper construction of
trenches to form gaps, &c.

2. The construction of a Support
line has been commenced in
the form of retrenchments, in places
where the possibility of the Enemy
driving matter them most urgent.
This has been completed fit for

occupation on the following
sections:-

① Behind ~~C6~~ C1 to left flank of ~~C8~~ C2.

② Left flank of ~~C9~~ C3 behind ~~C6~~ C4 and C5.

③ Behind ~~C6~~ C16 and ~~C7~~ C17.

④ In course of construction behind C18 and C19.

The wet nature of the ground makes it necessary to revet and board almost all trenches before they can be considered fit for occupation.

3. Very considerable damage has been done by the enemy's minenwerfer to some of the parapets especially in the cases of C4 and C5 already reported. It is suggested that some of the new trench mortars are necessary to retaliate, and

in the length of line held by the brigade. 4 of these could be freely and usefully employed.

4. A long communication trench from C5 to BODMIN COPSE has been dug through, but in view of new construction work, no men can be spared at present to deepen and strengthen it as a really safe avenue of approach.

Communication trenches are also in progress
① Back from C7 to Dumbarton Lakes Wood.
② Inverness copse to C 18
③ Glencorse Wood & C 25
④ The existing one from Glencorse Wood to Inverness Copse is much improved

5. 1st Subsidiary Line. Machine Gun emplacements have been constructed at

① S.E. of Stirling Castle

② E ¾ N by E of Stirling Castle near the MENIN Road.

③ S.W. Corner of GLENCORSE Wood.

The tripods are kept in position and guns are kept ready to mount at short notice.

19/4/15

A.H.Baker B.General
Comdg 8th I.B.

SECRET.

G.O.C.,
8th Infantry Brigade.

The attached letter by 5th Corps Commander is forwarded for your information and necessary action as regards your section of the defence line.

Please submit your first report on the lines suggested by 22nd April.

As regards Artillery questions you will no doubt consult with your artillery zone commander. Should you require further assistance on any point arising out of the problem set forth by Sir Herbert Plumer the General Staff of the Division, the G.O.C. R.A. and the C.R.E. will be ready to help you, in *every* possible way if you wish it.

14th April, 1915.

Lt-Colonel, G.S.,
27th Division.

V Corps.
G.X. 770.

27th Divn.
G.S. 541.

27th Division.

It is hoped that in the new area allotted to the Corps opportunities for offensive action will occur. How far we may be able to take advantage of these opportunities must depend in the first instance on the instructions we may receive from superior authority, but it is incumbent on us to be prepared for such action and to have definite plans as to where and how it should be carried out.

Within each Divisional area each Brigade Commander of a section of the defence line should consider the most suitable point or points in his section for offensive action.

These points should be selected as :-

I. Being of themselves of tactical importance.
II. Leading up to advantageous developments.
III. Being of tactical value to the enemy.

and after the points have been selected proposals should be submitted for attacking these stating :-

I. The method of attack.
II. The strength of the force to be employed.
III. The artillery support required.
IV. The preliminary measures necessary prior to the actual attack.

Such statements must necessarily include reports on the ground generally, the places for assembling troops detailed for the assault, Artillery positions, the strength and weakness of the points in the enemy's lines selected for attack, measures against counter-attack, etc., etc.

All these require throughout the whole section,

(2)

continuous reconnaissances and observations, in order to obtain and record the detailed information necessary.

Details as to the varying activity of the enemy's artillery and infantry from day to day, the work on his trenches carried out, the particular points strengthened, the hours of working, times of relief, the amount of rifle fire by day and night, the number of shells fired into an area day by day are all useful when received from several different sources and pieced together and are matters on which information can be obtained in a variety of ways calling for individual enterprise and intelligence.

Reports on such points can be submitted periodically or when received at the discretion of the G.O.C. Divisions and will be duly collated and tabulated at Corps Head Quarters, the object in view being to adopt every possible expedient to obtain as complete a knowledge as possible of the ground and disposition of the enemy on our immediate front.

13/4/1915.

Sd. Herbert Plumer, Lieut.General,
Commanding   Vth Corps.

Copy for
War Diary

COPY.

Headquarters,
    81st Infantry Brigade.

    The G.O.C. Division wishes me to express to you how deeply he appreciates the devotion to duty and power of endurance which you and the troops of your brigade have shown during the recent operations.

    The manner in which every battalion has fought and the cheerful way in which all ranks have worked in the reconstruction of the position deserves the highest praise.

    It must be a satisfaction to all ranks to feel that they have right well upheld the traditions of their respective regiments.

    The G.O.C. congratulates you and your Brigade on the results of your month's work.

(sd) H.L. Reed, Lt. Col. G.S.
27th Division.

18th May, 1915.

References:- Vth Corps G.X. 770.
27th Divn. G.S. 541.

Reference :-, Sketch attached and 1/40,000 YPRES (Sheet 28)

THE PROBLEM OF OFFENSIVE ACTION AS REGARDS THE CENTRE SECTION, 27th DIVISION.
Report by G.O.C. 81st Infantry Brigade.

22nd April, 1915.

INTRODUCTION. 1. As the whole line of defence of the 27th Division forms the apex of a big salient in the general line of defence, an advance does not seem to offer any advantages except as part of a larger strategical plan. As regards the northern theatre, no tactical action in front of the centre section can be effective except to bring us in line with the left of the 80th Infantry Brigade. To the South and South-East a possible first strategical objective would be MENIN and the crossings over the River LYS as far as WARNETON.

TOPOGRAPHY. 2. The distinctive features of the Centre Section are:-
A. Ridges and Spurs.
(i) The STIRLING CASTLE Ridge running S. to N. along GREEN JACKET RIDE - STIRLING CASTLE - FITZCLARENCE FARM - POLYGONE WOOD.
This ridge covers the approaches from YPRES to all our trenches up to
From S.E. of SANCTUARY WOOD - 1000 yds. from trenches.
From S.E. of GLENCORSE WOOD - 400 yds. from our trenches
From points between CLAPHAM JUNCTION and GLENCORSE WOOD, the country to the N.W. of YPRES can be seen for some miles.

(ii) The VELDHOEK RIDGE.
Along this ridge the German 2nd line and possibly his real 1st line of defence runs.
This runs N. and S. from the STIRLING CASTLE Ridge which it joins by a col between GLENCORSE WOOD and POLYGONE WOOD and is a some feet lower than it throughout its length.

(iii) The CHELUVELT Spur and the POLDERHOEK Spur running out from the VELDHOEK Ridge.
These are undoubtedly of great tactical importance to the enemy.

B. Streams and Valleys.
The STIRLING CASTLE Ridge forms a Watershed, all the streams N.W. of it running to the River YSER and those S.E. of it to the River LYS. The most important of the latter are:
(i) RENTEL BEEK between the German 1st Line Trenches on our left and the POLDERHOEK RIDGE and thence N. of and almost parallel to the MENIN Road till it joins the LYS just N. of MENIN.
(ii) SCHERRIABEEK, a tributary of the RENTEL BEEK, runs due E. between the POLDERHOEK SPUR and CHELUVELT SPUR.
(iii) BASSEVILLEBEEK separates the STIRLING CASTLE RIDGE and VELDHOEK - ZANDVOORDE RIDGE and running South just E. of HOUTHEM joins the LYS near COMINES.

In

In the valley of this stream are the 1st Line trenches of both sides (our numbers C.17 to C.1.)

(iv) The CHELUVELT BEEK which starts from the CHELUVELT Spur and runs nearly due S. some 150 yards East of ZANDWOORDE
These streams are small in themselves but considering the boggy nature of the country may become serious tactical obstacles.

C. Woods.
(a). In our possession:-
   i. SHREWSBURY FORREST.
   ii. BODMIN COPSE.
   iii. INVERNESS COPSE and DUMBARTON LAKES WOOD.
   iv. GLENCORSE WOOD.
   v. POLYGONE WOOD
   vi. SANCTUARY WOOD.
   vii. HOOGE CHATEAU WOOD.

These give us power to mass very large forces comparatively near our 1st Line (see statement of present accommodation in trenches and dug-outs from 300 yds. to 400 yds. from the enemy's 1st Line trenches).

(b). In possession of the enemy.
The wooded ridges E. of BASSEVILLE BEEK gives the enemy a partially covered approach to his 1st Line trenches.
His 2nd Line trenches on the VELDHOEK Ridge is along the E. edge of this wood (see para. 2)
The ridge itself with the wood forms a formidable obsracle to a direct advance, as the ground on the ridge is much broken with a tangle of fallen trees, shell holes and wire. The enemy's wire is difficult to detect for this reason.

3. Tactical objectives.
Whatever the strategical objectives, the first tactical objective of an advance or attack along the front of this section must be the VELDHOEK RIDGE whether it is intended to push on to CHELUVELT or not. In either case a simultaneous attack on the POLDERHOEK ridge from the North seems a necessity.
It is suggested that the line VELDHOEK RIDGE - S¹ to ZANDEVOORDE should form the primary objective of a larger scheme than is under consideration.

4. Method of attack on the VELDHOEK RIDGE.
Owing to the difficulties of an initial advance S. of the MENIN Road it is considered that the first attack should be a joint attack by the 81st and 80th Brigades on the line VELDHOEK - POLDERHOEK from the line GLENCORSE WOOD - POLYGONE WOOD. Further consideration than has been possible at present of the enemy's possible lines of defence behind his first line is necessary before the flanks of the objective and other details can be suggested, but in order to break through his first line the following proposals are put forward.

5. Strength of the Force to be employed.
Leaving out of consideration any attack from the front occupied by the 80th Infantry Brigade, on the POLDHOEK RIDGE, which should, however, be part of the same operation, it is suggested that one Infantry Brigade would be required for an attack on VELDHOEK from a front S.W. corner GLENCORSE WOOD - a point just N. of VERBEEK FARM. The actual line

from

from which an attack should start is left for consideration.

6. **The artillery support required.**

(i) The formation of the line with the right angle turn about BLACK WATCH CORNER is very favourable for a cross enfilade fire and the STIRLING CASTLE RIDGE allows guns to be placed in position at close ranges for this purpose and it is suggested that field guns should be placed 500 or 600 yards N. of VERBEEK FARM to enfilade the enemy's trenches in front of the 81st Infantry Brigade and in the neighbourhood of STIRLING CASTLE to enfilade their line in front of POLYGONE WOOD.

For this purpose it is proposed a brigade of 18 prs. each should be allotted, each battery being given a section of the line to enfilade e.g. the brigade N. of VERBEEK FARM to enfilade the German Line from BLACK WATCH CORNER S. for 2000 yards, i.e. opposit C.4 trench.

(ii) Other batteries as placed at present to be employed to cover the front in zones as at present paying special attention to the German 2nd Line on VELDHOEK RIDGE as defined above and to take on the approaches of the German supports and reserves.

(iii) **Heavy batteries.**
Heavy batteries and howitzers would be required for the following targets:-
  (a). The strong point at BLACK WATCH CORNER.
  (b). NORTHAMPTON FARM.
  (c). The bit of 2nd Line NORTHAMPTON FARM to the MENIN Road.
  (d). The German 2nd Line S. of the MENIN ROAD.
  (e). The houses on the MENIN ROAD VELDHOEK to GHELUVELT.
  (f). VELDHOEK Village.
  (g). GHELUVELT and area round it. The enemy's possible positions about GHELUVELT are not known at present.
  (h). Between GHELUVELT and MENIN.
  (i). MENIN itself and approaches from MENIN and district to GHELUVELT — a suitable target for 15-inch and 9.2 guns and other heavy guns.

(iv). The position and nature of the trenches is favourable for placing light field guns and mountain guns right in first line trenches.

7. **Preliminary measures.**
The enemy's first line opposite this section contains some strong points which would require special consideration before launching an attack.

From North to South as far as the MENIN Road these are:-
  (a) BLACK WATCH CORNER - Machine Guns position.
  (b) NORTHAMPTON FARM.
  (c) The strong barricade and position at the Cross roads S. of the V of VELDHOEK.

Against (a) and (b) it is possible that mining operations would be most effective to start an attack. It has been

calculated

calculated that at least one month's preparation would be necessary for this to be effective.

In absence of mining operations a systematic artillery bombardment with heavy howitzers would be necessary.

Other preliminary measures to be considered:-

(i). Destruction of enemy's obstacles.
(ii). Construction of more trenches behind our first line for the assembly of the attacking force.
(iii) Construction of more dug-outs and trenches for the supports and reserves.
(iv). More communication trenches from GLENCORSE WOOD to the trenches.
(v). Cutting necessary gaps in our own wire without unnecessarily drawing the enemy's attention.
(vi). Bridging and ladders
    (a) To get over our own parapets.
    (b) To bridge the network of old trenches which exists.

(vii) Formation of advanced R.E. Depots close behind the trenches and depots of bombs.
(viii) The proper training of bombing parties in the assault which requires time for instruction and a large supply of bombs to practise with.
(ix) The registration of artillery targets which should be spread over some weeks.

(x). Aeroplane photographs of the whole area as far back as possible, and any other means of obtaining information such as agents to be employed.

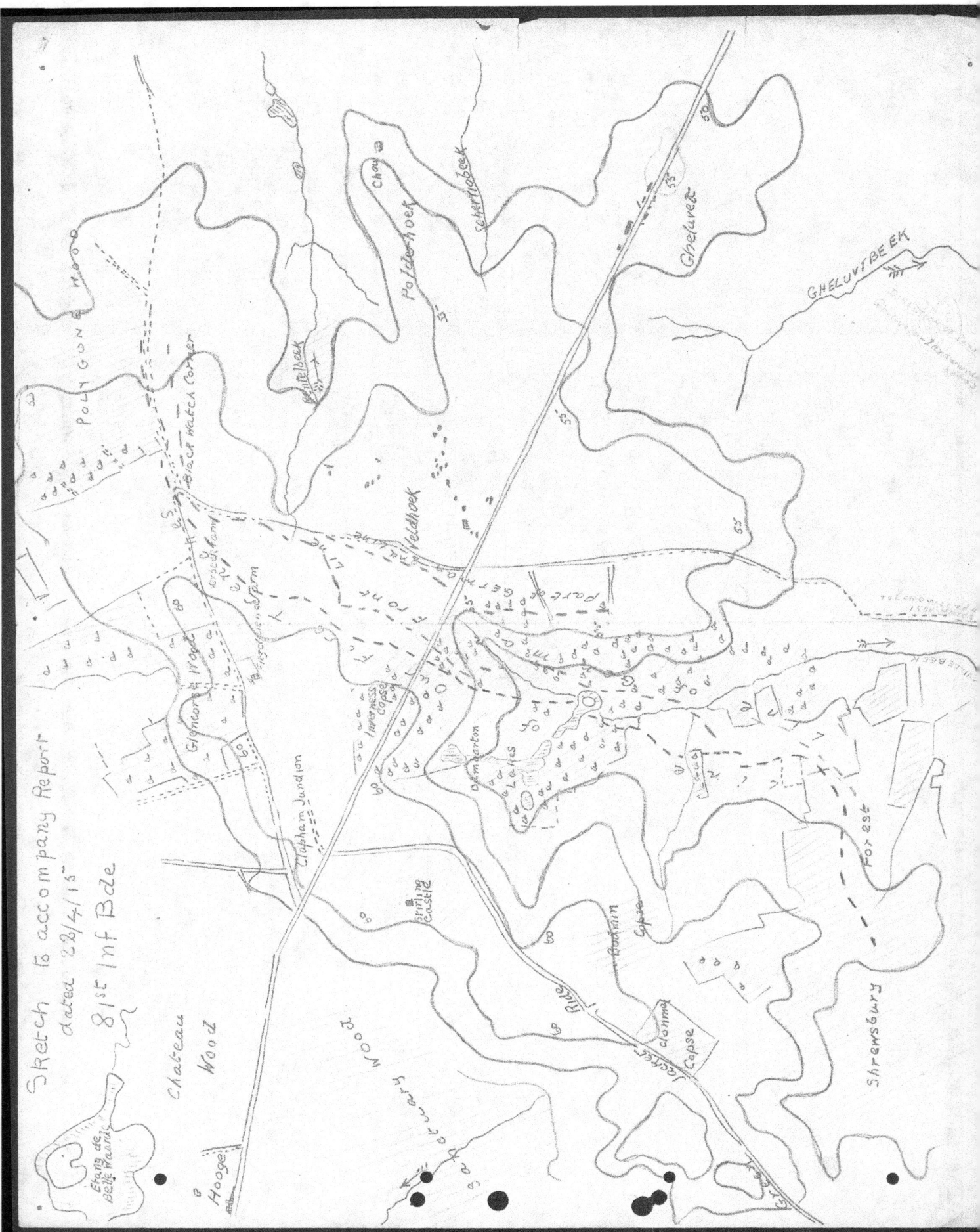

A.77.3

Report
On Leendra Creek
Section 97 pml
11th April
16th April
22nd April

27th Division.

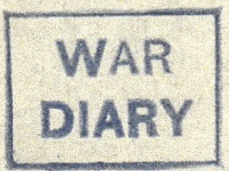

B. H. Q. 81st INFANTRY BRIGADE.

May

1 9 1 5

Attached:-

Operation Orders.
Casualties.
Reports on Bridges.
Maps.

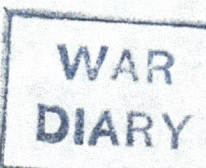

WAR DIARY
or
INTELLIGENCE SUMMARY
(Erase heading not required.)

Army Form C. 2118.

Hour, Date, Place	Summary of Events and Information	Remarks and references to Appendices
1st May	Disposition of Bde as follows:— In the Trenches — 1 R. Scots, 1 Argylls, 9 Argylls. In Support 2 Coys and 2 Platoons Gloucesters at SANCTUARY WOOD remainder in the Trenches of 1 Argylls and of 1 R. Scots — (No5Cg 15 Cr 2.) 9 R. Scots were attached to 80th and 82nd Bde — H.Q. & 2 Coys to 82nd, remaining 2 Coys under Senior major to 80th Bde. — 2nd Cameron H'rs formed Divisional reserve. After working on new line near FREZENBURG and near POTIJZE returned to bivouacs in ZOUVE WOOD about 1 a.m. Brigade was informed verbally that it had been relieved from our present front line of trenches probably on night of his 3rd/4th May.	

Army Form C. 2118.

WAR DIARY
or
INTELLIGENCE SUMMARY
(Erase heading not required.)

Instructions regarding War Diaries and Intelligence Summaries are contained in F. S. Regs., Part II. and the Staff Manual respectively. Title pages will be prepared in manuscript.

Hour, Date, Place	Summary of Events and Information	Remarks and references to Appendices
2nd. May	Camerons and Gloucesters worked on second line Trenches in SANCTUARY WOOD when possible by day. In afternoon owing to severe fighting both Camerons and 9th R. Scots ordered to POTIJZE to report to Divnl. Hd. Qrs. after remaining there in reserve both battalions returned before dawn 3rd May.	

WAR DIARY or INTELLIGENCE SUMMARY

Army Form C. 2118.

Hour, Date, Place	Summary of Events and Information	Remarks and references to Appendices
3rd May 3·45 pm	Camerons flourishing and 9th R Scots at work on new line which in many places was well worth ready for occupation. (2 cos) Germans reported to have pierced 28th Divn. at one point Camerons and 9 R Scots ordered to march to VERLDREN HOEK under Lt. Col. CAMPBELL and report to G.O.C. 85th Infy Bde. During night 3rd/4th the Bde retired from trenches in squares J 14 c and 20 b to a new line prepared in SANCTUARY WOOD squares J 13 c and 19 a The new line was taken up by the support companies of 1 Argylls 9 Argylls and 1 R Scots – During the retirement Snipers and Scouts were in the old Trenches in order to deceive the enemy and to report if the retirement was being followed up. The new line was very incomplete as the Camerons and 9th R Scots were ordered to join 85th Infy Bde while still working on this line leaving only 2 Coys of the Gloucesters to help the R.E. result the line was not nearly so good as it might have been especially as regards clearing the  field fields of fire, mounting fresh grass, and also establishments	See Map 2. For Retirement See Operation Orders and 27th Divn. Operation Order No 46 issued 2 May q.v

WAR DIARY

3rd May (Cont'd) | Arrangements had been made with the knots covered and with R.E. assistance for the following work, which was unfortunately not carried out.

1. Cutting roads in thick copse in J19.C.2.7 to 2.9.
2. Cutting strips in grass and undergrowth in front of the assumed salient about J14.6.8.
3. Clearing thick copse and undergrowth on the left front of this assumed salient.
4. Knocking down at least part of the South wall of Stirling Castle.
5. Clearing the undergrowth and advances for fire in the Stirling Castle Woods.
6. Constructing STIRLING CASTLE, the Strong and Some of the recent buildings on the MENIN ROAD.
7. Filling in old trenches in front of our lines and removing wire which might be of use to the enemy.

In the vain to send Pat Cameron and 9th R. Scot't the 26th C.L.I. only 2 Coys Gloucesters remaining any force was fitly available to hold the front line trenches.

Army Form C. 2118.

WAR DIARY
or
INTELLIGENCE SUMMARY

(Erase heading not required.)

Instructions regarding War Diaries and Intelligence Summaries are contained in F. S. Regs., Part II. and the Staff Manual respectively. Title pages will be prepared in manuscript.

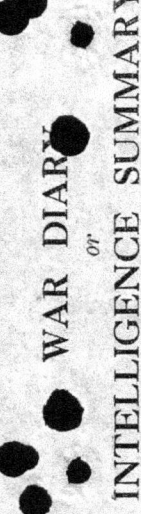

Hour, Date, Place	Summary of Events and Information	Remarks and references to Appendices
Night 3rd/4th May	The withdrawal from the 1st line was effected without a hitch and no casualties.^x Relief was reported complete at 2 a.m. (last man left the Trenches at 12.15 a.m.) – A few Scouts and Snipers were left out in the front of our line – Enemy continued to shoot at our trenches and sent up flares till after 3.10 a.m. At 7 a.m. first report received verbally from 1st Argylls that enemy were advancing chiefly towards wood known as STIRLING CASTLE, but also from BODMIN COPSE and towards CLAPHAM JUNCTION Enemy suffered considerable losses in attempting to establish his line on Ridge 60 about 350 to 500 yds from our new trenches - estimated along our front at 150 to 200 – Cameron and 9 R.Scots only returned at 12.30 a.m. and very tired. So line Trenches were occupied by 1st A.& S.H. ...... 2 Coys - Right. Gloucesters ..... 2 Coys - Centre 9th Argylls .... 1st Coys 2 - Left 1st R.Scots .... 1 Coy	x / men 1st R. Scots was afterwards reported wounded. (1/10000 Local Map)

Army Form C. 2118.

WAR DIARY
or
INTELLIGENCE SUMMARY

(Erase heading not required.)

Instructions regarding War Diaries and Intelligence Summaries are contained in F. S. Regs., Part II. and the Staff Manual respectively. Title pages will be prepared in manuscript.

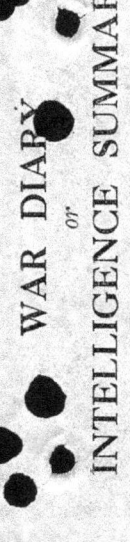

Hour, Date, Place	Summary of Events and Information	Remarks and references to Appendices
4th May to ZOUAVE WOOD 1st R Scots moved to H16a West of YPRES*	Disposition of Troops as follows — In the Trenches 1st Argylls on the Right — Gloucesters in the Centre — 9th Argylls and 1st R. Scots on left. Camerons in Reserve at ZOUAVE WOOD. 9th R. Scots in SANCTUARY WOOD. On the night 4/5 the following reliefs took place 2nd Cameron Hdrs relieved 9th Argylls and 1st R. Scots 9th R. Scots relieved 1st Argylls 1st Argylls to left went to SANCTUARY WOOD, and 9th ASH ⊗ 1st R Scots from to ZOUAVE WOOD (H16a West of YPRES *) Very severe bombardment of our Trenches and supports all day up to 5 P.M — Enemy made no advance since morning but appeared to be entrenching on line Track running S.W. to N.E. Square J19 thence North in front of CHATEAU J. 13D to Point just West of Road Junction J. 13 B.D. — Enemy presented frequent Targets at Ranges of 250 to 500 Yds. Bn Hd Qrs moved from H00&E to SANCTUARY WOOD Staff Capt from POTIJZE to BUSSEBOOM	* 1st R Scots the above 25 days without rest of which 22 were in the Trenches — The last 9 consecutive 1st and 9th Argylls were each 14 days in the front line — The former with 3 coys out of 4 continually in the fire Trenches — 9th Argylls had always 2 coys in fire Trenches and 2 in support Ref 1/40,000 map BELGIUM Sheet 28

Army Form C. 2118.

WAR DIARY
or
INTELLIGENCE SUMMARY
(Erase heading not required.)

Instructions regarding War Diaries and Intelligence Summaries are contained in F.S. Regs., Part II. and the Staff Manual respectively. Title pages will be prepared in manuscript.

Hour, Date, Place	Summary of Events and Information	Remarks and references to Appendices
5th May	Our 1st line Trenches subjected to a heavy bombardment by enemy's artillery from dawn. Our reply very inadequate and ineffective as the artillery had not registered new Targets and had not laid out wires from their new Hd Qrs. — Casualties from artillery fire were heavy — Enemy reported to have attacked but were repulsed near C.22.13 at 3.20 am (4.4 hin) heard at 10.5 am that enemy had rushed Hill 60 — (5" hin) under cover of gas, and later that they had recaptured our trenches. On right of the 82nd I.B. 82nd Bde reported enemy gathering there and apparently preparing to attack. A.S.H. were warned at 1.10 pm to get in touch with the 82nd I.B. received in case of our having to send them support. Enemy artillery bombardment was kept up at intervals till dark. A machine gun of Bn was put of out of action by a direct hit.	

1247 W 3299 200,000 (E) 8/14 J.B.C. & A. Forms/C. 2118/11.

WAR DIARY or INTELLIGENCE SUMMARY

Army Form C. 2118.

(Erase heading not required.)

Instructions regarding War Diaries and Intelligence Summaries are contained in F. S. Regs., Part II. and the Staff Manual respectively. Title pages will be prepared in manuscript.

Hour, Date, Place	Summary of Events and Information	Remarks and references to Appendices
May 6th.	Situation unchanged — Heavy shelling at intervals and little rifle fire — Enemy continuing fire started again at dawn. In STIRLING CASTLE ridge fear them advancing. Training Stations and our casualties still severe. One company strenuous hot. 18 casualties before 1 p.m. in the trenches. Q.M. 2nd Div. supplied prepared that more troops should be sent west of YPRES to escape shell fire. Major in prisoners to have our parents troops under close hand. ① In case of attack which opposed boards any day. ② All the ground between YPRES and our trenches under heavy shell fire and last off was under direct observation. ③ No large working parties as horses were required every night to bog and improve defences.	

Army Form C. 2118.

WAR DIARY
or
INTELLIGENCE SUMMARY

(Erase heading not required.)

Instructions regarding War Diaries and Intelligence Summaries are contained in F. S. Regs., Part II. and the Staff Manual respectively. Title pages will be prepared in manuscript.

Hour, Date, Place	Summary of Events and Information	Remarks and references to Appendices
7th May	A quieter day and it would appear enemy had withdrawn some artillery. Work on supporting points behind our line continued. Our artillery fire was much more effective today, than any day since we have been very occupied. Up to this date enemy have been very active in digging and has most 2 or 3 forward lines in front & in through up in all cases complete.	see App. 5.

Army Form C. 2118.

WAR DIARY or INTELLIGENCE SUMMARY

(Erase heading not required.)

Instructions regarding War Diaries and Intelligence Summaries are contained in F.S. Regs., Part II. and the Staff Manual respectively. Title pages will be prepared in manuscript.

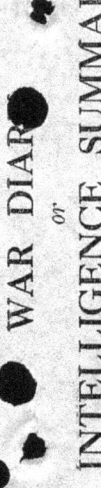

Hour, Date, Place	Summary of Events and Information	Remarks and references to Appendices
6.45 am 8th May	After a particularly quiet night our Trenches and Supports were subject to a very severe bombardment in touch by telephone with all Bns in front line — Shelling especially severe North of MENIN ROAD	
7.40 am	92nd Bde report all night in front of them and most shelling further North —	
7.50 am	Lost touch with 80th and 92nd Bde by Telephone — Gas was smelt —	
8.30 am	M.G. and rifle fire on our front and left of us — Artillery fire much quieter — Our Guns pratically ceased fire —	
8.45 am	Bombardment commenced again	
9.15 am	Bombardment very severe — A shell hit Bde Hd. Qr. and all lines to Bns were broken	
9.30 am	A good many 4th K.R.R. returning trench fitupto 4 K.R.R. returned with M.G. and did well in stopping M.G. Lt P.E.GRIFFIN men from going back.	

Army Form C. 2118.

WAR DIARY or INTELLIGENCE SUMMARY

(Erase heading not required.)

Instructions regarding War Diaries and Intelligence Summaries are contained in F. S. Regs, Part II. and the Staff Manual respectively. Title pages will be prepared in manuscript.

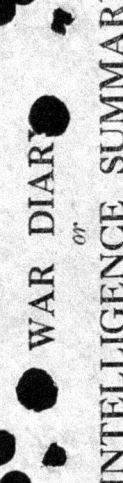

Hour, Date, Place	Summary of Events and Information	Remarks and references to Appendices
10.15 am 8th May	9th Argylls ordered up and occupied trench just in front of Bde Hd. Qrs on Right of Lake with Lewis machine guns Christie.	
10.40 am	More Rifle and M.G. fire	
11.8 am	Verbal message from 27 Divn. asking situation on left - Capt POWER sent to Bn Hd Qrs. 4th R.B. to ascertain situation -	See B.M. 100
12.5 pm	1st Argylls move to support PPCLI about 12.5 pm.	
1.30 pm	9th Argylls ordered to occupy 2nd line North of BELLEWARDE LAKE as far as railway crossing I 6.C	
3 pm.	OC 9th Argylls reports line N of Lake to railway held by 1 Coy A.S.H. 3 Platoons 4th R.B. 1 Coy A.S.H. right to left.	
4.45 pm	1st Coys Leinsters and 2 Coys R.I.F. placed at our disposal in SANCTUARY WOOD	
8.45 pm	1st R.Scots message from VLAMERTINGHE to take place of 1st A.S.H. who went left until arrival of 1st L.B.	
12.55 am 9th	1st R Scots arrived in SANCTUARY WOOD but at 3 am 27th Div ordered them to return to G.H.Q. line	

WAR DIARY

8th May 1915 (cont.)

A day of very heavy shelling from 6.45 am to 7 pm. Actually no attack was made in our line South of MENIN road, but an attack seemed probable at any hour.

9 am. Report of enemy massing to attack right of 28th div. and also a strong enemy from 27th div (about 12,000) showed that 28th div had evacuated a line running from their first line trenches to a line running through VERLORENHOEK South the lake Pk 80. Pk 80th Bde suffered severely as did 84 Cameron, and 84th protonged his left to Pk 6 hols front line. The enemy advancing from Zonnebeke & WESTHOEK. 2 corps G.O.C H. ordered 2nd line scots Pk to take about 1000 on and 4th R.B. promised to him further support if they required. This was all sent in meanwhile (12,000) he whole of Pk 1st A.H. was ordered by his division to reinforce Pk 80th Brigade N of the lake.

In still fears attack on Gheluvelt and Cameron and has only 2 corps Q A.H left in reserve. There corps were ordered by the div to assist 80th Bde N of the lake and support about 1.30 pm.

3½ left Lewistm 152nd Pom, flewed at an aufstal. Then chances at 5 pm. an Pd. O'Brien reported an attack on the Elverinctms at 5 pm to 1½ corps Lewistm and 2 corps Rd. Rusticins but through his Artillery from presented continued the very severe attack. Then a feint was made. Lewistm and R.L. Pons was never to pit in touch with the Elverinctms and Pk Rlcr, in case of attack and to reoccupy our 2nd line behind them the in Zeruion west up of refering and returned 15 thus pres hreistm 7.82 Rd. cst 12.30 am and yours came under orders of 82. Rd at 1.45 am.

WAR DIARY or INTELLIGENCE SUMMARY

Army Form C. 2118.

(Erase heading not required.)

Instructions regarding War Diaries and Intelligence Summaries are contained in F. S. Regs., Part II. and the Staff Manual respectively. Title pages will be prepared in manuscript.

Hour, Date, Place	Summary of Events and Information	Remarks and references to Appendices
12.55 am 9th.	Coys of Leinsters and R.I.F returned to 82nd Bde on arrival of 1 R. Scots.	
3 am.	1 R. Scots ordered to occupy portion of G.H.Q. line allotted to Bde. I 16	
3.30 am	Bde Hd Qrs moved from HOOGE to SANCTUARY WOOD I 24.b-3.4 Same Bn in Trenches as yesterday 9th Argylls in Bde Reserve at ZOUAVE WOOD. I 18. c.D. 1st Argylls under G.O.C. 80th Bde.	As shown in Rough Sketch enclosed.
10.35 am	After severe bombardment of nearly 2 hrs. Germans advanced against the centre Bn 2 Glouc. R. and half of the advanced trench was blown in by heavy artillery but enemy was repulsed — Our line was not penetrated but line did not slacken	
11.20 am	27th Division were well done Gloucesters do it again.	
3 pm	Enemy again attacked Gloucesters and succeeded in establishing themselves in a portion of the salient	

WAR DIARY or **INTELLIGENCE SUMMARY**

Army Form C. 2118.

(Erase heading not required.)

Hour, Date, Place	Summary of Events and Information	Remarks and references to Appendices
3 pm. 9th May	2 Coys 9th Argylls put into 2nd line to support Gloucesters Major R. Connor Gloucesters reinforced front line with 1½ Coys – Bombing Parties attacked both flanks of the German and counter attack regained part of lost Trench	MAJOR R. CONNOR reported missing – Subsequently reported prisoner
4 pm	2nd Counter attack took place but fallen trees and our own wire proved a formidable obstacle and with German machine Guns on both flanks and at the apex counter attack broke down – Colonel TULLOH killed 40 men killed & 90 wounded – Another counter attack ordered by 9th Argylls but on personal reconnaissance by Genl. CROKER he decided that it would be very costly and if successful German Heavy Guns could always shell us out again –	
5.40 pm	1 R. Scots order up from G.H.Q. line to ZOUAVE WOOD in order to relieve Gloucesters during night Imperious [?] to start mining operations against the advanced French line relieved by the 27th Inf. Bde.	

9th May '15.   An Attack 8th & 1st 13.
Yesterday, 8th Div. 80th Bde. owing to the 28th Bn redrawn. had commenced a new 1st line East as West of RAILWAY WOOD to protect their left. It was pointed out that the right than 8 1st line intimate —
At 3.15 am, informed that 28th new combination had taken to resume their front line, and that 80th Bde NZ the lake had already retired to the line (they complete.) running from the West-End of BELLEWAARDE lake.
The Coy. 4th KRR. came close. Perhaps about his mor. which left his Regt. (S of the lake) liable to be taken in reverse.   GS. 650 27½ bis
Investigation the 4th KRR. had informed servants from Shell trenches on the 8th and though orders to hold on to their present trenches it was doubtful if they would stand a German attack. with their left and "Bean Copse" —
Brigade HQ. were also exposed to fire from a rear point N of the lake and at 3.30am _____ went to SANCTUARY WOOD- MCCAUGRAN (till in HOOGE) being informed on the way —

The attack on the advanced French line by the Germans from about 6.30 am, a large number of Germans seen in concentration on the advanced French opposite STIRLING CASTLE, Thereon. Bursts of rifle and machine gun fire were opened on the same French between the salvos of heavy artillery fire until a German attack was launched from the East and South.

7th May 1915:
Contd.

War Diary 2/ L.B.

Our telephone communication had broken down and his first information regarding his attack reached by Bgs H.A. from its Inf Bde. The attack had been repulsed and though the advanced lines had been badly damaged by shells, no Germans had penetrated. This was corroborated by an R.A. observer who returned from the advanced trench at

10 a.m.

The advanced trench was occupied held by 3 platoons. Each Coy temporarily to arrive was split to 10 men each. The left platoon was entirely destroyed (2 Aplin & twenty wounded) and 3 men returning to the main trench about 7am. The centre platoon was cut off by the trench being blown in on each side of them. About the right platoon, 71.P. & twenty handled[?] were able to inflict heavy losses on the advancing Germans (aided by a machine gun). Between 7am and 9am the bulk of the enemy retired and it was thought the attack had been repulsed. The 2 Coys Leinsters in support prepared to meet an attack and 2 Coys Leinsters but from 8.30-9.30am were placed in position to support in the 2nd line. The enemy's losses in this attack alone were placed at 350 killed. The firing slackened to some extent between 9 and 10 am (at Pres Kpl 11.20 am
Reports received

9th May 1915:
Camp

9th May 1915: showed that some of the Enemy had formed a footing in the Advanced Trench on the left, and entering the circuit Trenches and open (on the top?) had

Enfilading machine guns in ones & twos places.
Attacks by bombing parties failed to turn the Germans out of the left arm cliff, and a counterattack with Artillery preparation was ordered at 3 p.m.
Meanwhile fire between 10 a.m. and 10.45 a.m. another German attack was launched from STIRLING CASTLE by about 4 Coys against the right of the Camerons and left of the Gloucesters. This was easily repulsed by gun, rifle and machine gun fire and soon became dangerous.
The Flanaskin counterattack was launched at 3.30 p.m., preceded by artillery fire, and supported by rifle and machine gun fire by the Camerons on the left. The counterattack failed to gain the crest. On the right part of the trench was reoccupied by the first line, but owing to the general supports could not be got up in time to extend the gain, and efforts on the left the first line was killed or wounded. In the left it Ramsay succeeded in reaching a point 10 yards from the Enemy, and commenced bombing them, but with cannon at hand to support him he had finally to withdraw.

Major Knox 9th

About 4 pm reports received from Capt 'Guy' Knox
showed that the attack had failed. Capt 'Guy' Knox
killed, Knox's Coy & Keshis both missing and
believed killed. Capt Spen wounded, the battalion
being in command of Capt Neary. Mr Fahan
Trist made a personal reconnaissance with his
Lt Col A.A.Q. (Mr J. Clarke) and was chiefly with
a view to a further combination. He found
was most unfortunate. A mass of broken wire
and shell holes anyone made a further advance
on any front line impossible, and fires and
our men were prevented the flanks being
turned. Brigadier decided to run up the advanced
finish altogether, and to attempt to make
it untenable by mining.   Lt BM
                                              167

4.30 pm
The Gloucester casualties are 40 killed
and 90 wounded & missing. The Colonel
was killed. The Lieup Knox (Conner) it afterwards
transpired has been taken prisoner in attempting
to venture his advanced trench in the morning.
Knox's trench has regained a foot the right of his
lines and was able to rejoin with a dozen
survivors about 7 pm
It is difficult to estimate the German losses but they
were probably up two three to 800 killed during the day.

WAR DIARY or INTELLIGENCE SUMMARY

Army Form C. 2118.

Hour, Date, Place	Summary of Events and Information	Remarks and references to Appendices
3.30 am 10th May	Relief of Gloucesters by 1 R. Scots completed	
12 Noon	Situation reported critical by OC Camerons — 2 Coys 9th Argylls sent to support 4 K.R.R. under orders of OC Camerons —	
12.35 pm	4. K.R.R. Trenches blown in by artillery — Men now holding 2nd line Trenches just in front of HOOGE — OC Camerons placed 2 Coys Argylls in new trench I 18 b 1.5 to 9 —	
1 pm	2 Coys Jernakas placed under our orders as Reserve — Gloucesters in G.H.Q line —	
1.25 pm	Germans reported attacking 1 R Scots	
1.30 pm	Germans attacking 2 Cameron Hdqrs.	
1.50 pm	OC Camerons reported his left flank open and his men North of MENIN ROAD forced to retire — Troops South of MENIN ROAD ordered to maintain their position at all costs	
2.40 pm	OC Camerons reports his left fallen back to support Trenches — 9th Argylls still in hand — Centre and Right holding on — No counter attack considered advisable	

Army Form C. 2118.

WAR DIARY
or
INTELLIGENCE SUMMARY

(Erase heading not required.)

Instructions regarding War Diaries and Intelligence Summaries are contained in F. S. Regs., Part II. and the Staff Manual respectively. Title pages will be prepared in manuscript.

Hour, Date, Place	Summary of Events and Information	Remarks and references to Appendices
3 p.m. 10 May	Colonel CLARKE commanding 9th Argylls reported killed.	
10.35 p.m.	Orders issued for the withdrawal of the 4th K.R.R. to H.16a	

10.6 May 915.

After a short respite, the enemy concentrated a heavy artillery fire on the trenches N of the MENIN road. The bombardment was continuous up till 11.30 a 12 noon when the enemy were reported to be reinforcing from direction of WESTHOEK.

At 12.15 pm. the Commdrs reported estimation of 4" KRR serious and two additional support at hand from the 80th Bde. Two Coys 9th A&SH were sent to Lt. Cameron to be used in conjunction with 4th KRR.

12.15 pm. Lt. Cameron reports 4" KRR blown but their trenches which were behind the consecrated total as far as the Lake the trench now being collected in the 2nd line (Cavalry Trenches)

Remaining 2 Coys 9th A&SH Kingston placed under Lt. Cameron and at 12.30 hrs 2 Coys Seaforths 82nd I.B. were placed at our disposal as Bgade Reserve —

1pm. The situation was critical. Enemy still looking on but bombardment increasing anything, and Lt. Cameron unable to get reinforcements up to his trenches to make good heavy casualties. His 2 platoons N of the MENIN road seemed to with'drawn to conform with the 4th KRR Trenches

10th May 91- (cont)

Irish
South of the Road nearest Coëri.

South of the Road nearest 2d hors on at our Coëri.

Between 1 and 3 p.m. heavy rain and often most severe bombardment. The enemy attacked the Cameroons South of the road but were repulsed with heavy loss. Enemy infantry advanced into the road, the evacuated trenches and at 5 p.m. were reported entrenching them at our line. The Cameroons South of the road were founding and preventing his Germans in the same line. On the N. were of the "road" — the road was cut through without a trench at each extr. A counter attack to regain the trenches N. of road was ordered, but at Commission and 2nd RIFR true against this because

① It would be crossing in rain owing to the difficulties approaches through a mass of fallen trees, and the difficulty of artillery preparation
② The trenches, if regained, could be rendered untenable by artillery fire at any time owing to their superior observation-
③ Unless the line was retired N. of the Lake it would always be liable to enfilade and reverse fire

3

Hostile

to 4 May 15 . 6 pm | The enemy again using gas made a last-apparent effort to capture the trench south of the road. By this time during a cessation of the Artillery fire the G.O.C. A.H. had been able to get a company up the Jim Trenches to support the Connaughts and mainly by the resistance the German attack were finally repulsed with loss —

It is difficult to estimate the enemy's losses but, whenever it was possible to remain in trenches and face their infantry attacks with rifle and machine gun fire, their close formation & their infantry caused him to suffer very severely and when, as on more than one occasion today our artillery were also able to assist, their attacks were decimated —

About 6 pm | The German was ordered a line of trenches to dig through CHATEAU WOOD as close as possible in front (?) our old trenches (now in German hands) with a view to saving all the tps south of the road.

For this purpose the 1st A.H. (2 coys) 3rd R.S.R. and

G.O. 832
27th Div.

To O.C. Army
(Cavalry)

4th Rg. Brigade has been placed under orders of the
OC 81st Bde. The 1st Weener & 17th & 2nd Cav Rg to assist.
Reconnaissances by Mhine Ft Coft and R.E. showed
that the state of the ground, and esp. the many fallen
trees made the digging impracticable in the time
available. It was therefore arranged to hold
the 2nd Line (now occupied by the 80th Inf Bde) as
far South as SANCTUARY WOOD and thence to
improve a existing communication trench to
connect with our present front line in the
N.E. corner of SANCTUARY WOOD.   See Map 2(d-e)
Withdrawing the Camerons from the trench South
of the Menin Road as far as SANCTUARY WOOD.
This work was under O.C. Camerons –
The Pt R. Scots on the Camerons right has a
counterattack (first day) to further German
attacks was made from the advanced trench, where
the situation was temporary. Their Lf. Company
with machine guns well placed to command the open
ground between STIRLING CASTLE keep and our
trenches greatly assisted in stopping the attack on
the Camerons.

The 4th A Scots were not attacked
A congratulatory telegram was received from the Corps Commander GR835

11:25 am

Army Form C. 2118.

WAR DIARY
or
INTELLIGENCE SUMMARY
(Erase heading not required.)

Instructions regarding War Diaries and Intelligence Summaries are contained in F.S. Regs., Part II. and the Staff Manual respectively. Title pages will be prepared in manuscript.

Hour, Date, Place	Summary of Events and Information	Remarks and references to Appendices
7.50am 11th May	9th R. Scots and 1 R Scots in same position as yesterday. Camerons on left of 1st R. Scots as far as new trenches I 15b 9.2. 1st Argylls thence across MENIN ROAD to clump of trees – All the above formed their own supports and 1 Argylls 1 Coy near level crossing I 11 b (still under 60th R.B.) 4 R.B. in trenches on left of 1st Argylls (on Pilkem Rd) supported by 3rd K.R.R. Any on R.B. West of LAKE. 9th Argylls in ZOUAVE WOOD about I 15 d. in Brigade Reserve. Lenisters in 52nd in Support Bn Argents about I 24 b 2.2	
10 am to 11 am	Germans attacked 1 R Scots left and Camerons – Repulsed with losses – Gas used against Camerons but with little ill effect – 2 Bns Germans caught in close formation by M.G. – 1 M.G. fired 15 belts before Sgt. I/C was blown up – Estimated loss 600 Germans. 2 Coys Leinesters reinforce Camerons.	
4.30 pm.	Camerons repulse another German attack. Camerons eventually shelled out and forced to retire to 2nd line. [?] Lieut. Colonel Campbell 2nd Camerons was wounded	

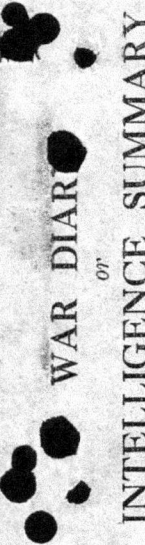

Army Form C. 2118.

WAR DIARY
or
INTELLIGENCE SUMMARY
(Erase heading not required.)

Instructions regarding War Diaries and Intelligence Summaries are contained in F. S. Regs., Part II. and the Staff Manual respectively. Title pages will be prepared in manuscript.

Hour, Date, Place	Summary of Events and Information	Remarks and references to Appendices
12.30 a.m. 12th May	Counter attack by Leinsters – Hill captured but not Trench about 1 a.m. – Hill and Trench finally captured	
3 a.m.	at point of bayonet. Major Conyers 2/c Leinsters seriously wounded and heavy casualties – Gloucesters supporting on left – Leinsters driven out by the enemy and fall back to 2nd line –	
5.50 a.m	Gloucesters with 1 Coy retake crest of hill and drive out Germans from Trench at point of bayonet – but forced to retire owing to M.G. cross fire and enfilade fire – 2 platoons Gloucester again attack hill and some of 400 to 500 Germans the latter were caught in close formations at short Range – Gloucesters finally forced to retire and crest of hill remained unoccupied by either side	

11th May 1915.

War Diary 8.5.15.

The 1st Tans along the North Edge of Sauchbury Wood formed a night-ought scheme on the North East Corner of the wood, and the holding of the Enemy trenches formed along the Menin Road as well as the STIRLING CASTLE map gave him a great advantage in establishing observation.

At 5.30 am the situation was quiet, but soon after, an intermittent shell fire was commenced by the Enemy which increased in intensity till about 7am. The fire was whole front of the Camerons and 1st A.& S.H. on each side of the Menin road. At 7am. the trenches in the easiest angle of the N.E. Corner of the wood was the target of a concentrated artillery and machine gun fire. Gas was then used against both Camerons and Argylls but the wind prevented much damage from this front of the Salien — the Germans from then prevented his advance in large numbers supporting heavy losses especially from the A.& S.H. in the trenches just South —

On the Main Road —

By 10 a.m. the centre of the Cameroons had fallen back. Their Krupp Quick-firers in. and by 11 a.m. the O.C. right wing of Cripps' leading his trench to badly damaged by shells as to be unable in his opinion to hold them against the ------ of his men to a commanding trench in rear. Part of the ----- ------- was occupied by Germans who however found themselves under an enfilade fire from ------ and machine guns.

Lt Col. Campbell (O.C. Cameroons) was now wounded and it at this 1st A.H. assumed command of the C.B. — Stoheroxxxxx

All the rest of the day, attempts were made by the Germans to occupy and hold the North-East and North East corner of Sanctuary Wood. Eventual attack on the initiative of Company Commanders were frequently made by the Cameroons 1st A.H. and 1st R.Regt, the by it P.A.H. 1st A.H. fairs every to this ------ being wounded. ------ by Captain Roberts

3.

Another by Lieut. Young's Squadron to originate with the Cameron's (successful) only to front the French was evident and culminated in daylight.

Captain McCall's Company (Cameron's) counterattack successfully twice but was driven out again by heavy shell fire and gas - this allowed the enemy to occupy the North East Corner of the Wood and might have exposed the three Coys of Pt R'devts and 9th R'devts to Enfilade and scalp cross fire. A Supporting Company of the Pt R'devts had been warned to be in readiness to protect their left flank - a reconnaissance by Lt Scott showed that the Germans were reoccupying the Trenches vacated by the Cameron's in force - Captain Farquharson's company at one counterattacked, assisted by the Cameron's, who at once turned again on finding assistance, and drove out the Germans, reoccupied and never lost the trench under heavy fire.

11th Evng 9.15 –

8/pr Evng 8 p.m. 13

During the morning Lt. Ff. Adj. Munn rejoined Christie who formed the Brigade Reserve in Zouave Wood had been very heavy during shelled (I saw two or 3 too large H.E. shells fell in the wood above in a short space of time). The trench had been heavily in the previous two supporting the 80th Bn and the Canadians. They were very heavy ^[losses]^ Some 200 men to one Posn. the task of tpgttng ^[supporting]^ and working at all costs his supporting force in Zouave Wood so save the Enemy succeeded in breaking the front line. Two companies Kentish were again given to us as Brigade Reserve and there were placed in the Jun. line behind the Canadians. These Platoons were eventually sent up to the firing trenches, and are excellent work in steadying the Canadians, and fell up Gaps – By 6.30pm the Evenness had been driven out of all our trenches except in the Loch Zach corner of Sanctuary Wood where they were reported to have a footing and Dr. Whiting

7 pm.

11.4.May 915. | in our own trench between first firing, and the Menin Road.
The Remaining 2 coys Devonshire were now placed at our disposal and being the only fresh troops available were ordered to hook on immediately to right the three trenches at 6 p.m.

Working parties were hard at it the B[attalio]n however being organised to dig a retrenchment behind the line of the Three (about 100 yards behind the cusp of the wood) which would start [?] from the angle of the salient and not be so subject to observed artillery fire —

About 7.30 p.m. the counterattack was postponed by one of the Division who rang up the 2:0 Gloucesters from the 83rd [Brigade?] to assist.
The Gloucesters arrived about 9.30 p.m. and further delay was necessary to allow reconnaissance and organise the attack and working parties at rest —

12.4.May 915. | The attack commenced at 12.20 a.m. 12:th and Two companies Devons (under Major Evingzer[?])

12 h Mar
(Contd)

W Coy remain 8" J.B.

were to carry out the assault. The Seweslers following up to protect the left flank assaulting Trenches facing North. Sir Pt. R. Scott was to front the right flank and arrive by him.

The first attack reached the Crest of the hill but failed to reach the trench, which was found to be strongly occupied. A second attack Coe by Major Congreve in person) famed the trench and drove out the enemy. Little loss. Major Congreve was mortally wounded—

It was now 2.30am and too late to dig a entrenchment before daylight..

The trenches were therefore ordered to hold the ground won by leaving a thin line of men just behind the crest, and the Gloucesters to hold the rise of the hill on their left. The bulk of troops to the rise to have ready to attack of the enemy again attempted to reoccupy our old Trenches.

12th May (cont'd) | on hearing daylight. The enemy concentrated a heavy artillery and machine gun fire on the Lincolns who with crews to the 2nd Lincs Captain Jones (Lincolns) keeping the Lincolns retiring at once counterattacked, and captured the trenches on the top of the hill beginning 12 n 15 — in the trench and driving off the remainder.

At 4.45 am he was forced to withdraw under a heavy artillery and cross M gun fire —

At 5.20 am the enemy were seen to approach in force. Captain Jones' Company again attacked, occupied the crest of the hill and drove dispersed 400 n 500 Germans with loss. A field company of Engineers (under Captain Barth) was now sent to assist Captain Jones Company (inhabits men were exhausted). It was the Germans occupied the crest trench in a fresh German attack before it developed but was then too forced to withdraw on receipt of the artillery and Mg. fire.

7

8.

12th May contd.

The enemy's trenches were reported as being
for 24 hours, and no further German counter-
was attempted.

8 pm.
At night a party of Sappers & Miners with
a working party of the 2nd Gurkhas continued
working further to the south of the line, while
digging the retrenchment. Joining the top of
the 15pdr trench to the trench held by the 2nd A.S.A.
This work was subsequently placed under
O.C. 1st RSch: and was energetically
carried on. In 2 or 3 nights work -

The enemy meanwhile were working on an
old trench south of the Main Road;
and approaching the trenches held by
digging. Their working parties frequently
exposed themselves and on the 13th and
following days lost many casualties from
the fire of our snipers and artillery.
No attempts on the 11th and 11½pm to move the Turco-German
efforts against the 81st Brn. by the Germans.

Army Form C. 2118.

WAR DIARY
or
INTELLIGENCE SUMMARY
(Erase heading not required.)

Instructions regarding War Diaries and Intelligence Summaries are contained in F. S. Regs, Part II. and the Staff Manual respectively. Title pages will be prepared in manuscript.

Hour, Date, Place	Summary of Events and Information	Remarks and references to Appendices
4 am. 13th May	Heavy bombardment on our left — and on HOOGE village from 4 am to 4 pm. Our front was thought during the day and few casualties — R.I.F. were to have relieved Camerons but were ordered to support 80th Bde left Flank — During night 13th/14th retrenchments in SANCTUARY WOOD were continued —	

Army Form C. 2118.

WAR DIARY
or
INTELLIGENCE SUMMARY
(Erase heading not required.)

Instructions regarding War Diaries and Intelligence Summaries are contained in F. S. Regs., Part II. and the Staff Manual respectively. Title pages will be prepared in manuscript.

Hour, Date, Place	Summary of Events and Information	Remarks and references to Appendices
14th May	No attacks – Gloucesters relieved Lewis Gun in new French connecting 1st R. Scots and Camerons trenches becoming Bde. Reserve –	F.E.

Army Form C. 2118.

WAR DIARY
or
INTELLIGENCE SUMMARY
(Erase heading not required.)

Instructions regarding War Diaries and Intelligence Summaries are contained in F. S. Regs., Part II. and the Staff Manual respectively. Title pages will be prepared in manuscript.

Hour, Date, Place	Summary of Events and Information	Remarks and references to Appendices
15th May	Disposition of Troops in Trenches — Right Sector 9th R. Scots I 24 D 8.9 to J 19 A 4.6 Centre Sector 1st R. Scots & Gloucesters to J 13 C 5.8 Left Sector 1st Argylls & Camerons to J 18 B 7.6 H.Q. right and centre sector Bns. are here near each other in J 24 B 7.6 H.Q. 1st Argylls and Camerons at HOOGE in old so 2nd Bde H.Q. I 18 B 4.3	

WAR DIARY
or
INTELLIGENCE SUMMARY

Army Form C. 2118.

Hour, Date, Place	Summary of Events and Information	Remarks and references to Appendices
16th May	A Quiet day — Bn Hd Qrs moved to N.W. corner of ZILLEBEKE LAKE to about I.21.A.9.9. Enfiladen and S.Erskin RE came to examine the N.E. and S.E. corners of SANCTUARY WOOD with a view to knowing whether they aeclined to be feasible. Operations were to be commenced without delay under to STOCHER.	

Army Form C. 2118.

WAR DIARY
or
INTELLIGENCE SUMMARY

(Erase heading not required.)

Instructions regarding War Diaries and Intelligence Summaries are contained in F. S. Regs, Part II. and the Staff Manual respectively. Title pages will be prepared in manuscript.

Hour, Date, Place	Summary of Events and Information	Remarks and references to Appendices
17th May	All available Troops employed on 2nd line constructed in SANCTUARY WOOD. Cavalry officers arrived at 9 p.m. to be shown Trench as the Bde was being relieved on the following night. Divisional Wagin accompanied representative from Staff 9th Cav Regt to H.Q. Cheveuxins Retcht and 14 au9	

Army Form C. 2118.

WAR DIARY
or
INTELLIGENCE SUMMARY

(Erase heading not required.)

Instructions regarding War Diaries and Intelligence Summaries are contained in F. S. Regs., Part II. and the Staff Manual respectively. Title pages will be prepared in manuscript.

Hour, Date, Place	Summary of Events and Information	Remarks and references to Appendices
13th May	On the Night 18th/19th the Bde with the exception of the 1st and 9th R Scots were relieved by cavalry and went into rest near BUSSEBOOM – 1st and 9th R Scots were attached to the 82nd Bde.	Summary of casualties (to be typed)

27th DIVISION.

Statement of Casualties 81st Infantry Brigade, during fighting from 22nd April to 15th May 1915.

Brigade.	Unit.	Officers.				Other Ranks.				Remarks.
		Kd.	Wd.	Missg.	Total.	Kd.	Wd.	Missg.	Total.	
81st I.B.	1st Rl. Scots.	5	3	-	8	45	236	-	281	* Major Cross.
	2nd Gloster Regt.	3	4	1	8	79	321	18	418	(Was taken prisoner in succeeding week)
	2nd Cameron Highrs.	4	15	-	19	34	232	49	315	x*
	1st A. & S. Highrs.	3	5	1	9	38	162	25	225	x
	9th Royal Scots.	2	5	-	7	22	184	10	216	
	9th A. & S. Highrs.	5	9	-	14	34	270	42	346	
		22	42	1	65	252	1405	144	1801	

Army Form C. 2118.

WAR DIARY
or
INTELLIGENCE SUMMARY
(Erase heading not required.)

Instructions regarding War Diaries and Intelligence Summaries are contained in F. S. Regs., Part II. and the Staff Manual respectively. Title pages will be prepared in manuscript.

Hour, Date, Place	Summary of Events and Information	Remarks and references to Appendices
19th to 22nd May	Bttn in Reserve near BUSSEBOOM – 1st and 9th R.Scots attached to 82nd Bde. On Night 22nd/23rd May 1st and 9th R.Scots were relieved by the Welsh Regt and K.O.Y.L.I. respectively and returned to billeting area near BUSSEBOOM.	RG

Army Form C. 2118.

WAR DIARY
or
INTELLIGENCE SUMMARY

(Erase heading not required.)

Instructions regarding War Diaries and Intelligence Summaries are contained in F. S. Regs., Part II. and the Staff Manual respectively. Title pages will be prepared in manuscript.

Hour, Date, Place	Summary of Events and Information	Remarks and references to Appendices
23rd May to 24th	Bde Remained at rest in bivouacs near BUSSEBOOM	

Army Form C. 2118.

WAR DIARY
or
INTELLIGENCE SUMMARY
(Erase heading not required.)

Instructions regarding War Diaries and Intelligence Summaries are contained in F. S. Regs., Part II. and the Staff Manual respectively. Title pages will be prepared in manuscript.

Hour, Date, Place	Summary of Events and Information	Remarks and references to Appendices
25th May to 27th	Bate marched from BUSSEBOOM to VLAMERTINGHE on the afternoon of the 25th and were placed in Divisional Reserve - The remainder in Huts at VLAMERTINGHE until the morning of the 28th.	

WAR DIARY or INTELLIGENCE SUMMARY

Army Form C. 2118.

(Erase heading not required.)

Instructions regarding War Diaries and Intelligence Summaries are contained in F.S. Regs., Part II. and the Staff Manual respectively. Title pages will be prepared in manuscript.

Hour, Date, Place	Summary of Events and Information	Remarks and references to Appendices
5 am 28th May	The Bde marched to LOCRE arriving at 10 am. and proceeded to Billets	PG

Army Form C. 2118.

WAR DIARY
or
INTELLIGENCE SUMMARY

(Erase heading not required.)

Instructions regarding War Diaries and Intelligence Summaries are contained in F. S. Regs., Part II. and the Staff Manual respectively. Title pages will be prepared in manuscript.

Hour, Date, Place	Summary of Events and Information	Remarks and references to Appendices
5am 29th May	The left LOCRE and arrived in billeting area S.W. of STEENWERCK at 10am.	R.G.

Army Form C. 2118.

WAR DIARY
or
INTELLIGENCE SUMMARY

(Erase heading not required.)

Instructions regarding War Diaries and Intelligence Summaries are contained in F. S. Regs., Part II. and the Staff Manual respectively. Title pages will be prepared in manuscript.

Hour, Date, Place	Summary of Events and Information	Remarks and references to Appendices
30th May	The Bde marched from STEENWERCK to ARMENTIERES and relieved the 16th Infy Bde and part of the 17th Infy Bde in the Trenches — The Bde was distributed as under In the Trenches 1st Argylls 1st R. Scots 2nd Gloucesters In Billets at Armentieres 2nd Cameron Hdrs. 9th R. Scots (Meerut Divl. Reserve)	

Army Form C. 2118.

WAR DIARY
or
INTELLIGENCE SUMMARY
(Erase heading not required.)

Instructions regarding War Diaries and Intelligence Summaries are contained in F. S. Regs., Part II. and the Staff Manual respectively. Title pages will be prepared in manuscript.

Hour, Date, Place	Summary of Events and Information	Remarks and references to Appendices
31st May	9th R. Scots were detailed to form Divisional Reserve.	

J.W. Walsh Lt. Col.
Cmdg. 1st Infy. Bde.

CASUALTIES

Casualties 8th & 9th May.

	Officers					Other Ranks				Total Casualties
	K	W	M	Total		K	W	M	Total	
1st R.Scots 4-12 Ap.	1	x	—	1	Captain Ef Johnston	4	30	—	34	35 } 269
16 Ap - 9th May	x	x	x	x	x	x	x	x	x	122? x
9th May - 22nd May	1	1	—	2	Lt Young 2/Lt Copeland	30	100	—	130	132
2/ Inniskilling	3	4	1	8	Capt Farquharson	79	321	18	418	426
2/ Connaught 21st Ap – 18th May (casualties in trenches)	7	16	—	23		128	480	50	658	681
1st A.&S.H.										
2nd Ap – 8 May	x	x	x	x		x	x	x	x	(no statement from reported)
8th – 18th May	3	5	—	8	K Lt Clarke Capt Poddens DSO 2nd Lt G.Alp	75 205	25		300	300 } 308 spinous
9th R.Scots F										
18 – 27 Ap.	—	6	—	6	Capt Jayton Bell Green	17	119	6	142	148 } 276
28 Ap – 18 May	2	2	—	4	+ 1st Sept, 2Lt in trenches	25	89	—	114	118
9th A.&H.	x	x	x	x		x	x	x	x	346 x ? 2795

OPERATION

ORDERS

Copy No. 1

81st INFANTRY BDE. ORDER No. 50

1. The Brigade will march to YPRES to-morrow and take over a section of trenches from the French 17th Division to-morrow evening 4th instant. March table is attached.

2. The 2nd Cameron Highlanders, 1st A. & S. Highlanders and 9th A. & S. Highlanders will take over trenches 51 to 77 inclusive as arranged with officers Commanding battalions.
   The 81st Brigade are responsible for the defence of the gap between the 82nd Infy. Brigade and trench 51.
   The 9th Royal Scots, less 2 Companies will take over half the accommodation for the centre battalion in close support in the wood at J. 15 c. under arrangements made with G.O.C. 82nd Infantry Brigade.
   The 2nd Gloucesters will be in close support at POTIJZE with 1 Company just W. of Lake BELLEWAARDE and one company under O.C. 1st A. & S. Highlanders in GLENCORSE WOOD.
   On leaving YPRES battalions will march by trench parties from right to left.

3. An Officer and an Interpreter will go to the cross roads I 8. c. East of YPRES, 5 minutes in advance of each company to find their French guides and save checking at this point.
   Extra Interpreters will join battalions in YPRES.

4. As much R.E. material and ammunition as possible is being stored to-night at Hd. Qrs. of battalions in the trenches.
   O.C. 9th Royal Scots will inform O.C. 2nd Camerons and 1st A. & S. Highlanders by wire what ammunition, R.E. Stores and water have been taken up and Officers Commdg. Battalions will arrange to take up anything further necessary after the relief.

5. From 8 p.m. 4th inst. till 10 a.m. 5th inst. the brigade will be under command of the G.O.C. French 17th Division.

6. Refilling point to-morrow WESTOUTRE as usual and men will carry rations for the 5th inst on the march.

7. Brigade Headquarters during the relief to-morrow will be at HOOGE.

(Sd) L. Holland

Captain,
Bde. Major 81st Infy. Bde.

Issued at 7.45 p.m.

Copy No.

81st Infantry Brigade Operation Order
No. 51.

1. The Brigade will continue its march to-morrow to billeting area S.W. of STEENWERCK via BAILLEUL.

2. Starting point Road Junction TRENT 23 YPRES, Sq. S.9.a

Order of march:-

  1st A. & S.H.   5-40 a.m.
  2nd Gloucester Regt.   5-45 a.m.
  2nd Camerons.   5-50 a.m.
  1st Rl. Scots.   5-55 a.m.
  9th Rl. Scots.   5-58 a.m.
  Bde. Amn. Col.   6-5 a.m.

Baggage Section Train under an officer of Coy. A.S.C. and Transport Officer of 1st Rl. Scots pass the starting point at 6-30 a.m.

  81st Fd. Ambulance.   6-15 a.m.

3. The Brigade will pass the G.O.C. 3rd Corps at the Road Junction S. 27 a.

         L. HOWLAND, Captain,
       Brigade Major 81st Inf. Bde.

No. 1

81st INFANTRY BRIGADE OPERATION ORDER
No. 52.

29th May, 1915.

1.   The 81st Infantry Brigade will relieve the 16th Infantry Brigade and part of the 17th Infantry Brigade in the trenches to-morrow evening, 30th inst. as explained to Officers Commanding Battalions.

2.   The 1st A. & S. Highlanders, 1st Rl. Scots and 2nd Gloucesters will march to-morrow to bivouac in square H. 5.a. leaving present bivouacs as follows:-

    1st A. & S.H.   1-30 p.m.
    1st R. Scots.   1-30 p.m.
    2nd Gloucesters.   1-30 p.m.

Route - BAC St. MAUR - ERQUINGHEM - LYS.

3.   The above battalions will march to relief as follows:-
Starting point - ROAD JUNCTION H. 5.b. 3.2.

    1st A. & S.H.   7-15 p.m.
    1st R. Scots.   7-30 p.m.
    2nd Gloucesters.   8   p.m.

Adjutants will go to H.Q. 16th Infantry Brigade a quarter of an hour ahead of their battalions.

4.   Machine guns will leave the bivouac in H. 5 a. at 4-30 p.m., 1st A. & S.H. leading and proceed to 16th Infantry Brigade Headquarters in order to carry out their relief in daylight.

5.   The 2nd Camerons and 9th Rl. Scots will be in reserve. Further orders will be issued regarding their move and also of all transport not required for the relief.

                                                                              Captain,

Issued 6 p.m.   Bde. Major 81st Infy. Brigade.

AFTER ORDERS

1.   The 81st Fd. Ambulance moves to ERQUINGHEM-LYS at 6 a.m. on 30th inst and takes over medical arrangements from 16th Fd. Ambulance to-morrow morning.

2.   Refilling point to-morrow as for to-day.

                                                   (sd) L.H. Capt.
                                                            B.M.

Copy No. 3

27th Division Operation Order No. 46.

2nd May 1915

(1) In order to shorten the line now held to the East of YPRES, 27th 28th and Canadian Divisions will withdraw on the night of 3rd/4th to a line I 30 c - Eastern edge of SANCTUARY WOOD - Eastern corner of ETANG BELLEWAARDE - ARRET (J 1 a), - FREZENBERG - farm in C 22 b - farm in C 15 c where the French right rests.

(2) The 27th Division will occupy their section of the line as follows:—

85th Brigade From present 5th Division trench line on I 30 c to where the new trench line crosses the fence East of the house marked in J 19 c 1.7 inclusive (Scale 1/10000).

81st Brigade From this fence not inclusive to fence 30 yards South of MENIN ROAD in J 13 a.

80th Brigade From the left of 81st Brigade to the track J 7 a 8.8 (West of WESTHOEK) not inclusive.

The 28th Division continues the line Northwards.

GOC Brigades will arrange the exact points of union and will occupy their sections with their Reserve troops on night 3rd/4th. All movements in this connection to be completed by 9 p.m.

(3) All roads and tracks South of the track from J 7 b - level crossing I 11 b to MENIN ROAD in I 9 d are at the disposal of this division for the move.

(4) The artillery will begin withdrawal at 8-30 p.m.

(5) The withdrawal of the infantry of 27th Division and 28th Division will take place in three successive parties.

(a) First parties — Half the troops in the trench line.
(b) Second parties — Half the remainder.
(c) Third parties — The troops still remaining followed by the three or four men who are left till the last in each trench.

(a) First Parties

At 9 p.m. the infantry of the 28th Division will begin to withdraw and will reach the following line by 10 p.m. - N.W. corner of POLYGONE WOOD

(J9a 5'.4) - subsidiary line to present trench line about 10.20 to 8.8.

9.p.m. The First Parties 80th Brigade holding trenches from L.1. to the left will be withdrawn to the line L.1. — N.W. corner POLYGONE WOOD moving in conjunction with the 28th Division. They will not move West of that line till 10-30 p.m.

10.30.p.m. First Parties of 80th and 81st Inf. Bdes will withdraw through the new trench line moving in conjunction with 28th Division and with one another. The First parties 82nd Brigade will move at same time in succession from the left under brigade arrangements and in touch with 81st Brigade.

(b) Second Parties.

10.30.p.m. The Second Party 80th Brigade will move to the line L.1. — N.W. corner of POLYGONE WOOD in touch with 28th Division arriving at 11.30 p.m. and halt till 12 midnight.

12 midnight Second Parties 80th 81st and 82nd Brigades will withdraw in same manner as ordered for First Parties, withdrawal to be completed by 1 a.m.

12 midnight (c) The Third Party 80th Brigade followed by 3 or 4 men left in each trench will withdraw through the line L.1. — N.W. corner POLYGONE WOOD moving in conjunction with 28th Division.

1.30 a.m. The Third Parties 81st and 82nd Brigades will withdraw in conjunction with the 80th Bde, withdrawal to be completed by 1.45 a.m.

(d) It is intended to move two battalions 80th Brigade, one battalion 81st Brigade and one or one and a half battalions 82nd Brigade to the West of YPRES, but as it will be daylight before the rearmost parties of these battalions are clear of new trench line and formed up it is inadvisable to move them West of YPRES that day, therefore, the battalions moving West of YPRES will take shelter for the day (4th May) as follows:-
1. Battn 80th Brigade in G.H.Q. 2nd Line in Square I.10.
1. " " " " . " " " - South of MENIN Road Square I 16 b.

The battalions of 81st and 82nd Brigades will be sheltered in rear of their own areas under brigade arrangements.

Orders for further withdrawal of these battalions will be issued on the morning of 4th May.

(6) All movements to be completed by 3.30 a.m. The 28th Division is responsible for the timing of the movement. The 27th Division will regulate its withdrawal by that of 28th and will keep in close touch with it throughout, the Canadian Division conforming on the left of the 28th.

(7) If, before or during the withdrawal, the action of the enemy makes it advisable to postpone or delay it, the division which becomes aware of the reasons for such delay will immediately inform both the other divisions as well as Force Headquarters, and failing special instructions will conform to the movements of the 28th Division.

(8) The new trench line will be reconnoitred tonight and all approaches thereto from present trench line carefully marked and passages made through existing wire.

(9) All transport not absolutely required for the above operations will move West of YPRES tonight, moving after 12 m.n. to squares H.7 and H.8.

(10) All ranks should be warned that the success of the operation depends upon perfect quiet and concealment of movement.

(11) Communication between divisional headquarters in H.18 a & c and brigade headquarters will be established by 4 pm 3rd May. The exact hour of transfer of Report Centre will be notified later.

R. H. Hare
L.Col. GS
27th Division

Issued at 1-45 pm.

SECRET

81st Infantry Brigade Operation Order Z

3rd May. 1915.

(1). The 81st Infantry Brigade will occupy the Centre Section of the new line as explained on the ground to O.C. Battalions. Troops to be in position at 9 p.m. tonight 3rd inst.

(2) The 1st Subsidiary Line from S of STIRLING CASTLE to the trench just N of CLAPHAM JUNCTION inclusive, will be occupied by ½ Coy each of the Gloucesters and 1st Royal Scots Support Coys at the same hour. These will withdraw after the 3rd Trench Parties have passed.

The O.C. 9th A.S.H. will arrange to hold the edge of GLENCORSE WOOD till his trenches are vacated by the 3rd parties.

(3). The withdrawal of the Infantry from the old line will be carried out as follows:-

(a) All remaining S.A.A., bombs, tools, pumps, and stoves will be withdrawn by parties from trenches and support companies immediately after dark and carried to the Brigade Advance Depot SANCTUARY WOOD.

10.30 p.m. (b) First Trench Party — half the men in trenches — will begin to withdraw at 10.30 p.m. and go straight to bivouacs in SANCTUARY or ZOUAVE WOODS.

12 midnight to 1 a.m. 4th inst (c) Second Trench Party. Half the Remainder - will withdraw as above.

Amended by B.M. 96 ½ 2nd 13 - Parties all go at 12 mid 3rd 4 men at 12.15 a.m.

(d) The Remainder — Third Trench Party — will withdraw from the trenches leaving 3 or 4 men with flares in each trench. This movement will be done in conjunction with the 80th Brigade, and will be completed by 1.30 a.m. The left of the 9th A.S.H. moving at the same time as the right of the 80th Brigade. Three or four men with flares will be left in each trench who will withdraw by 1.45 a.m.

(4) The O.C. 9th A.S.H. will keep in constant touch with the Right Battalion 80th Infantry Brigade on his left.

The First Party 80th Brigade moves to the line Trench L.1. - N.W of POLYGONE WOOD at 10 p.m. and leaves this line at 10.30 p.m.

The Second Trench Party 80th Brigade reaches the same line at 11.30 p.m. and leaves at 12 midnight.

The Third Trench Party 80th Brigade begins to leave the trenches on its left at 12 midnight and leaves the same line in conjunction with the 3rd party 9th A.S.H.

(5) O.C. Battalions will arrange to report at once the arrival behind the new line of each party and the last few men.

(6) The importance of absolute silence during the operation must be impressed on all.

(7) Brigade Headquarters during the movement will remain at HOOGE CHATEAU, and will afterwards be established at the ECOLE DE BIEN FAISANCE at square I 9 C.

+ afterwards Answered Hd. remained at HOOGE till 9/5/15.

Issued at.

Sh Captain,
Brigade Major, 81st Infantry Bde.

Secret 8 P. 18 D 8 . Y post.
8 p.

1. The 27th Division have been ordered to withdraw to new line of trenches tomorrow night 3rd/4th inst.

2. In view of this the following steps will be taken tonight.

(a) Machine guns belonging to affiliated battalions will be returned to them from the fire trenches immediately after dark.

(b) As many footboards, firing platforms, latrine seats, rifle racks as possible will be withdrawn tonight and placed in an advanced brigade store being formed in Sanctuary Wood near I 18 D 8.5.

(c) All bombs, grenades, S.A.A. and tools surplus to probable requirements for 48 hours will be withdrawn to the same place before dawn.

(d) French explosives will be withdrawn or buried tonight, detonators in a separate place.

3. Company Officers and guides from each platoon will reconnoitre lines by which they can withdraw and note the gaps in the wire of the 1st Subsidiary Line and the new Line. This will be done in the dark as well as in daylight. Fresh gaps may be cut if necessary but these must be reported.

4. The new line will be taken up by

Right Sector — 9th R. Scots
Centre Sector — 2nd Gloucesters
Left Sector — 2nd Camerons.

5. These battalions will ~~forthwith~~ (a) place in the new fire trenches tonight.
(1) Machine Gun Dugouts (and commence building emplacements).
(2) S.A.A. Bombs.

(b) Before dark tomorrow Communication Trenches will be sited and marked so as to be defiladed from Stirling Castle Ridge.

(c) ~~Also~~ have old trenches and dug outs within 100 yards of the fire trenches filled in before daylight 4th inst.

~~After withdrawal tomorrow night the 1st R Scots will bivouac in Sanctuary Wood and move to west of YPRES on the night 4/5.
The 1st ~~aft~~ will bivouac in ZOUAVE Wood
The 9th as H will be bivouac in~~

6. Battalions leaving trenches tomorrow night must be prepared to bivouac in SANCTUARY or ZOUAVE Woods.

Thulett

REPORT ON

BRIDGES

SECRET

G.X. 911.

Report on Bridges across YPRES CANAL

in Square I, 13 and 19.

----

1. Reference attached sketch, the bridge are lettered from A. to H.

2. Bridges A. C. H. are trestle bridges suitable for Infantry in fours and field guns. Approaches over hard ground at present passable for all arms, but probably very heavy in wet weather.

3. Bridges B. and G. are main road bridges. B. is suitable for all types transport. G. has been somewhat damaged as flanges ot left girder (looking East) has been cut near point of support. Would probably not be safe for continuous stream of heavy traffic.

4. D. and F. Bridges are suitable for all types of transport. F. Bridge is slightly out of repair. but repairs are being carried out. Approaches by rough unmetalled tracks which would cut up in rough weather.

5. Bridge E. at ECLUSE No. 9. Planks have been laid across to form foot bridge. Passable for Infantry in single file.

6. All bridges are in view of high ground to South in possession of Germans, particularly B. and G. (the main road bridges).

(sigd.) J.D.D.BRANCKER,
Captain,
G.S.O. (3) 5th Division.

Head Quarters
81st Infantry Bde.

The above are forwarded to you for your information & retention. Acknowledge by wire

27/Div.
3/5/15.

SECRET   App 2.

Report on Bridges across YPRES CANAL
in Square I, 13 and 19.

(1).   Bridges A.C.H are trestle bridges suitable for infantry in fours and field guns. Approaches over hard ground at present passable for all arms, but probably very heavy in wet weather.

(2).   Bridges B & G are main road bridges. B is suitable for all types transport. G has been somewhat damaged, as flange of left girder (looking East) has been cut near point of support. Would probably not be safe for continuous stream of heavy traffic.

(3).   D & F Bridges are suitable for all types of transport. F Bridge is slightly out of repair, but repairs are being carried out. Approaches by rough unmetalled tracks which would cut up in rough weather.

(4).   Bridge E at ECLUSE No 9. Planks have been laid across to form foot bridge. Passable for Infantry in single file.

(5).   All bridges are in view of high ground to South in possession of Germans, particularly B and G. (the main road bridges).

Sd. W. G. D. Brancker,
Capt.
G.S.O. (3) 5th Division

CROSSINGS ZILLEBEKE

SKETCH OF G.H.Q. LINE

"A" Form. Army Form C. 2121.

MESSAGES AND SIGNALS.

TO: G.O.C. 81st Brigade

Sender's Number: D 21 Day of Month: 8 AAA

I enclose sketch of crossings on ZILLEBEKE also sketch of 81st Brigade area GHQ line AAA I went back to Army outs at Railway Crossing but found they were untenable So after keeping Gunners with they found my Coy returned to dug outs on 81st Brigade area of GHQ line I6a9.8 AAA Please you left me to call and see you through AAA Have you any stores the infantry have taken more of mine today AAA

From: O/C "A" Horace Reed Coy R.E.
Time: 7-5 pm

(signature)

B.M. 17A /UNITS 81st L.B. 74

1. Reference attached the following will be the order of withdrawing
   (1) Close Support Battalion will go straight to occupy its portion of the G.H.Q. line.

2. The prepared supporting points are allotted as follows
   (a) and (b) Centre battalion in trenches
   (c) and (d) Right   "   "   "
   (e) and (f) Left   "   "   "

3. Lines of Retirement
   Left Battn. Left Boundary (North) — Straight line to crossroads at centre of square I.10
   Southern Boundary — Straight line Centre Battn. to Menin Road Level Crossing
   Centre Bn. Thence South to where the junction Lash crosses the junction of I.16 A and B
   Right Battn. thence South to the centre of square I.16

4. On the Close Support battalion retires to the GHQ line. The support companies of Bowen in trenches will take up supporting points and such trenches in the old 2nd Subsidiary line as are in their zones.

5. At a given hour the Coys will begin to withdraw from the fire trenches keeping touch with Battln on their left —

6. If the enemy presses closely supports should be prepared to charge with the bayonet but not be led back into machine gun fire. Limit of charge say 40 or 50 yards.

7. An officer of one can be chosen and about 6 NCOs & men to be attached to flank coys of battalions of 80th and 82nd Bdes to keep our flank battalions informed of their movements.

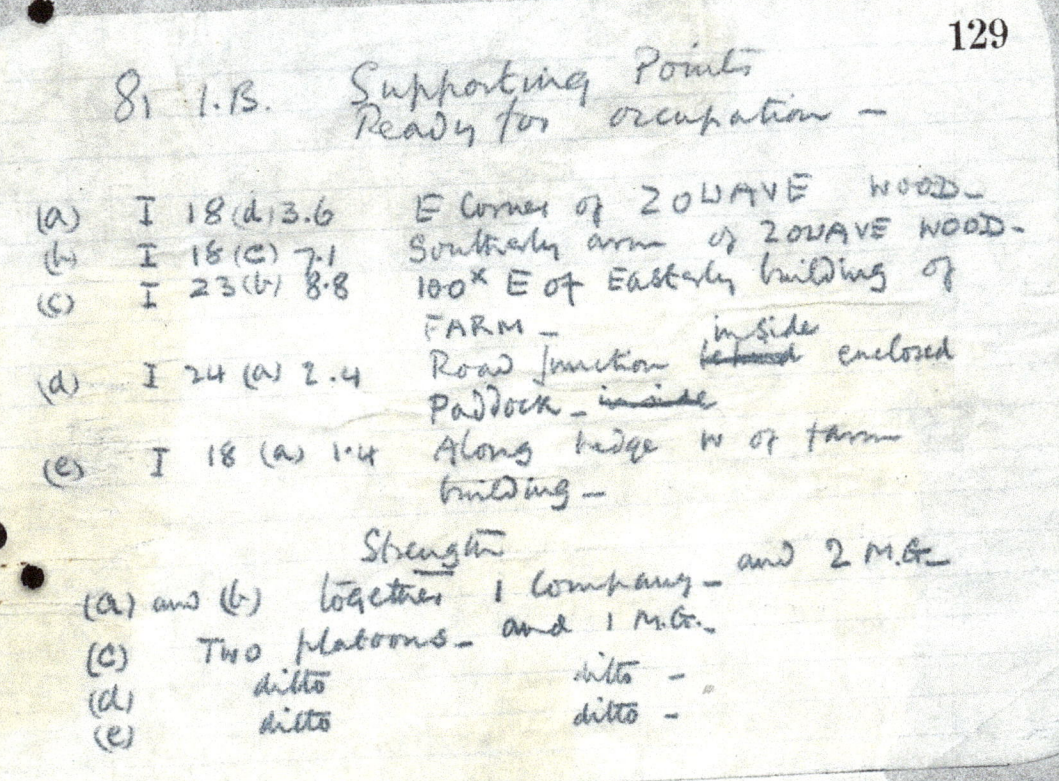

81 I.B. Supporting Points
Ready for occupation —

(a) I 18 (d) 3.6   E Corner of ZOUAVE WOOD —
(b) I 18 (c) 7.1   Southerly arm of ZOUAVE WOOD —
(c) I 23 (b) 8.8   100ˣ E of Easterly building of FARM —
(d) I 24 (a) 2.4   Road Junction inside enclosed Paddock —
(e) I 18 (a) 1.4   Along hedge W of farm building —

Strength
(a) and (b) together 1 Company — and 2 M.G.
(c) Two platoons — and 1 M.G.
(d) ditto   ditto —
(e) ditto   ditto —

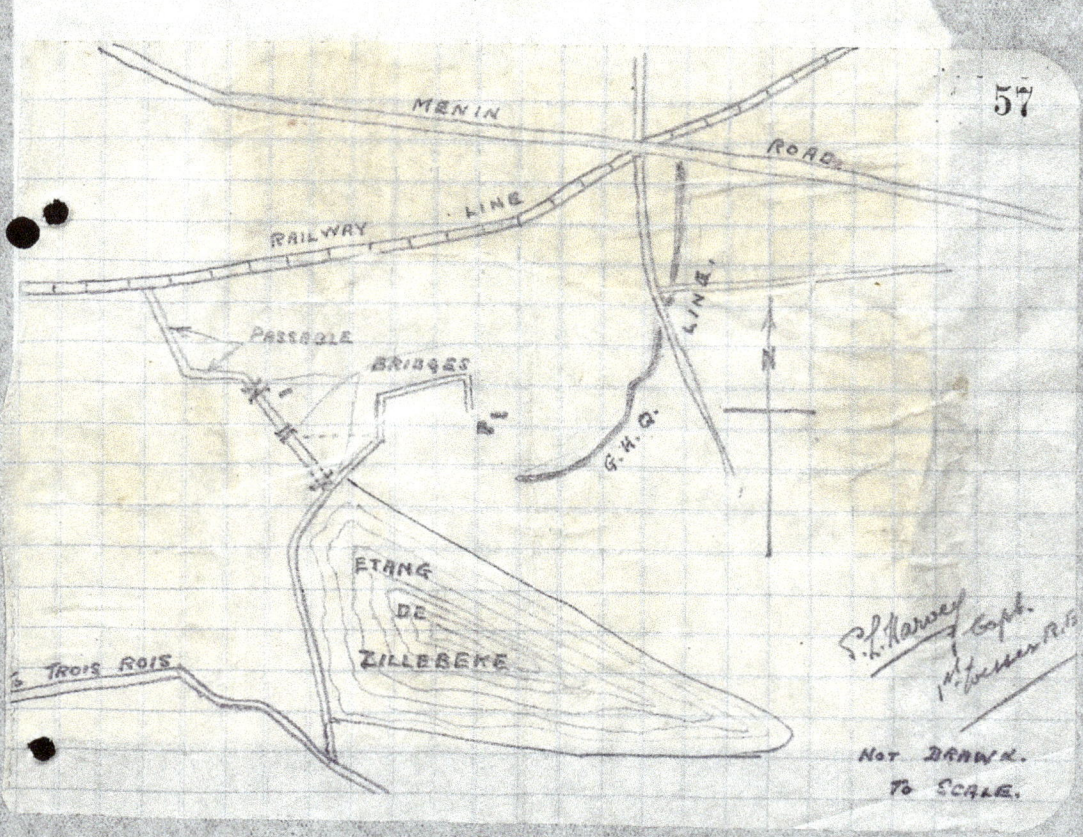

Not drawn to scale.

8. Gaps in wire to be reconnoitred and marked on maps.

9. No retirement at all without definite orders.

9/5/15.   S Howard Caxton(?)
          BM 81st L.B

Issue(?)
Cameron 6. 30pm

Secret

Identification Trace for use with Artillery Maps.

92nd Div Section at G.H.Q line.

YPRES

Scale 1/5000

HOOGE
Bellewarde Lake
ZOUAVE WOOD
MENIN ROAD

M A P S

Situation of line after withdrawal.

OUTLINE OF V CORPS AREA.

81st Brigade dispositions to 4th May.

   "   "   Situation 4th May.

   "   "   " 14th-17th May.

Headquarters,

    81st Infantry Brigade.

    The G.O.C. Division wishes me to express to you how deeply he appreciates the devotion to duty and power of endurance which you and the troops of your Brigade have shown during the recent operations.

    The manner in which every Battalion has fought and the cheerful way in which all ranks have worked in the reconstruction of the position deserves the highest praise.

    It must be a satisfaction to all ranks to feel that they have right well upheld the traditions of their respective regiments.

    The G.O.C. congratulates you and your Brigade on the results of your month's work.

18th May, 1915.
                                                      G.S.,
                                           27th Division.

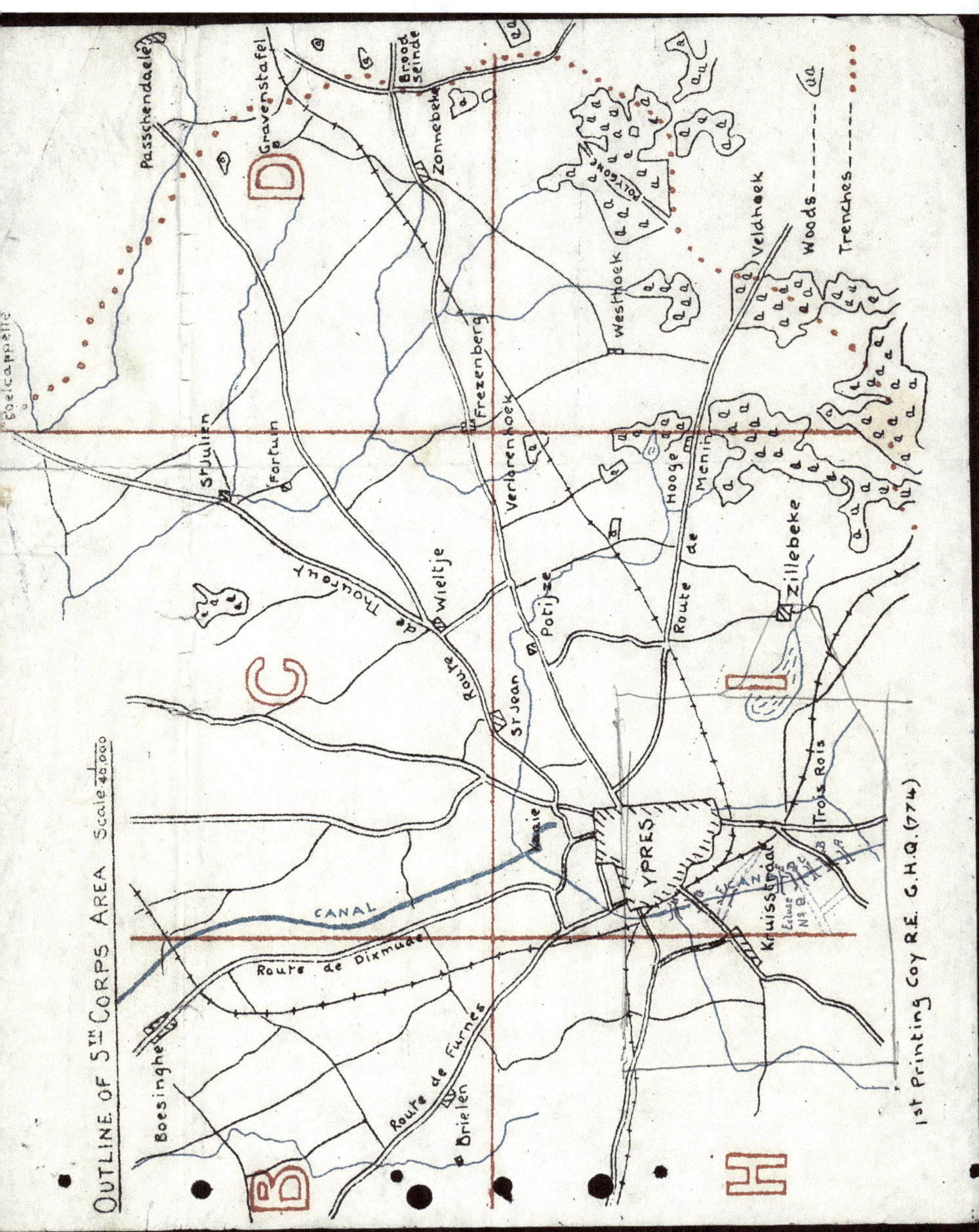

App 2

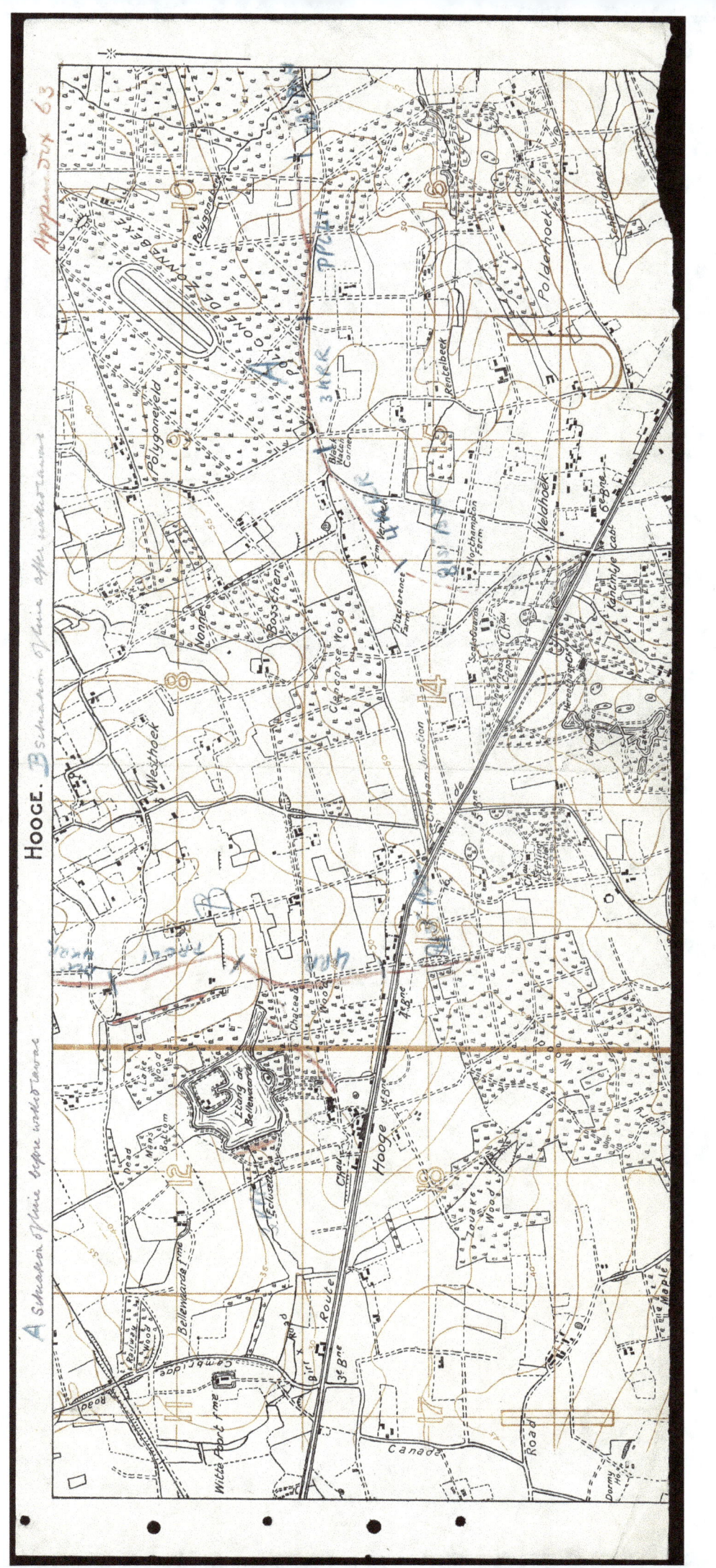

27th Division.

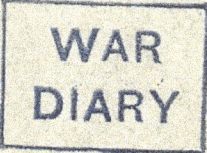

B. H. Q.   81st INFANTRY BRIGADE

June

1 9 1 5

Attached:
Brigade O.O. No. 53.
Sketch.

WAR DIARY

WAR DIARY
or
INTELLIGENCE SUMMARY

(Erase heading not required.)

Army Form C. 2118.

Hour, Date, Place 1915	Summary of Events and Information	Remarks and references to Appendices
1st May June ARMENTIERES	The Bde was distributed as under:— In the Trenches — From left to Right 1st R. Scots — 2nd Gloucesters — 1st Argylls Line of Trenches approximately from I 21 c 2.8 through RUE DU BOIS and I 16 central to I 10 d 10.4 Billeted in ARMENTIERES 2nd Camerons and 9th R. Scots — 9th R. Scots formed Divisional Reserve — Night 1st/2nd the Bde handed over the Rue Du BOIS defences to the 19th Bde — These were the Trenches occupied by the 1st Argylls — The Argylls moved to the left of our line and took over a new portion from 2 Coys the Rifle Bde — line from left to Right was as follows — 1st Argylls — 1st R. Scots — 2nd Gloucesters line of Trenches approximately from I 21 a 10.8 through 16 Central I 11 a 5.5	Ref. 1/40,000 map Sheet 36 BELGIUM

Army Form C. 2118.

WAR DIARY
or
INTELLIGENCE SUMMARY

(*Erase heading not required.*)

Instructions regarding War Diaries and Intelligence Summaries are contained in F. S. Regs., Part II. and the Staff Manual respectively. Title pages will be prepared in manuscript.

Hour, Date, Place	Summary of Events and Information	Remarks and references to Appendices
2nd May June	A quiet day – Situation normal – Nothing to report –	PG
3rd May June	Situation still unchanged – Camerons relieved the 1st R. Scots in the Trenches. 1 R Scots took over Camerons billets in Armentières and were placed in Divnl. Reserve.	PG

Army Form C. 2118.

WAR DIARY
or
INTELLIGENCE SUMMARY
(Erase heading not required.)

Instructions regarding War Diaries and Intelligence Summaries are contained in F. S. Regs., Part II. and the Staff Manual respectively. Title pages will be prepared in manuscript.

Hour, Date, Place	Summary of Events and Information	Remarks and references to Appendices
4th May June	A quiet day – a little sniping otherwise situation unchanged –	PG
5th May June	Situation unchanged.	PG
6th May June	Situation normal – # Brigadier decided to construct a 2nd line for use if necessary in the case of attack – 200 men detailed nightly to work on the 2nd line.	See sketch map attached PG

Army Form C. 2118.

WAR DIARY
or
INTELLIGENCE SUMMARY
(Erase heading not required.)

Instructions regarding War Diaries and Intelligence Summaries are contained in F. S. Regs., Part II. and the Staff Manual respectively. Title pages will be prepared in manuscript.

Hour, Date, Place	Summary of Events and Information	Remarks and references to Appendices
7th June ARMENTIERES	Corps Commander Major General PULTENEY inspected 1st R. Scots and 9th R. Scots — 2nd Lieut L. J. BARLEY lectured to 1st R. Scots and 9th R. Scots on asphyxiating gases.	RG
8th June ARMENTIERES	Night 8th/9th 3 Coys 9th R. Scots relieved 3 Coys 1st Argylls 8th R. Scots relieved 2nd Camerons 1st Argylls formed Divisional Reserve in ARMENTIERES — 1 Coy 9th R. Scots supplied Guards and Fire Piquet and one attached to 2nd Camerons — 2nd Camerons formed Bde Reserve at ARMENTIERES	RG
9th June	Lecture by 2nd Lieut L. J. BARLEY to 2nd Camerons and 1st Argylls on asphyxiating gases Work continued on 2nd line.	RG

1247 W 3299 200,000 (E) 8/14 J.B.C. & A. Forms/C. 2118/11.

Army Form C. 2118.

WAR DIARY
or
INTELLIGENCE SUMMARY

(Erase heading not required.)

Instructions regarding War Diaries and Intelligence Summaries are contained in F. S. Regs., Part II. and the Staff Manual respectively. Title pages will be prepared in manuscript.

Hour, Date, Place 1915	Summary of Events and Information	Remarks and references to Appendices
10th June ARMENTIERES	The 9th R. Fusiliers 36th Infy Bde arrived in ARMENTIERES at 10 am and were attached to the 13th Infy Bde for instruction — Work continued on 2nd line defences	PG
11th June	A quiet day except for a little shelling — Work continued on 2nd line	PG
12th June	Situation unchanged — In the Night 12th/13th "3 Coys 10th Argylls" relieved 3 Coys Glosters — Glosters marched to ARMENTIERES and became Divisional Reserve.	PG

Army Form C. 2118.

WAR DIARY
or
INTELLIGENCE SUMMARY

(Erase heading not required.)

Instructions regarding War Diaries and Intelligence Summaries are contained in F. S. Regs., Part II. and the Staff Manual respectively. Title pages will be prepared in manuscript.

Hour, Date, Place	Summary of Events and Information	Remarks and references to Appendices
13th June	Situation unchanged – Work continued on 2nd line defences	RG
14th June	A quiet day – Night 14th/15th 3 Coys Camerons relieved 3 Coys 1st R Scots	RG
15th June	Situation normal – Work continued on 2nd line – Officers patrol reported enemy cutting grass and making entanglements – 9th R Fusiliers joined the left of the Bde at 3.40pm on conclusion of attachment –	RG
16th June	Enemy shelled our communication Trenches and 2nd line defences but did little damage. – Work continued on line defences – Germans shelled all haystacks in rear of our near CHAPELLE D'ARMENTIERES and set them on Fire. German searchlight reported to be continually displaying the following letters – SITE SITE AB LIB	Lieut. N. MACDONALD 9th R Scots reported missing. This officer went out with a reconnoitring patrol on night 15th/16th RG

1247 W 3299 200,000 (E) 8/14 J.B.C. &A. Forms/C. 2118/11.

Army Form C. 2118.

WAR DIARY
or
INTELLIGENCE SUMMARY

(Erase heading not required.)

Instructions regarding War Diaries and Intelligence Summaries are contained in F. S. Regs., Part II. and the Staff Manual respectively. Title pages will be prepared in manuscript.

Hour, Date, Place	Summary of Events and Information	Remarks and references to Appendices
17th May June	Patrol sent out failed to find any sign of LIEUT. MACDONALD — Situation unchanged	PG
18th May June	Night 18/19th Gloucesters relieved Argylls — All quiet to our front —	PG
19th May June	Stong search light from direction of the interspersed with working parties cutting grass in front of our Trenches otherwise situation unchanged —	PG

Army Form C. 2118.

WAR DIARY
or
INTELLIGENCE SUMMARY

(Erase heading not required.)

Instructions regarding War Diaries and Intelligence Summaries are contained in F. S. Regs., Part II. and the Staff Manual respectively. Title pages will be prepared in manuscript.

Hour, Date, Place	Summary of Events and Information	Remarks and references to Appendices
20th June	6th Bn The Buffs arrived at ARMENTIERES and were attached to the Bde for instruction — Night 20th/21st R. Scots relieved 2nd Camerons in the Trenches — Camerons proceeded to Billets in ARMENTIERES	PG
21st June	H.D. Horses substituted for L.D. horses in Battalion & Travelling Kitchens. — Work continued on 2nd Line — OC Divnl. Train inspected all 1st Line Transport.	PG
22nd June	Situation unchanged	PG

Army Form C. 2118.

WAR DIARY
or
INTELLIGENCE SUMMARY
(Erase heading not required.)

Instructions regarding War Diaries and Intelligence Summaries are contained in F. S. Regs., Part II. and the Staff Manual respectively. Title pages will be prepared in manuscript.

Hour, Date, Place	Summary of Events and Information	Remarks and references to Appendices
23rd June	A quiet day - Nothing to Report	JPG
24th June	Situation unchanged - Night 24th/25th 1st Argylls relieved 2/Gloucesters in the Trenches - 2nd Gloucesters proceeded to billets in ARMENTIERES. 6th Buffs completed their attachment and moved off at 5 p.m.	JPG
25th June	Situation Normal	JPG

Army Form C. 2118.

WAR DIARY
or
INTELLIGENCE SUMMARY
(Erase heading not required.)

Instructions regarding War Diaries and Intelligence Summaries are contained in F. S. Regs., Part II. and the Staff Manual respectively. Title pages will be prepared in manuscript.

Hour, Date, Place	Summary of Events and Information	Remarks and references to Appendices
26th June	Work continued on 2nd line	Readjustment of Trenches Trench Gloucesters } 60 to 63 inclusive Argylls } 4th R Scots } 64 Camerons } 65 to 68 inclusive 1st R Scots } This was final position by June 30th JRG
27th June	Situation unchanged — Night 27th/28th 1st R Scots relieved were relieved in the Trenches by 2nd Camerons. 1st R Scots moved to Billets at ARMENTIERES. Night 27th/28th line Readjusted Bar took over Trenches 60 to 68 as per attached map	
28th June	Work continued on 2nd line — Situation normal	JRG
29th June	Work continued on 2nd line — Situation normal	JRG
30th June	Situation unchanged — Work continued on 2nd line Night 30th/1st Gloucesters relieved Argylls in Trenches	JRG

Copy No. 1

81ST INFANTRY BRIGADE OPERATION ORDER.

No. 53.

1. The front held by 27th Division will be readjusted as follows:-
   The 19th Brigade will hold from the BOIS GRENIER - BRIDOUX Road to trench 59 (both inclusive).
   The 81st Brigade will hold from trench 60 to trench 68 (both inclusive).
   The 80th Brigade will hold from trench 69 to trench 79 (both inclusive).
   The 82nd Brigade will hold from trench 80 to trench 89, RIVER LYS (both inclusive).

   The 81st Brigade front will be divided as follows :-

   Right Sector. (Trenches 60,61,62,63.) (Bn. H.Q. in dug-outs in rear of trench 62) Held by 2nd Bn. Gloucestershire Regiment and 1st Bn. A. & S. Highrs.

   Centre Sector. (Trench 64.) (Bn. H.Q. in dug-outs in ORCHARD) Held by 9th Bn. The Royal Scots.

   Left Sector. (Trenches 65,66,67,68.) (Bn. H.Q. Fme DU BIEZ) Held by 1st Bn. The Royal Scots and 2nd Bn. Cameron Highrs.

   All moves will be complete by 3 a.m. on 28th inst.

2. There will be no change in the position of Divisional or Brigade Headquarters.

   The Brigade will be supported by the same group of artillery as before.

3. Batteries will support sectors as under :-

   Right Sector. 133rd Battery R.F.A.
   Centre Sector. 98th Battery R.F.A.
   Left Sector. 132nd Battery R.F.A.

4. Officers Commanding Battalions will arrange to have any trenches they are unacquainted with reconnoitred by afternoon 27th inst.

5. The relief of 1st Bn. The Royal Scots by 2nd Bn. Cameron Highrs will now take place on night 27th/28th and not on night of 26th/27th as stated in letter No. 81/659 dated 14.6.15.

6. On relief by 80th Brigade the companies 9th Royal Scots holding trench 73 will return to billets in ARMENTIERES using the PORT EGAL AVENUE.
   On relief by 80th Brigade the companies 1st Royal Scots will leave trenches 72,71,70,69, by "LOTHIAN ROAD AVENUE".
   On relief by 2nd Bn. Cameron Highrs., the companies 1st Bn. The Royal Scots holding trench 68 will leave by "LEITH WALK".

7. 2nd Camerons will use "COWGATE" and "LEITH WALK" avenues for purposes of relieving trenches 65,66,67,68.

8. 9th Royal Scots will use "WINE STREET" for purpose of relieving trench 64.

9. "RAILWAY AVENUE" and "HAYSTACK AVENUE" will be used by Battalion 19th Brigade on relief.

10. Units will report to Brigade Headquarters as soon as relief is complete and their battalions in position.

11. Officers of 80th Brigade will visit trenches 69, 70, 71, 72, and 73 on the afternoon June 26th.

12. Relieving companies of 80th Brigade will arrive in front line trenches about 9-30 p.m. on night June 27th/28th.

M. Henderson
Captain.

26.6.15. for Brigade Major, 81st Infantry Brigade.

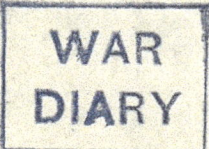

B. H. Q.   81st INFANTRY BRIGADE

July

1 9 1 5

Army Form C. 2118.

WAR DIARY
or INTELLIGENCE SUMMARY
(Erase heading not required.)

Instructions regarding War Diaries and Intelligence Summaries are contained in F. S. Regs., Part II. and the Staff Manual respectively. Title pages will be prepared in manuscript.

Hour, Date, Place	Summary of Events and Information	Remarks and references to Appendices
ARMENTIERES.		
1st JULY	Enemy quiet; work of improving support line. Construction of August S6. continued.	For distribution of units see MAP "A".
2nd JULY	Situation unchanged, work continued.	Right Sector 2nd GLOS } Trenches 60, 61, 62, 63 or 1st A.&S.H. Right Sector Support: 1 Company 2nd GLOS } Subsidiary line near or 1st A. & S.H. DESPLANQUE ESTAMINET.
3rd JULY	Work continued. 1st ROYAL SCOTS relieved 2nd CAMERONS in left sector at 8.30 p.m.	Centre Sector. 3. Platoons 9th ROYAL SCOTS } Trench 64. Centre Sector Support 5 Platoons 9th ROYAL SCOTS SS64
4th JULY	Additional Communication trenches from the trench to support line commenced every 50 yards. Enemy quiet.	Left Sector 1st ROYAL SCOTS } Trenches 65, 66, 67, 68. or 2nd CAMERONS Left Sector Support 1 Company } Subsidiary line at 1st ROYAL SCOTS CH. D'ARMENTIERES.
5th JULY	Enemy more active both with snipers and artillery. Work on support line continued.	
6th JULY	Enemy's aircraft and artillery active. Work continued. 1st A & S. Highlanders relieved 2nd GLOUCESTERSHIRES in left sector.	2nd CAMERONS

Army Form C. 2118.

WAR DIARY
or
INTELLIGENCE SUMMARY
(Erase heading not required.)

Instructions regarding War Diaries and Intelligence Summaries are contained in F. S. Regs., Part II. and the Staff Manual respectively. Title pages will be prepared in manuscript.

Hour, Date, Place	Summary of Events and Information	Remarks and references to Appendices
ARMENTIERES 7th July. 1915.	Enemy Quiet. Work on support line continued, wiring Commenced.	Same
8th July 1915.	Enemy Quiet. Work Continued. ASYLUM at ARMENTIERES -F.S. & Town itself shelled during the evening.	Same
9th July 1915	Enemy Quiet. 2/CAMERONS relieved 1st ROYAL SCOTS in Right Left Sector	Same
10th July 1915.	Enemy Quiet. Work on support line & Communication Continued.	Same
11 July 1915.	Work Continued.	Same
12 July 1915.	Enemy Quiet. 2/GLOUCESTERSHIRES relieved 1st A. & S. HIGHLANDERS in Right Sector	Same
13 July 1915	Enemy Quiet.	Same
14 July 1915	Enemy Quiet in trenches. ARMENTIERES heavily Shelled from 11am to 1 pm and intermittently during afternoon.	Same
15 July 1915.	Enemy Quiet. 2/Camerons relieved by 1st R. SCOTS in Centre Left Sector.	Same

Army Form C. 2118.

WAR DIARY
or
INTELLIGENCE SUMMARY
(Erase heading not required.)

Instructions regarding War Diaries and Intelligence Summaries are contained in F.S. Regs., Part II. and the Staff Manual respectively. Title pages will be prepared in manuscript.

Hour, Date, Place	Summary of Events and Information	Remarks and references to Appendices
ARMENTIERES.		
16 July 1915.	Enemy quiet, work in trenches continued.	
17 July 1915	Trenches 67 & 68 were taken over by 151st Inf. Bde at 9 p.m. The boundary between 1st & 2nd Army becoming LILLE-ARMENTIERES RD to level crossing (I.i.c) & thence along STEENWERK Railway. 81st Inf. Bde became part of 1st Army.	DISTRIBUTION OF UNITS R. Sector. Tch. 61. 62. 3 Coys 2/GLOSTERS with 1 Coy in Support in Subsidiary Line. Centre Sector. Tch. 63. 2 Coys 9th R. Scots. Left Sector. Tch. 64. 65. 66. 3 Coys 1st R. Scots with 1 Coy in support in subsidiary line. Bde Reserve. 1. A. & S. H. 2/GLOUCESTERSHIRES. 2 Coys 9th R. Scots.
18 July 1915.	Enemy quiet, work in trenches continued. 1st A & S. H. relieved 2nd Gloucestershires in Right Sector. Situation normal.	
19 July 1915		
20 July 1915	Trench 59 taken over by 1st A. & S. H. 1 Coy 2 Gloucestershires brought into Subsidiary line in Support of 1st A. & S. H.	DISTRIBUTION OF UNITS R. Sector. 1. A. & S. H. with 1 Coy 2/Glos in support in Subsidiary line. Centre Sector as above. Bde Reserve. 2/Camerons 2/Gloucestershires (less 1 Coy). 2 Coy 9th R. Scots.
21 July 1915.	2nd Camerons relieved 1st R. Scots in Left Sector	
22 July 1915.	Enemy commenced firing Rifle Grenades into Trench. They were replied to with Trench Mortars & Rifle Grenades and silenced.	

Army Form C. 2118.

WAR DIARY
or
INTELLIGENCE SUMMARY
(Erase heading not required.)

Instructions regarding War Diaries and Intelligence Summaries are contained in F.S. Regs., Part II. and the Staff Manual respectively. Title pages will be prepared in manuscript.

Hour, Date, Place	Summary of Events and Information	Remarks and references to Appendices
ARMENTIERES		
23 July 1915	Enemy inactive. Work continued on Support line and Communication Breastworks (continued)	Two.
24 July 1915	Work continued	Two
25 July 1915	Work continued. 2 GLOUCESTERSHIRES relieved 1st R. & S.M. in Right Sector at 9 p.m.	Two.
26 July 1915	Work continued. From 1pm to 3.30pm Enemy bombarded BOIS GRENIER line, from DESROSIERES to RUE ROAD.	Two. Two.
27 July 1915	Work continued. Enemy inactive. 1st R. Scots relieved 4 Cameroons in ① Left Sector	Two Two
28 July 1915	Work continued, defences of Communication avenues.	Two
29 July 1915	Work Continued	Two
30 July 1915	Work Continued	Two
31 July 1915	Work continued. At 6.20pm a minor operation was carried out by "B" Group R.F.A. & attached batteries, the 2/GLOUCESTERS & 9th R. Scots cooperating with rifle and machine gun fire, & French mortars	Two

Br. General.
Commanding 81st Infantry Brigade.
1-8-15.

To Head Quarters,

        27th Division.

With reference to your G.S.660, dated 7-7-15, I beg to report as follows:-

(a). DEFENSIVE OPERATIONS.
    (1). A support line must be constructed sufficiently near the fire trench to admit of the withdrawal of part of the Garrison during bombardment, with sufficient communication trenches for that part to return by immediately the Infantry attack commences.
    It has been found that dugouts in the breastworks themselves are a source of weakness.
    A design of a splinter proof roof found usefull is attached.

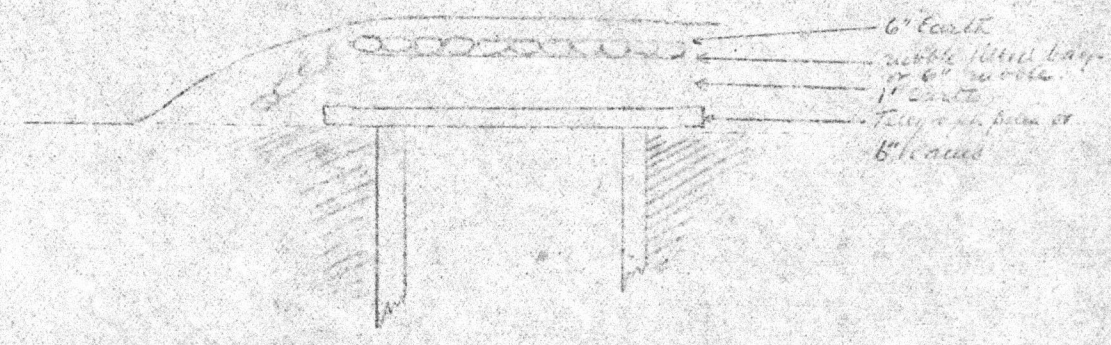

    (2). The principal essentials appear to be:-

        (a). A liberal supply of Machine guns, in good positions, sited especially with a view to the utilization of obstacles both natural & artificial.

        (b). Sufficient splinter proof dugouts for the whole garrison.

    (3). For local counterattacks by the supports in trenches a prearranged scheme is essential, especially in the case of gas and mine attacks, to ensure immediate counterattack in the case of a lodgement of the enemy in the fire trench. The provision of suitable jumping off places must be arranged.
    A similar arrangement for organization of a counter-attack by the Brigade Reserve must be made, as regards jumping off place, equipment with sandbags, bombs, etc.

    (4).(a). Alarms.
        Gongs for immediately spreading the alarm among the men in the trenches.
        Prearranged telephone messages to inform neighbouring units and R.A.
        Light signals in case of telephonic communication breaking down.

        (b). Methods of dispersing gas.
        Vermoral sprayers and ordinary sprayers from force pumps.
        Fire boxes or braziers a short way down communication trenches.
        Fans made of sandbags etc:.

        (c). Organisation of defence.
        The formation of a previously arranged plan to br-

(4).(c).bring supporting and reserve troops into the most
favourable position to counterattack any part of
the front line should the enemys attack be succ-
-essful.

(b).OFFENSIVE OPERATIONS.

As the Brigade under my command has not yet been employed
on offensive operations other than counterattacks,I can
only state the arrangements now provided in my present
line.

(1).Ample room can be found for assaulting troops in the
support trenches,(50 to 150 yards in rear of fire
trench),and in small breastworks specially constructed
for a previous operation.
Sufficient communication trenches from support line
are either constructed or under construction.

(2).There are now existing in the left sector several saps
connected together,beyond the wire,by a trench;and in
the right sector,seven saps.
Short ladders suitable for four men to go up at a time,
or better still ramps would have to be provided in
addition.

(3).The following appliances were made and tested with a
view to attack,and some few of them still remain.
Bridges:- 12 foot by 18 inches made of wood &
wirenetting.
Heavy ladders:-12 ft by 2ft made of wood.
Hen coop ladders:-wooden,with slats,and a grapple
at the end.
Mats:-Of stout canvas,6 ft by 3ft,quilted.

(4).I am unable to state anything on this heading.

(5).The only points I am able to mention are:-
(A).The necessity of carrying a proportion of sandbags
shovels,etc with the assaulting columns.
(B).The necessity of creating depots of sandbags,wire,
bombs,S.A.A.tools,etc:,at the nearest possible
points to the enemy.

(c).GENERAL.
(I).(a).Within the Battalion.
Special points must be selected before at which
telephonic communication with the Battalion H Q
will be established if possible.
Orderlies must also be arranged at the above
communication centres.
Arrangements must also be made for visual signall-
-ing whereever possible.
(b).From Battalion to Brigade.
A carefully laid system of wires must be made the
fire trench from which the attack is to be made,
before it commences,and wherever possible the wire
should be laid out in front of that trench as far
as possible in the direction of the prearranged
communication centres, of BN.H.Q.
A system of orderlies and wherever possible visual
signalling must likewise be arranged.

(2).All working parties for special purposes such as beg-
-ining communication trenches from the captured line,
placing localities in a state of defence,must be arr-
-anged beforehand,& tools carried up by them for the
purpose.

(c). (3) I am unable to give any information.

(4). A machine gun in buildings, if accurately located, is best dealt with by artillery.
In the open air or in breastworks, either by the concentrated fire of opposing machine guns or by rifle fire.

H.H.Crocker
Brig. General,
9th July, 1915.   Commanding 81st Infy. Brigade.

B

BREASTWORK
FIRE TRENCH
COMMUNICATION TRENCH
BATTALION HD QRS

B

27th Division.

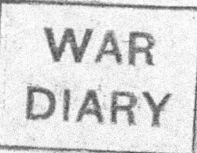

B.H.Q. 81st INFANTRY BRIGADE

August

1915

Attached:
Bde. O.Os. Nos. 53 and 55.
Sketches.

ORIGINAL

Army Form C. 2118.

WAR DIARY
or
INTELLIGENCE SUMMARY
(Erase heading not required.)

Instructions regarding War Diaries and Intelligence Summaries are contained in F.S. Regs., Part II. and the Staff Manual respectively. Title pages will be prepared in manuscript.

Hour, Date, Place	Summary of Events and Information	Remarks and references to Appendices
ARMENTIERES.		
1. August 1915.	Work carried on in trenches, enemy inactive	Nil.
2. Aug 1915.	81st Inf. Bde relieved by 80th Inf/Bde at 8-30 p.m. The 81st Inf. Bde goes into Divisional Reserve at ERQUINGHEIM.	Nil
	Billets as under:—	
	1. R. Scots. FORT ROMPU	Operation Order No 53 Attached.
	2 GLOUCESTERS H.1.6.2.7.	Appendix I
	2 CAMERON H'RS. H.3.6.6.1. ⎫ Sheet 36.	
	1. A. & S. H'RS JESUS FARM. ⎬	
	9. R. SCOTS. PETIT MOULIN. ⎭	
	Divisional Reserve. Period of Rest.	
ERQUINGHEIM.		
3. Aug 1915.	—— do ——	Nil
4. Aug 1915.	—— do ——	Nil
5. Aug 1915.	—— do ——	Nil
6. Aug 1915.	—— do ——	Nil

Army Form C. 2118.

WAR DIARY
or
INTELLIGENCE SUMMARY
(Erase heading not required.)

Instructions regarding War Diaries and Intelligence Summaries are contained in F. S. Regs., Part II. and the Staff Manual respectively. Title pages will be prepared in manuscript.

Hour, Date, Place	Summary of Events and Information	Remarks and references to Appendices
ERQUINGHEIM		
7. Aug 1915.	Divisional Reserve, Period of Rest.	Rwo.
8. Aug 1915.	do	Rwo
9. Aug 1915.	Work Commenced on BOIS GRENIER defences by 1st & S.H. 11th & 2/ Gloucestershires, & 9th Royal Scots	Rwo
10. Aug 1915.	Work Commenced on RA VESEE defences by 1st R. Scots, & 2/ Camerons. Work commenced on the ROLANDERIE Farm posts, and continued at BOIS GRENIER. Visit of Sir DOUGLAS HAIG to I.Q. of Bn.	Rwo
11. Aug 1915.	Work on the 3 posts continued	Rwo
12. Aug 1915.	do	Rwo.
13. Aug 1915.	do	
14. Aug 1915.	do	Rwo.
15. Aug 1915.	Work on BOIS GRENIER POST 1 KA VESEE stopped 3am Relieved 52nd Inf. Bde in the trenches from I.31.d. 1.9. to I.20.d.8.6. at 7.45 p.m.	Rwo. See appendix II.
16. Aug 1915.	Relief completed 10.50 pm. Bn. I.Q. RUE MARLE.	Rwo.

Army Form C. 2118.

WAR DIARY
or
INTELLIGENCE SUMMARY
(Erase heading not required.)

Instructions regarding War Diaries and Intelligence Summaries are contained in F. S. Regs., Part II. and the Staff Manual respectively. Title pages will be prepared in manuscript.

Hour, Date, Place	Summary of Events and Information	Remarks and references to Appendices
RUE MARLE. ARMENTIERES. 17 Aug 1915.	Work commenced on Trenches & Communication avenues. Enemy very quiet	Two
18. Aug 1915.	Work continued. Line extended on right by taking over sector as far as I.31.c.3.7. from 2nd Inf. Bde. Relay completed 10.45 p.m. from front line to trenches	See Appendix III. Two
19. Aug 1915.	Enemy very quiet, work continued	Two
20 Aug 1915.	Continued. Enemy quiet, work continued	Two
21 Aug 1915.	do	Two
22 Aug 1915.	do — 1/4th A.C.K.I. attached this	Two
23 Aug 1915.	Enemy quiet, working parties available. See also Relieved 7.49 & 7.50 Communication 1st Royal Scots relieved by CAMERONS in Sect D. at 9 pm	Two

Army Form C. 2118.

WAR DIARY
or
INTELLIGENCE SUMMARY

(Erase heading not required.)

Instructions regarding War Diaries and Intelligence Summaries are contained in F. S. Regs., Part II. and the Staff Manual respectively. Title pages will be prepared in manuscript.

Hour, Date, Place	Summary of Events and Information	Remarks and references to Appendices
RUE MARLE, ARMENTIERES. 24 August 1915.	Enemy quiet, work continue	two.
25 Aug 1915.	do	two
26 Aug 1915.	do	two.
27 Aug 1915	do	two.

WAR DIARY
or
INTELLIGENCE SUMMARY

Army Form C. 2118.

Hour, Date, Place	Summary of Events and Information	Remarks and references to Appendices
RUE MARLE ARMENTIERES 28th August	7th D.C.L.I. left the Brigade having completed their six days attachment.	RG
29th August	Situation unchanged.	RG
30th August	Camerons relieved the Argylls in Sector B with 1 Coy in Bn Reserve. 1 Coy Gloucesters from Bn Reserve relieved 1 Coy Argylls in the BOIS GRENIER LINE. Argylls complete Bn went into billets in RUE DELETTREE forming Bde Reserve with 1 Coy Camerons in RUE DU BIEZ	RG
31st August	2 Coys 9th R.Scots relieved 2 Coys 9th R.Scots in Sector "C"	RG

J.W. Lister Lieut.
3rd Gunner
County 8th July Bde

8/9/15

Secret   Copy No. 1

81st Infantry Brigade Operation Order No. 53.

Reference Sheet 36.   31st July, 1915

1. Information.	1. The 80th I.Bde. will relieve the 81st I.B. on night 2/3rd August.
2. Distribution.	2. **Right Sector.**
	1st K.S.L.I. & 1 Coy. 4th R.B. will relieve 2/Gloster Regt. and the Coy. 1st A. & S.Hrs. supporting them.
	Centre Sector.
	2 Coys. P.P.C.L.I. will relieve 2 Coys. 9th R.Scots.
	Left Sector.
	The 3rd K.R.R.C. will relieve the H.Q. and the 3 Coys. 1st R.Scots in the Front line.
	One Coy. 4th K.R.R.C. will relieve the Coy. of the 1st R.Scots in the SS, and BOIS GRENIER LINE.
3. Times & Sequence of Relief.	3. Leading Companies of relieving troops of each sector will arrive at the undermentioned places, where guides will meet them, as under:-
	(a) For R. Sector. At Road Angle 300 yds. S. of DESPLANQUE FARM at 8.30 pm.
	(b) For C. Sector. H.Q. 81st I.B. at 9.30 pm
	(c) For L. Sector. H.Q. 81st I.B. at 8.0 pm.
	In all cases the number of guides and the intervals between Companies arriving will be arranged direct between the representatives of Units; except that the troops relieving the Left Sector must be clear of H.Q.81st I.B. by 9.25 pm.
4. Avenues of relief and withdrawal.	4. All troops both relieving and withdrawing must move by the allotted route.
	(a) To and from R. Sector. Via DESPLANQUE FARM--BOIS GRENIER ROAD--LA VESEE--GRISPOT--RUE DE BIEZ.
	(b) To and from Centre & Left Sectors. Via CHAPELLE D'ARMENTIERES ----SECHE RUE.
5. Visit of respresentatives	5. Representatives of relieving units will arrive at Bn. H.Q. in the trenches at about 10 a.m. tomorrow.
6. Billets.	6. The u/m billets are allotted.

UNIT	PLACE	UNIT EVACUATING.
1st R.Scots	Huts, FORT ROMPU	3rd K.R.R.C.
9th R.Scots	PETIT MOULIN H3a.	P.P.C.L.I.
2nd Glosters	H.1.b.2.7.	1st K.S.L.I.
2nd Camerons	H.3.b.6.1.	4th K.R.R.C.
1st A.&S.Hrs.	JESUS FM.B.26.d.	4th R.B.

Troops of the 81st I.B. in billets will vacate their billets at 3 p.m.
Order have been issued as regards advanced billeting parties
Troops from trenches will move direct to billets

2.

7. Trench Stores.	7. All Trench Arms & Equipment and trench stores will be handed over, Log Books and Inventory Boards will be made up to date and handed over. Copies of the lists of stores, arms, etc. as shewn by the Battalion Log Book will be forwarded to this office by 12 noon 2nd. The O.C. 1st Royal Scots and O.C. Support Coy. in BOIS GRENIER line near DESPLANQUE Farm will report the number of rounds there are in BDE reserve dumps at COWGATE AVENUE, and near DESPLANQUE respectively at the same hour.
8. Reports.	8. Bde. H.Q. will remain in its present position till the relief is complete, when it will remove to a house 100 yards S. of ERQUINGHEIM CHURCH. O.C. Units will report at latter place as soon as their unit is complete in its new billets.

                              [signature]   Captain,

Brigade Major, 81st Infantry Brigade.

Issued At

```
Copy No. 1  ..................... to WAR DIARY.
    "    2  ..................... to File
    "    3  by orderly .........to O.C. 1st R.Scots
    "    4     "    "  ..........to O.C. 9th R.Scots.
    "    5     "    "  ..........to O.C. 2nd Glosters.
    "    6     "    "  ..........to O.C. 2nd Camerons.
    "    7     "    "  ..........to O.C. 1st A.&S. hrs.
    "    8     "    "  ..........to G.O.C. 80th Infy. Bde.
```

War Diary II

S E C R E T.   Copy No. 1.

81st Infantry Brigade Operation Order No 55.

Ref; Sheet 36. I/40000.   14th Aug 1915.

1. Information. 1. The 81st Inf;Bde; will relieve the 82nd Inf;Bde in the trenches on Monday Next 16th inst as under:-

Ist A.&.S.H. will relieve Ist Leins in T50---T53.R.Sector.
9th R.Scots, ,, ,, 5th Cambs in T54.Centre Sector.
2nd Camerons ,, ,, (Ist R.Irish Regt in T55---T58) L.Sector
                              (5th Cambs. in T55.

I Coy 2nd Glouc,Regt will relieve I Coy Ist D.C.L.I. at BOIS GRENIER.

2. Times. 2. Reliefs will commence as under:-

Head of 2nd Camerons to be at entrance of PARK ROW AV: 8-15 p.m.

Head of 9th R.Scots to be at entrance of SHAFTESBURY AV: 8-15 p.m.

Head of Ist A.&.S.H. to be at entrance of SHAFTESBURY AV: 8-45 p.m.

The Coy of the 2nd Glouc;Regt will relieve the Coy of the Ist D.C.L.I. at an hour to be arranged by the O.C.Ist A.&.S.H. as convenient to him.

Coys should follow one another at such intervals as Bn; Commanders consideradvisable

3. Routes 3. The Ist A.&.S.H. will use RUE DU BIEZ---RUE DES CHARLES------BOIS GRENIER ROAD.OR the road from RUE DES CHARLES in H.24.c. meeting GRISPOT---BOIS GRENIER ROAD in H.24.d. 4.5. and thence by made track to SHAFTESBURY AVENUE in I.19.c.

The 9th R.Scots will also use the above route. they should arrange to cross the ERQUINGHEIM BRIDGE in front of the 2nd Camerons.

The 2nd Camerons will arrange to use the RUE DES ACQUETS---GRISPOT---LA VESEE ROAD.

4. Guides. 4. All arrangements for guides will be made direct by the O.C. Battalions.

5. Billets. 5. The Ist R.Scots will take over the billets of the Ist R. Irish Fus; in RUE DE BIEZ, leaving their present billet at 2-30 p.m. & using the RUE DE LA LYS---RUE DU BIEZ.

The 9th R Scots (less 2 Coys), will take over the billets of 5th Cambs in RUE DELPIERRE, leaving their present billet at 3-15 p.m. & using route ERQUINGHEIM BR:---RUE DU MOULIN.

The 2nd Glouc Regt (less I Coy), will take over the billets of the 2nd D.C.L.I. in RUE DELETTRE, leaving their present billets at 3-15 p.m.& using the route ERQUINGHEIM BR:

2.

                                                                                                  ERQUINGHEIM

5. Billets, contd; 5. BR --- Road running S through H.10.b,& d.to H.16.b.2.9.
                         --- Road running S.E. through H 16.b.& d. and H.17.c.

6. Brigade H.Q.   6. All reports should be sent to Bde H.Q. at ERQUINGHEIM
                      up to 9 p.m. after which to the RUE MARLE.

7. Trench stores. 7. All trench stores and reserve S.A.A. will be taken over
                      except Very Pistols and Rifles with telescopic sights.

8. Reports.   8. All units will report as soon as they have taken o
                      over successfully.

                                                                                                                                        [signature]   Captain.
                                                                      Bde Major 81st Infantry Brigade.

Issued at 2.3. p.m.   Copy No.   By.   To.

Copy No.	By.	To.
1.		War Diary.
2.		File.
3.	cyclist ord;	27th Division.
4.	,, ,,	82nd Brigade.
5.	,, ,,	O.C.1st R.Scots.
6.	,, ,,	,, 9th ,,
7.	,, ,,	,, 2nd Glouc;Regt.
8.	,, ,,	,, 2nd Camerons,
9.	,, ,,	,, 1st A.& S.H.

①

DISTRIBUTION OF UNITS.

TRENCHES.

Right Sector, (T.50 - T.53). 1st A.&.S.H. (or 2nd Glouc: R.)
  1 Coy 2nd Glouc Regt, (or 1st A.&.S.H.) in support
  in the BOIS GRENIER POST.

Centre sector, (T.54.). 2 Coys 9th Royal Scots.

Left Sector. (T55 - T.58.). 2nd Camerons. (or 1st R.Scots.).

BRIGADE RESERVE.

2nd Glouc Regt, (or 1st A.&.S.H.), Less 1 coy, RUE DELETTRE.

2 Coys 9th Royal Scots.   RUE DELPIERRE.

1st Royal Scots, (or 2nd Camerons).   RUE DU BIEZ.

RELIEFS.

Reliefs will take place as under:-

Right Sector. 16th, 23rd, 30th Aug;. 6ht & 13th September.

Centre Sector. As arranged by O.C.9th R.Scots, but not to
  clash with other reliefs.

Left Sector. 16th, 22nd, 28th August, 5th, & 13th September.

Cancelled Kus
18/8/15

15-8-15.   [signature] Captain.
                                            Bde Maj. 81st Inf Bde.

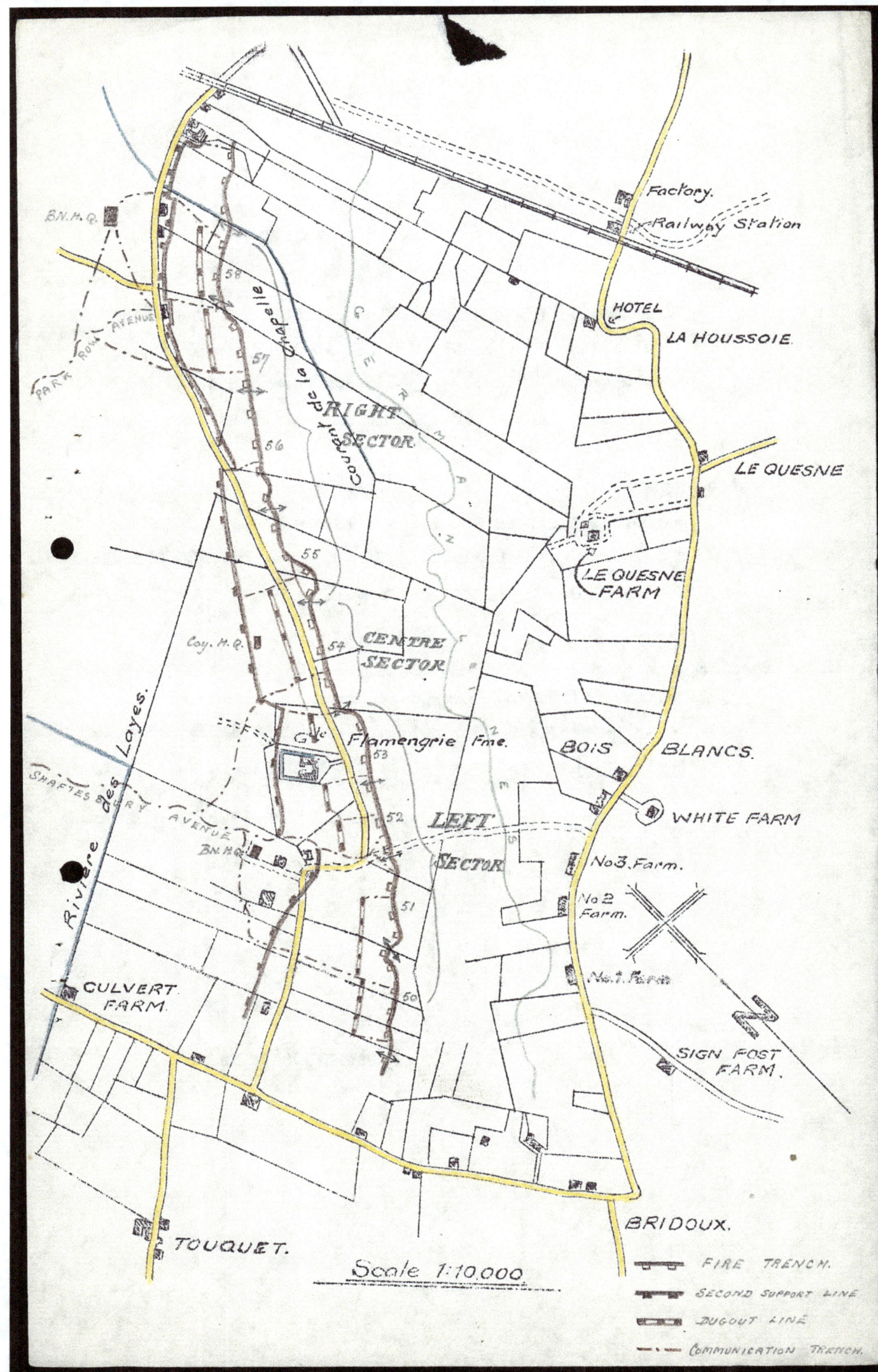

81st Infantry Brigade.

- DISTRIBUTION OF UNITS. -

Sectors will comprise the following trenches.-

Sector A. T.48, T.49, T.50.　　　3 Coys.
,, B. T.51, T.52, T.53.　　　3 Coys.
,, C. T.54.　　　2 Coys.
,, D. T.55, T.56, T.57, T.58. 4 Coys.

Reliefs will take place on the following dates.-

Sector A. A. & S. Hrs. relieve GLOSTERS on 6th Sept.
,, B. CAMERONS ,, A. & S.H. on 30th August.
,, C. Under arrangements of O.C. 9th R.Scots.
,, D. 1st R.SCOTS relieve CAMERONS on 23rd August.

BOIS GRENIER POST will be held as under. -

18th - 23rd August.　GLOUCESTERS　　(1 Coy).
24th - 30th ,,　　A.& S. HRS.　　(,,).
31st Aug- 6th Sept.　GLOUCESTERS　　(,,).
7th - 13th Sept.　　CAMERONS　　　(,,).

BRIGADE RESERVE will be comprised as under, -

18th - 23rd August.　1st R.SCOTS - 1 Coy. A.& S.H.-2 Coys.9/R.S.
24th - 30th ,,　　2nd CAMERONS - 1 Coy. GLOSTERS- - do. -
31st Aug.- 6th Sept. 1st A. & S.H.- 1 Coy. CAMERONS- - do. -
7th - 13th SEpt.　　2nd GLOSTERS - 1 Coy. A.& S. Hrs- do. -

SECTOR.	16th - 23rd August.	24th - 30th August.	31st August - 6th Sept.	7th - 13th Sept.
A.	GLOUCESTERS (15)	GLOUCESTERS (21)	GLOUCESTERS (21).	ARGYLLS (21).
B.	ARGYLLS (23)	ARGYLLS (21)	CAMERONS (21)	CAMERONS (21).
C.	9th R.SCOTS (14)	9th R.SCOTS (14)	9th R.SCOTS (14)	9th R.SCOTS (14).
D.	CAMERONS (28).	1st R.SCOTS (28).	1st R.SCOTS (28)	1st R.SCOTS (28).
BOIS GRENIER POST	GLOUCESTERS (7)	ARGYLLS (7)	GLOUCESTERS (7)	CAMERONS (7).

The figures in brackets denote the number of nights of companies in the trenches.

e.g. A complete Bn. in trenches for one week equals 4 Coys. x 7 days. (28).

27th Division

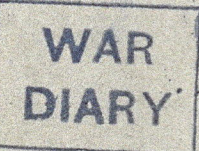

B. H. Q. 81st INFANTRY BRIGADE.

October

1 9 1 5

Attached:
Appendices I, II, III and IV

WAR DIARY

INTELLIGENCE SUMMARY

(Erase heading not required.)

Hour, Date, Place	Summary of Events and Information	Remarks and references to Appendices
PROYART.		Distribution of units
1. Oct. 1915.	In Divisional Reserve.	Bde H.Q. "PROYART" 1. R. Scots MORCOURT 2. GLOUC, RGT, MORCOURT 2. Camerons PROYART 1. A.S.H. ABANCOURT 9. R. Scots ABANCOURT Tens
2. Oct. 1915.	— do —	
3. Oct. 1915.	— do —	
4. Oct. 1915.	Relieved the 82nd Inf Bde on the DOMPIERRE – FAY SECTOR of trenches. Relief complete by 1 p.m.	Distribution of units Bde H.Q. CHUIGNOLLES 2/Gloucesters. R. Secteur Tranches 1. R. Scots L. Secteur " 9. R. Scots Local Reserve at FONTAINE LES CAPPY and CHUIGNES BDE RESERVE 2 Camerons PROYART 1. A.S.H. CHUIGNOLLES See Appendix I two

INTELLIGENCE SUMMARY

Instructions regarding War Diaries and Intelligence Summaries are contained in F.S. Regs, Part II. and the Staff Manual respectively. Title pages will be prepared in manuscript.

(Erase heading not required.)

Hour, Date, Place	Summary of Events and Information	Remarks and references to Appendices
CHUIGNOLLES.		
5. Oct. 1915.	Enemy quiet, two small mines exploded	Nil.
6. Oct. 1915.	Enemy most active. About 200 shells fired into the trenches, a mine was exploded near German lines in front of G1 at about 9.5 p.m. No damage done, 8th R. Scots Fus. trenches attacked. See.	Nil.
7. Oct. 1915.	Enemy active. Mine exploded F2 about 4 p.m. No damage done	Nil.
8. Oct. 1915.	2 Camerons relieved 1 R. Scots & 1 A & S.H. 2/Gloucester at 10 a.m. Enemy quiet.	Nil.
9. Oct. 1915.	Enemy quiet.	Nil.
10. Oct. 1915.	Attached enemy 8th R. Scots trenches. Craters. Enemy quiet.	Nil.

INTELLIGENCE SUMMARY

Instructions regarding War Diaries and Intelligence Summaries are contained in F. S. Regs., Part II. and the Staff Manual respectively. Title pages will be prepared in manuscript.

(Erase heading not required.)

Hour, Date, Place	Summary of Events and Information	Remarks and references to Appendices
CRUIGNOLES 11 Oct 1915.	8th South Wales Borderers arrive for attachment to Bde. Enemy quiet	Enc.
12 Oct 1915.	1. R. Scots relieve 2/(Camerons in 11th Left Secto 2. Glouc. Regt relieve 1. A & S. H. in Right Sector. Enemy quiet except for trench mortars.	Enc.
13. Oct 1915.	At Brig HQ near F16 c 9.9.1. Enemy quiet. 1. Cor 9th R. Scots moved from CHUIGNES to REDUIT 99 to support left 2. Camerons transferred (temporarily) to 67th Inf Bde.	Enc. Enc.
14. Oct 1915	Enemy quiet	Enc.
15. Oct 1915.	Enemy quiet	Enc.
16. Oct 1915	1. A. & S. H. relieved 2/Glouc Regt in Right and 8. S.W.B. relieved 1. R Scots in Left	Enc.

INTELLIGENCE SUMMARY

or

(Erase heading not required.)

Instructions regarding War Diaries and Intelligence Summaries are contained in F. S. Regs, Part II. and the Staff Manual respectively. Title pages will be prepared in manuscript.

Hour, Date, Place	Summary of Events and Information	Remarks and references to Appendices
CHUIGNOLLES		
17 Oct 1915	Enemy quiet	See
18 Oct 1915	Enemy rather more active	See
19 Oct 1915	"	See
20 Oct 1915	2/Yorks Regt relieved 1. A&S.H. in Right Sector & 1st R. Scots relieved 2/S.W.B. in Left Sector. Attachment of 8. S.W.B. Classes 2nd Carriers return to 81st Bde and remains billeted at Cappy	See
21 Oct 1915	Enemy quiet	See
22 Oct 1915	Enemy quiet	See
23 Oct 1915	Enemy quiet	See

INTELLIGENCE SUMMARY

Instructions regarding War Diaries and Intelligence Summaries are contained in F. S. Regs., Part II. and the Staff Manual respectively. Title pages will be prepared in manuscript.

(Erase heading not required.)

Hour, Date, Place	Summary of Events and Information	Remarks and references to Appendices
CHUIGNOLLES 24 Oct 1915.	81st Inf. Bde relieved by 5e Regiment at Alfautieres, relief completed at 5.30 p.m. and Brigade went to MORCOURT & ABANCOURT. (see Appendix II).	Distribution of units:— 1.R.Scots — } MORCOURT 2/5 Lone Regt — } 1. A.& S.H. — } ABAN- 2 Camerons — } COURT 9. R.Scots — }
ABANCOURT. 25 Oct 1915.	81. Inf. Bde H.Q. moved to ABANCOURT at 9 a.m.	Euro.
26 Oct 1915.	Bde marched from MORCOURT & ABANCOURT (see appendix III). At 7 a.m. reached BOVES at 1.30 p.m.	Euro.
BOVES 27 Oct 1915.	81. I. B. Group marched to new Brigade area round SEUX arriving about 5 p.m.	Distribution of units:— 81. I. B. H.Q. SEUX 1. R. Scots SAISSEVAL 9. R. Scots BOURGAINVILLE 2. Glouc. R. SEUX 2. Camerons BOURGAINVILLE 1. A.& S.H. — do —

INTELLIGENCE SUMMARY

(Erase heading not required.)

Instructions regarding War Diaries and Intelligence Summaries are contained in F.S. Regs., Part II. and the Staff Manual respectively. Title pages will be prepared in manuscript.

Hour, Date, Place	Summary of Events and Information	Remarks and references to Appendices
FEUX.		Distribution of units
27 Oct. 1915.	Continued	20 Bde. R.F.A. BRIQUEMESNIL.
		1. Wessex R.E. SAISSEMONT.
		81. Fd. Amb. MONTENOY
		97 Coy. A.S.C. FROIXCOURT
28 Oct 1915.	2 sections moved to ST AUBIN. 81st Fd Ambulance to BOURGAINVILLE.	ditto.
29 Oct 1915.	At rest.) Capt. Reeve	ditto
30 Oct 1915.	Arrest.)	ditto
31 Oct 1915.	Arrest.	ditto

2/11/15:

J.A. Wilson
B. General
Comdg. 87th Inf. Bde.

Tracing of 81st Inf Bde
Trenches.
4. Oct. 1915

Fire trenches.
Communication trenches.

Tracing of 81st Inf Bde
Trenches
4 Oct 1915

Fire trenches Red
Communication trenches Green

SECRET   APPENDIX I.   Copy No....2....

81st Infantry Brigade Operation Order No. 59.

Preliminary Order.

Reference AMIENS SHEET.
1/10,000 Trench Maps.   30th September, 1915.

1. The 81st Infantry Brigade will relieve the 82nd Infy. Bde. on 4th October. The relief will probably take place by daylight.

2. Units will be distributed as under. –

Brigade Head Quarters at CHUIGNOLLES.
1st Royal Scots in trenches Left Sector relieving R. Irish Regt
2nd Gloucesters   "   "   Right   "   "   R. Irish Fusrs
2nd Camerons   in billets at PROYART (probably as now held)
1st A & S.Hrs. "   "   at CHUIGNOLLES relieving Leinster Regt.
9th Royal Scots in local reserve at CHATEAU FONTAINE LE CAPPY 2 Coy
                2 Coys. at CHUIGNES in relief of 5th Cambs. Regt.

3. The G.O.C. wishes a thorough preliminary reconnaissance of the trenches made by as many officers as possible of those units going into the trenches, and officers from all units to scout the routes to the communication trenches.

4. Detailed orders will be issued later as regards times, guides, etc.

                                    Captain,
            Brigade Major, 81st Infantry Brigade.

Issued at ....

Copy No. 1 to File.
  "   2 to War Diary.
  "   3 to 27th Divn. by Motor Cyclist.
  "   4 to 82nd Infy. Bde.   "   "
  "   5 to 1st Royal Scots by Cyclist Orderley
  "   6 to 2nd Camerons   "   "   "
  "   7 to 2nd Gloucesters "   "   "
  "   8 to 1st Argylls   "   "   "
  "   9 to 9th Royal Scots "   "   "

SECRET   Copy No......2....

81st Infantry Brigade Operation Order No. 59.

Reference AMIENS SHEET.
1/10,000 Trench Maps.   2nd October, 1915.

1. The relief as detailed in preliminary order of 30th will be carried out as under.

   (a) 2nd Gloucester Regt. will leave MORCOURT 6 a.m. via MERICOURT – road junction ½ mile S. of FROISSY – CHUIGNES to FONTAINE LE CAPPY.
   Guides of R. Irish Fusrs. will be at Bn. Hd.Qrs. in FONTAINE LE CAPPY at 10 a.m.
   This will allow about 1 hours halt for a meal at FONTAINE LE CAPPY.

   (b) 1st Royal Scots will leave MORCOURT at 6.30 a.m. via MERICOURT and FROISSY and thence by canal route to CAPPY.
   Guides of R. Irish Regt. will be at bridge in CAPPY at 10a.m.
   This will allow about 1 hours halt for a meal in CAPPY.

(NOTE – Cookers etc. have to go via BRAY. They should therefore if possible move off about 5.55 a.m. before 2nd Gloucester Regt.)

   (c) 9th Royal Scots will march so as to arrive at FONTAINE LE CAPPY at 12 noon leaving 2 companies and their transport at CHUIGNES.
   Moving via MERICOURT and road junction ½ mile S. of FROISSY.

   (d) The 1st A. & S. Hrs. will march so as to arrive at CHUIGNOLLES at 11.30 a.m. following the 9th Royal Scots by the same route.

   (e) The 2nd Cameron Highlanders will remain in their present billets. They will be under Command of G.O.C. 82nd Infy. Brigade from 8 a.m. until relief is complete for use in emergency.

2. Transport.
   That of units in trenches will move to dugout stables ½ mile S.E. of FROISSY. That of other units will be with units.

3. Machine Guns should accompany the leading company of units going into trenches. As they have a very long carry extra men s should be told off to help carry them up.

4. Precautions against coming into view.
   (a) Troops are forbidden to pass over the high ground ½ mile West of CHUIGNOLLES in daylight.
   (b) Watch must be kept for aircraft.
   (c) Units should march in parties of not more than 1 company after FROISSY road junction.
   (d) Care should be taken as to where the men of Gloucester Regt. have their meal.

5. Brigade Head Quarters will move to CHUIGNOLLES at 10.30 a.m

                                          Captain,
2.10.15   Brigade Major, 81st Infantry Brigade.

Copy No. 1 to File Copy No. 2 to War Diary Copy No.3.to Div.by DR
   ,,   4 to 82 I.B. ,,   5 to 1st R.S.   ,,   6 to 2nd Cams.
   ,,   7 to 2nd Glosters No. 8 to 1st Argylls No.9 to 9th R.S.

Copy No. 1 to File
"   2 to War Diary.
"   3 to 27th Divn. by Motor Cyclist.
"   4 to 82nd Inf. Bde.
"   5 to 1st Royal Scots by cyclist orderley.
"   6 to 2nd Camerons   ,,   ,,   ,,
"   7 to 2nd Gloucesters ,,   ,,   ,,
"   8 to 1st Argylls   ,,   ,,   ,,
"   9 to 9th Royal Scots ,,   ,,   ,,

SECRET.   APPENDIX 2   Copy No. 2

81st Infantry Brigade Operation Order No. 60.

PRELIMINARY ORDER.

21st October, 1915.

1. The 81st Infantry Brigade will be relieved by the French on night 24th/25th.

2. The destination of the Brigade is unknown but will entail two days march. MONTDIDDIER SHEETS should be taken into use.

3. Trench Stores will be handed over to the French except VERMOREL SPRAYERS, TOOLS, SNIPERSCOPES, WEST & REISEN BOMB THROWERS and Rifle Grenade Stands.
   The above stores with the exception of the VERMOREL SPRAYERS WEST & REISEN BOMB THROWERS and 10 picks and 40 shovels each for 1st Bn. Royal Scots and 2nd Bn. Gloucester Regt. will be collected and stacked as under. -
   From Right Sector and CHATEAU REDOUBT at Gloucester Regt. Hd. Qrs
   "   Left   "   REDOUBT 99   at 1st Royal Scots Hd.Qrs.
   They must be sent to above places in sufficient time to be returned by the empty ration limbers when they return tomorrow; The tools being sent to R.E.Park at FROISSY and remainder of stores to Bde. Hd.Qrs. Special instructions have been issued as regards bomb-throwers.
   The Vermorel Sprayers and the 50 tools which remain in the trenches will be evacuated on the 24th, further instructions will be sent. Any surplus tools of units in Brigade Reserve should also be returned to R.E.Park at FROISSY.

4. All S.A.A. except 120 rounds per man, 20 boxes per Bn. as Reserve, and 5,500 rounds per machine gun, will be collected and stacked as under by 8am, 23rd.
   From Right Sector and CHATEAU REDOUBT at Gloucester Regt.Hd.Qrs.
   "   Left   "   99   "   at 1st R.Scots Hd.Qrs.
   The O.C.1st Royal Scots and O.C. 2nd Gloucester Regt. will report by 9am, 23rd the number of boxes at their dumps to this office, when instructions will be issued as regards evacuating them.
   Note. This S.A.A. must be in full boxes, it will not be withdrawn from dumps until night of 23/24th and can be used in emergency.

5. Telephone wires will be left.

6. All grenades, except those in limbers, will be handed over.

                                          Captain,
Issued at 4.30 pm.   Brigade Major, 81st Infantry Brigade.

Copy No.1 to File.   Copy No. 6 to 1st Royal Scots.
  "   2 to War Diary.   "   7 to 9th Royal Scots.
  "   3 to 27th Divn.   "   8 to 2nd Gloucesters.
  "   4 to 81st Fd. Ambce.   "   9 to 2nd Cameron Hrs.
  "   5 to 97 Coy. A.S.C.   "   10 to 1st A. & S. Hrs.

S E C R E T.   Copy No. 2

81st Infantry Brigade Operation Order No. 60.

24/10/15

1. The relief will be carried out as per table attached.

2. On relief units will be billetted as under:-

   1st R.Scots) MORCOURT, same billets as previously
   2nd Glosters) occupied.

   9th R.Scots   ) WARFUSEE-ABANCOURT, same billetting area as
   1st A. & S. Hrs) was held before Bde. Hd.Qrs. and 2nd Cameron
   2nd Cameron Hrs) Highrs. moved to PROYART.

   1st Bn. A. & S. Hrs. will march from MERICOURT at 12 noon.
   2nd Cameron Highrs.   "   "   CAPPY   at 12 noon.

3. **Trench Stores.**
   (a) Vermorel sprayers will be carried empty on the limbered waggons of units.
   (b) Remaining tools and Braziers will be stacked where the railway line cuts fork road ½ mile S. of FROISSY at 12 noon, a small party being sent to load them on lorries.
   (c) Other trench stores will be handed over to the incoming units and the attached lists filled in, one copy being handed over to the relieving unit, the duplicate being receipted and sent to this office.
   (d)

4. **Maps.** All trench maps (i.e. 1/500, 1/10000 & 1/20,000) will be handed over.
   Those of Brigade Reserve units should be sent to this office.

5. **Blankets.** The instructions as regards blankets, in the memo. re S.A.A. are cancelled.
   Blankets will be sent to the spot where the railway cuts fork road ½ mile South of FROISSY, tied in bundles ready to load on lorries to take them to their new billets as under:-

   2nd Bn. Cameron Hrs.) at 8.15 a.m.
   9th Royal Scots   )   "
   ~~2nd Gloucester Regt.) at 10.30 a.m.~~
   ~~1st Bn. Royal Scots.)   "~~

   A loading party of one senior N.C.O. and 10 men should be sent who will accompany them. The N.C.O. must know where the blankets should be taken to in the new billets.
   The 1st Bn. A. & S. Hrs. must arrange to send their blankets by their own waggons wither in advance of or after the battalion.
   Separate instructions have been issued to 1st Royal Scots & 2nd Glosters

6. **Reports.** Units will report as soon as relief is complete.

7. Brigade Head Quarters will remain at CHUIGNOLLES until 9 am. 25th when it will move to its old place at ABANCOURT.

8. The Brigade will march to the vicinity of BOVES on 26th.

                                              [signature]
                                              Captain,
Issued at 7 pm.   Brigade Major, 81st Infantry Brigade.

Copy No.1 to File   Copy No.5 to 97 Coy. A.S.C.
  "   2 to War Diary   "   6 to 1st R.Scots.
  "   3 to 27th Divn.   "   7 to 9th R.Scots.
  "   4 to 81st Fd. Ambce.   "   8 to 2nd Gloucesters
           Copy No. 9 to 2nd Camerons.
             "   10 to 1st A. & S. Hrs.

TIME TABLE OF RELIEF.

1. Sector to be relieved.	2. Time relieving unit leaves CHUIGNOLLES.	3. Time Bn. Guide should report at Brigade Hd.Qrs.	4. Time and place at which Coy. Guides should meet unit.	5. Remarks.
Right	12 noon	11.55 a.m.	GLOUCESTER REGT. Head Qrs. at 1.30pm.	
Left	1 p.m.	12.55 p.m.	2.15 pm at FONTAINE LES CAPPY (where cookers were).	Unit will go in by the BOYAU DE LA GRANDE CEINTURE. 1st Bn. Royal Scots will withdraw by BOYAU LE GRANDE & CAPPY.
Local Reserve	2 p.m.	1.55 p.m.	3.15 p.m. at FONTAINE LES CAPPY (where cookers were).	

Notes. Battalion Guide (in column 3) should be an officer, if possible speaking French. Company Guides (in column 4) should be officers or Sergeants.

APPENDIX III

SECRET.   Copy No. 2

              81st Infantry Brigade - Operation Order No.61
NS & MONTDIDIER --
SHEETS.   25/10/14

1. The Brigade will march to the vicinity of BOVES tomorrow as under:-

  Starting point.   Most westerly road junction of WARFUSEE ABANCOURT.

  Times   Brigade Headquarters 7 a.m.
           2nd Camerons   7.10 a.m.
           1st Argyll & Sutherland Highlanders 8.5 a.m.
           9th Royal Scots   9 a.m.
           1st Royal Scots   9.45 a.m.
           2nd Gloucesters   10.40 a.m.

Intervals.

        The following intervals will be kept, between each Company five minutes, between each platoon 10 yards.
        An interval of fifteen minutes is allowed for between battalions.

Halts.

        The usual halt of ten minutes before each clock hour will be made. O.C. Units must ensure that no bodies of troops are moving between ten minutes before the hour and the hour. (i.e. no Company could start it's march at 9.50.)

        The strictest march discipline will be enforced.

        Units of the 22nd Division may wish to cross the route, should this be the case they must be given precedence.

Route.

        WARFUSEE - VILLIERS BRETONNEUX - PT 49 - ST. NICOLAS.

        Correct time should be obtained from 81st Infantry Bde. on evening of 25th.

2. A horse ambulance will accompany each of the following Units. It will report at their Headquarters at the hour named.

        1st Argyll & S.H. at 7.45 a.m. for 1st Argyll & S.H. and 2nd Camerons.
        1st Royal Scots at 7.30 a.m. for 1st Royal Scots and 9th Royal Scots.
        2nd Gloucesters at 8.30 a.m. for 2nd Gloucesters and overflow of above, if any..

3. Advanced Billeting Parties will meet the Staff Captain at MAIRIE BOVES at 10 a.m.
   They should consist of one Officer and five Other Ranks, if possible, with bicycles.

   Suitable parties under an Officer should also be sent by 20th Brigade R.F.A. and 2nd Wessex R.E., 81st Field Ambulance and 97th Company A.S.C.
   One Representative of these parties will be sent back to meet his Unit at Cross Road Pt.60, quarter of a mile N.E. of ST. NICHLAS.

4. Orderlies.

        On arrival at BOVES the Units of the 81st Infantry Brigade

(Brigade)

group other than the Infantry will send one cyclist orderly to be attached to the 81st Infantry Brigade Headquarters for duty.

5. Transport.

First Line Transport and Baggage Waggons will accompany Units.
One lorry per Battalion will be at ABANCOURT and MORCOURT DURING THE MORNING OF THE 28TH FOR THE CARRIAGE OF BLANKETS.
One N.C.O. and one man per battalion will travel with the blankets.

6. Brigade Headquarters will close at ABANCOURT at 6.30 a.m. on 26th. and re-open at BOVES at 1 p.m. Units will report number of men who fall out on line of march, on arrival.

7. S.A.A. Units requiring S.A.A. to complete, should send limbers to Brigade Headquarters, ABANCOURT, at 2 p.m. to-day, with a note shewing numbers of boxes required.

Issued at................ .... Captain,
Brigade Major, 81st Infantry Brigade.

Copy No. 1. to file.
" " 2. War Diary.
" " 3. To 27th Divn.
" " 4. 81st Field Ambulance.
" " 5. 20th Bde.R.F.A.
" " 6. 2nd Wessex Coy.R.E.
" " 7. 97th Coy. A.S.C.
" " 8. 1st Royal Scots.
" " 9. 9th Royal Scots.
" " 10. 2nd Gloucesters.
" " 11. 2nd Camerons.
" " 12. 1st Argylls.

FOR INFORMATION ONLY

Table of approximate times when units will reach
and clear certain points.

Unit	Leaves MORCOURT	Starts to clear WARFUSÉE-BEANCOURT (tail)	Clear Western end of WARFUSÉE-BEANCOURT 49. (11½ miles)	Head reaches H.W. (11½ miles)	Head reaches X roads N.E. ST.NICOLAS (12½ m.G)
51st I.B. HdQrs.	—	7 a.m.	7.5 a.m.	9.30 a.m.	10.10 a.m.
2nd Bn Camerons	—	7.10 a.m.	7.40 a.m.	10.10 a.m.	10.40 a.m.
1/6 A. & S.H.	—	8.5 a.m.	8.35 a.m.	11.5 a.m.	11.35 a.m.
9th R.S.	—	9 a.m.	9.30 a.m.	12 noon	12.30 p.m.
1st R. Scots (tail 8.30 a.m)		9.45 a.m.	10.25 a.m.	1.5 p.m.	1.35 p.m.
1st Gordons (tail 9.15 a.m)		10.40 a.m.	11.20 a.m.	1.50 p.m.	2.30 p.m.

The following amendments are made in Operation Order No.61 to-day.

Paragraph 1.
   Delete sub-paragraph "Times" and substitute:-

"Times"
Brigade Headquarters	7 a.m.
2nd Camerons	7.10 a.m.
1st Argyll & Sutherland Highlanders	7.35 a.m.
9th Royal Scots	8.10 a.m.
1st Royal Scots	8.35 a.m.
2nd Gloucesters	9.10 a.m.

Paragraph 1.
   Delete sub-paragraph "Intervals" and substitute:-

"Intervals"

The following intervals will be kept; between each Company two minutes, between each Platoon 10 yards.
An interval of five minutes is allowed for between Battalions.

Paragraph 2.
   Delete "7.45 a.m." and substitute "7.15 a.m."
   Delete "7.30 a.m." and substitute "6.50 a.m."
   Delete "8.30 a.m." and substitute "7.30 a.m."

Para. 6 For "28th" read "26th"

Issued at.....2.40pm.

                                     [signature]   Captain,
                              Brigade Major, 81st Infantry Brigade.

approximate only.
to be the approximate times between which will march
all the arrival points

Unit	Leaves MRCOURT	Arrives MRCOURT (N. edge)	Leaves N.E. of MRCOURT (N. edge)	Arrives ABONCOURT	Leaves ABONCOURT	Arrives N.E. of ABONCOURT (M. edge)	Leaves N.E. of ABONCOURT (M. edge)	Arrives Xroads NE NICOLAS (N½)
HQ & B.Bn	—	7 a.m.		7.5 a.m.		9.30 a.m.		10.10 a.m.
L.Gun	—	7.10 a.m.		7.15 a.m.		9.40 a.m.		10.20 a.m.
1st Bn	—	7.35 a.m.		7.55 a.m.		10.5 a.m.		10.35 a.m.
1K R Ln	—	8.10 a.m.		8.29 a.m.		10.40 a.m.		11.20 a.m.
1K Lan about 7pm		7.15 a.m.		7.30 a.m.		11.5 a.m.		11.35 a.m.
	7.45 a.m.	9.10 a.m.		9.25 a.m.		11.40 a.m.		12.20 p.m.

APPENDIX IV

SECRET. Copy No. 2

81st Infantry Brigade Group Operation Order No. 65.

26th October, 1915.

Units will march tomorrow to their new area as per march table attached.

Intervals for the Infantry units will be as under.-

Between each Company 50 - 100 yards.
" " platoon not more than 10 yards.

2. **Halts.** The usual hourly halt will be made. O.C. Units must ensure that this takes place at the right moment. Brigade time must be obtained.

The cookers must be with the First Line Transport and not sent on ahead. The duration of the halt for dinners is at the discretion of Battalion Commanders. The road must be cleared.

3. **Blankets.** Lorries for blankets will be at Head quarters of Infantry units at 7 a.m.

4. **Advanced billetting parties.** These should be sent forward under regimental arrangements.

5. **Ambulances.** Horse ambulances will report at Head quarters of units as under.-

Hd.Qrs. 1st A.& S. Highrs. for 9th R.Scots, 2nd Camerons, & 1st A.& S. Highrs. at 7.40 am

Hd.Qrs. 1st R.Scots for 1st R.Scots. at 9.15 am
Hd.Qrs. 2nd Gloucester Regt. for 2nd Bn. Gloucester Regt. at 10.25 am

They will remain with those units for night 27th/28th and rejoin 81st Field Ambulance at MONTENOY on 28th. They should have rations with them.

6. Brigade Head quarters will close at BOVES at 9am. and reopen at BEUX at 2pm.

7. **Reports.** Units will report numbers falling out by 10 a.m. 28th.

Captain,

Issued at 6 pm. Brigade Major, 81st Infantry Brigade.

Copy No. 1 to File.
" 2 to War Diary.
" 3 to 27th Division.
" 4 to 81st Fd. Amboe.
" 5 to 20th Bde. R.F.A.
" 6 to 2nd Wessex Coy R.E.
" 7 to 1st R.Scots.
" 8 to 9th R.Scots.
" 9 to 2nd Gloucesters.
" 10 to 2nd Camerons.
" 11 to A.& S. Highrs.
" 12 - 97 Coy A.S.C.

Unit	Starting Point	Time	Route	Destination	
9th Royal Scots	Road Junction of Boves-St Fuscien and Boves-Cagny Roads	7 a.m.	St Fuscien - Dury - Yers - Clairy - Pissy - Fluy	Bourgain-Ville	Halt for dinner should be made. Any place after Pissy
2nd Camerons		7.20 a.m.			
1st A.S.&H.		7.40 a.m.			Released any place after Clairy
81st Field Ambulance	(¼ mile North or E of Boves)	8.10 a.m.	St Fuscien - Dury - Vers - Clairy - Revelles - Fresnoy	Montenoy	Released any place after Bovelles
70th Bde R.F.A.		8.30 a.m.	St Fuscien - Dury - Saleux - Guignemicourt - Bovelles	Briquemes - Nil	
1st Royal Scots		9.15 a.m.	St Fuscien - Dury - Saleux - Guignemicourt - Bovelles	Saisseval	Between Guignemicourt & Bovelles
97th Coy A.S.C.		6 a.m.	St Fuscien - Dury - Saleux - Bovelles	Floxicourt	
2nd Wessex R.E.		10 a.m.	St Fuscien - Dury - Saleux - Guignemicourt - Bovelles	Saissemont	Released between Guignemicourt & Bovelles
H.Q. Snt Inf: Bde.		10.15 a.m.	— Do —	Seux	
2nd Gloucesters		10.25 a.m.	— Do —	Seux	Between Guignemicourt & Bovelles

27th Division

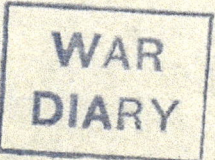

B. H. Q. 81st INFANTRY BRIGADE.

September

1 9 1 5

Attached:
Appendices I, II, III
and IV.

Army Form C. 2118.

WAR DIARY
or
INTELLIGENCE SUMMARY

(Erase heading not required.)

Instructions regarding War Diaries and Intelligence Summaries are contained in F. S. Regs., Part II. and the Staff Manual respectively. Title pages will be prepared in manuscript.

Hour, Date, Place	Summary of Events and Information	Remarks and references to Appendices
RUE MARLE ARMENTIERES		
1st Sept.	Situation unchanged. Night of 1/2nd. T48 and T49 were handed over to 25th Bde. Glouc. went into Bde Reserve with 1 Coy at BOIS GRENIER POST – Camerons took over T50 from Glouc with their Coy from Bde Reserve. Glouc went into Billets at ROLANDERIE FARM.	APPENDIX I. Distribution of Bns. &c R. Sector 2 Camerons C. Sector 9. R. Scots (less 2 Coy) L. Sector 1. R. Scots BOIS GRENIER POST: 1 Coy Glouc.
2nd Sept.		Bde Reserve (in billets) 1. A. & S. Highlanders 2 GLOUCESTERS (Less 1 Coy) 2 Coys 9. R. Scots.
2nd. Sept.	900 from Ration and 45,000 Rounds of S.A.A. were placed in the cellar of the HOSPICE H24d 2.1. (White House.)	
3rd Sept	Situation normal	
4th Sept	Enemy quiet	

Army Form C. 2118.

WAR DIARY
or
INTELLIGENCE SUMMARY

(Erase heading not required.)

Instructions regarding War Diaries and Intelligence Summaries are contained in F. S. Regs., Part II. and the Staff Manual respectively. Title pages will be prepared in manuscript.

Hour, Date, Place	Summary of Events and Information	Remarks and references to Appendices
RUE MARLE. ARMENTIERES. 5th Sept	Situation unchanged.	
6. Sept 1915.	Situation unchanged. 1st A. & S. H. relieved 2 Camerons in the Right Sector.	
7. Sept 1915.	Situation unchanged. Enemies more shelling	
8. Sept 1915.	Situation unchanged, many rifle grenades & shells in the morning. 10 Officers 91st Infantry Brigade arrived for instruction.	
9. Sept 1915	Situation unchanged, 10 Officers 91st Inf. Bde. depart. Two Battalions 69th Brfs.(?) 89th Yorks Bgr.(?) (?) to work Bde. arrive for instruction. 2/Cameron relieve 1st R. Scots in Left Sector.	
10 Sept 1915	Situation unchanged. M. G. Section of Yeomanry arrive for instruction	

Army Form C. 2118.

WAR DIARY
or
INTELLIGENCE SUMMARY

(Erase heading not required.)

Instructions regarding War Diaries and Intelligence Summaries are contained in F.S. Regs, Part II. and the Staff Manual respectively. Title pages will be prepared in manuscript.

Hour, Date, Place	Summary of Events and Information	Remarks and references to Appendices
RUE MARLE. ARMENTIERES		
11. Sept 1915.	Situation unchanged. Expenditure bomb to Durant	Leo
12 Sept 1915.	Situation unchanged. Attachment of 9 yorks Regt & 11 West yorks Cease, & attachment of 8 Yorks Regt & 10 West Riding commences	Leo
13. Sept 1915.	Situation unchanged. Yorkwry M.G. Sectn rejoins unit	Leo Leo
14 Sept 1915.	Situation unchanged	Leo
15. Sept 1915.	At 7pm the 69th Infantry Bde & 2 Coys of 25 Inf Bde were relieved by 61st Inf Bde in the trenches. The Bde marched in relief to Reserve Bde billetting area as under:— 81.I.B. H.Q. STEENWERCK 1. R. Scots. FORT ROMPU 9 R Scots PETIT MOULIN } Sheet 36 2 Gloucesters. L'HALLE BEAU N.W. 2 Queensowns. ERQUINGHEM 1 A FT. R. JESUS FARM	See Appendix II Leo

Army Form C. 2118.

WAR DIARY
or
INTELLIGENCE SUMMARY
(Erase heading not required.)

Instructions regarding War Diaries and Intelligence Summaries are contained in F.S. Regs., Part II. and the Staff Manual respectively. Title pages will be prepared in manuscript.

Hour, Date, Place	Summary of Events and Information	Remarks and references to Appendices
STEENWERCK. 16 Sept 1915.	Remained in billets at STEENWERCK.	Two.
VIEUX BERQUIN. 17 Sept 1915.	At 5:30 am the Bde marched to new billeting area round VIEUX BERQUIN, and at 10 am were billeted as under:— 81. 1.13. R.F.A. — VIEUX BERQUIN 1. R. Scots. — VERTE RUE } HAZEBROUCK 9. R. Scots. — VIEUX BERQUIN } SHEET 5A. 9 Glosters — Caudescure 7 Camerons — LA COURONNE 1. A.S.H. — BLEU	Appendix III.
18 Sept 1915.	Reviewed at VIEUX BERQUIN. Farewell Inspection by Sir William Pulteney Cmdg. 3rd Corps	Two.

WAR DIARY
or
INTELLIGENCE SUMMARY
(Erase heading not required.)

Army Form C. 2118.

Hour, Date, Place	Summary of Events and Information	Remarks and references to Appendices.
VIEUX BERQUIN. 19th Sept 1915.	6pm. Brigade commenced entraining for joining 12th Corps of 3rd Army.	See Appendix IV.
20th Sept 1915	Remainder of Brigade Entrained to join 12th Corps. Bde concentrated at ABANCOURT at 11.30 pm.	
ABANCOURT. 21st Sept 1915.	In Divisional Reserve at ABANCOURT.	
	do 1. R. Scots 9	
22 Sept 1915	21 Glouc Regt moved to MONCEAUX to new billets.	

Army Form C. 2118.

WAR DIARY
or
INTELLIGENCE SUMMARY
(Erase heading not required.)

Hour, Date, Place	Summary of Events and Information	Remarks and references to Appendices
ABANCOURT		
23 Sept 1915.	In Divisional Reserve.	—
24 Sept 1915.	———— do ————	—
25 Sept 1915.	———— do ————	—
26 Sept 1915.	Moved to Bitsch in PROYART.	—
PROYART		
27 Sept 1915.	Divisional Reserve. Bn. H.Q. moved to PROYART at 4 pm	—
28 Sept 1915.	In divisional Reserve	—
29 Sept 1915.	———— do ————	—
30 Sept 1915.	———— do ————	—

JWWh.
Br. General.
Commdg. 81st Infantry Brigade

APPENDIX I

Distribution of Units.

Sectors will comprise the following trenches.

Right Sector.	T.50 - T.53	1 Battalion.
Centre Sector.	T.54.	2 Coys.
Left Sector.	T.55 - T.58	1 Battalion.

BOIS GRENIER POST will be held by

    1 Coy. 2nd Bn. Gloucestershire Regt.

Brigade Reserve will be comprised as under.

    1 Battalion.

    1 Battalion (less 1 Coy)

    2 Companies 9th Rl. Scots.

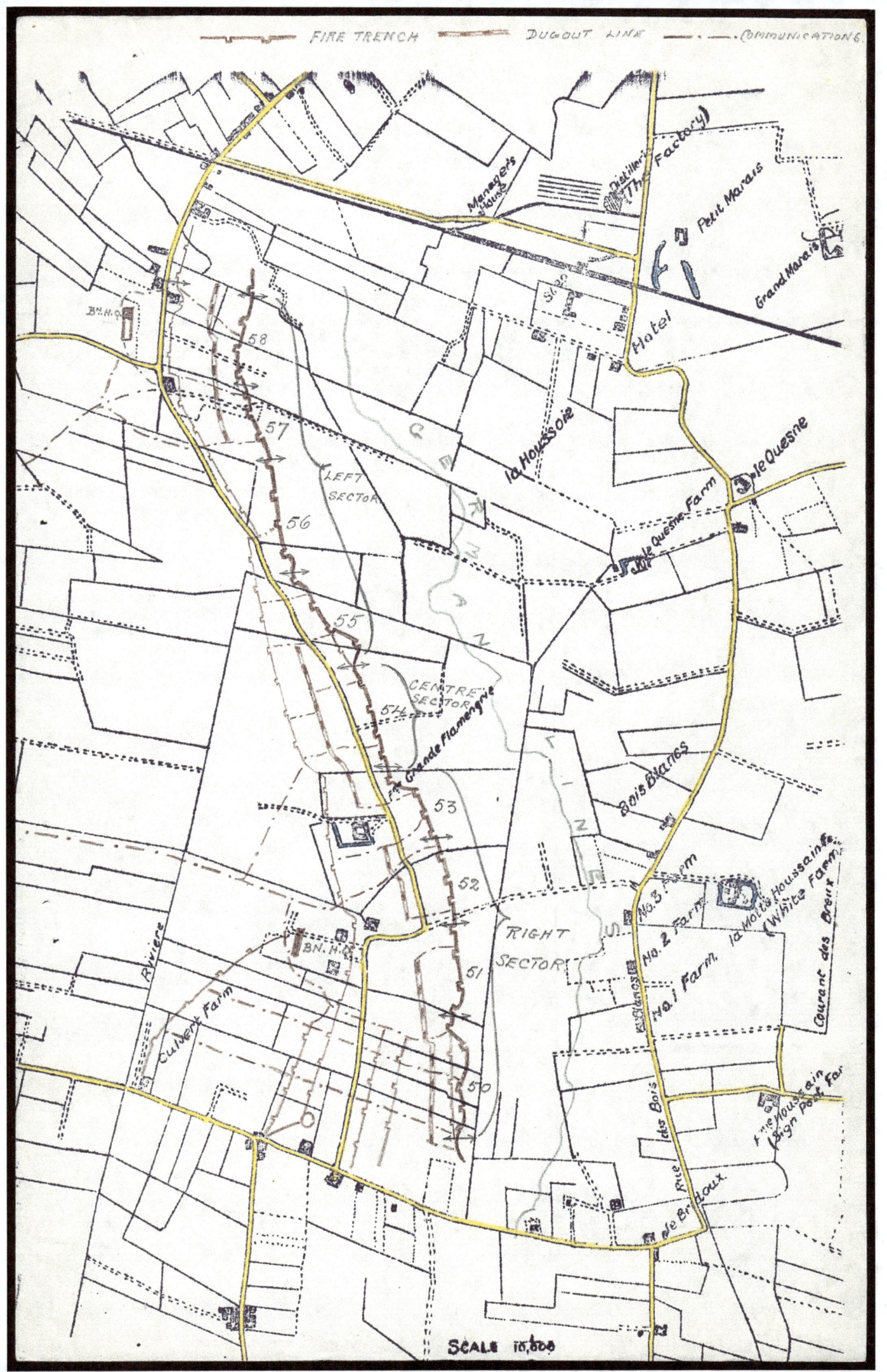

SECRET APPENDIX II   Copy No. 1.

81st Infantry Brigade Operation Order No 56.

PRELIMINARY ORDER.

12th Sept 1915.

1. The 69th Inf Bde will relieve the 81st Inf Bde / on the night 15/16th Sept.

2. The 81st Inf Bde may expect a move by rail on the 17th.

3. All units are warned that no extra Transport for carriage of stores or supplies can be provided, surplus kits which may have accumulated must be disposed of before the move. All surplus Ordnance stores are to be returned to railhead at BAC ST MAUR. Surplus supplies, other than those in defended p posts, will either be under drawn or returned to the S.S.O. at refilling point.

4. Instructions will be issued later as regards the carriage of blankets.

5. All supplies in defensive posts, trench stores, shelters, tents, etc; will be handed over to the incoming Brigade & receipts Taken.

6. Detailed orders will be issued later.

7. All leave is stopped until after the move. Officers and other ranks now on leave need not be recalled. Instructions will be issued later as to the date to which outstanding leave warrants, which are signed but have not yet become due, should be altered.

Issued at 10-30 a.m.

Captain.

Bde Major, 81st Infantry Brigade.

Copy No		to		By
1.		War Diary		....
2.	"	File.	"	....
3.	"	1st R. Scots.	"	cyclist.
4.	"	2/Gloucesters	"	"
5.	"	2/Camerons.	"	"
6.	"	1st A.S.H.	"	"
7.	"	9th R. Scots.	"	"
8.	"	27th Divn.	"	Motor cyclist.
9.	"	69th Bde.	"	" " "

SECRET.   Copy No... 1 ...

81st Infantry Brigade Operation Order No 56.

14th Sept '15.

1. The relief notified in Preliminary order issued 12th Sept will be carried out as per Table attached.

2. Units in billets will march to their new billets near STEEN--WERK as under;-
   2nd Gloucestershires will vacate billets at 4-10 p.m.
   1st Royal Scots.   ,,   ,,   ,,   ,, 4-20 p.m.
   both above Regiments will move via ERQUINGHEM BRIDGE.

   9th R.Scots will vacate their billets at 4 p.m. moving via BAC ST MAUR BRIDGE.

   Units in the trenches will march to their billets on relief by the most direct route.

   The exact location of the new billets will be notified to units by the Staff Captain who will conduct representatives to them tomorrow morning.

3. The Brigade will move to VIEUX BERQUIN (HAZEBRUCK SHEET 5A), on the 17th Sept, time of start about 5-30 a.m. March Table will be issued later.

4. Baggage Waggons will accompany their units.

5. Bde H.Q. will remain at RUE MARLE until relief is complete.

Issued at 12 noon.   [signature] Captain.
                                      Bde Major 81st Infantry Brigade.

    Copy No 1   to War Diary.
     ,,   ,, 2 ,, File.
     ,,   ,, 3. ,, 1st R.Scots.   by Cyclist.
     ,,   ,, 4. ,, 2nd Gloucesters.   ,,
     ,,   ,, 5. ,, 2nd Camerons.   ,,
     ,,   ,, 6. ,, 1st A.S.H.   ,,
     ,,   ,, 7. ,, 9th R.scots.   ,,
     ,,   ,, 8. ,, 27th Division.   ,,
     ,,   ,, 9. ,, 69th I.B.   by Motor Cyclist.
     ,,   ,,10. ,, 25th I.B.   ,,

TABLE OF RELIEFS 15/16 SEPT.

No of trench or Name of Post.	By Whom held.	By whom taken over.	No of guides required.	Time of relieving Coy to be at rendezvous where guides will meet it.	Place where guides will rendezvous
T50.	1st A.S.H.	1 Coy 25th I.B.	1 per Platoon	7-0 p.m.	Entrance of SHAFTES BURY AVENUE.
T51.	,,	,,	,,	7-25 p.m.	---do----
T52	,,	1 Coy 10th W.Riding Regt.	Coys at Present in the trenches, details to be arranged direct		
T53.	,,	---do----			
T54.	9th R.Scots.	1 Coy 10th W.Riding Regt.	1 per Platoon.	7-45 p.m.	Junction of roads H.24.d.5.5.
			Note. The O.C.9th R.Scots will arrange the intervals between Coys, and all details as regards relief.		
T55 to T58.	2nd Camerons.	8th Yorkshire Regt.	All details to be arranged direct between Officers Commanding		
BOIS GRENIER POST.	2nd Gloucesters	1 Coy 25th I.B.	1 per Platoon.	7-30 p.m.	BOIS GRENIER CH;.
BOIS GRENIER LINE FROM MOAT FARM. TO N.	NOT OCCUPIED.	1 Coy 10th W.Riding Regt.	Details arranged by 69th Inf; Bde;.		

SECRET.   Copy No....1....

APPENDIX III

81st Infantry Brigade Operation Order No.57

1. The 81st Infantry Brigade will move to new billetting area near VIEUX BERQUIN to-morrow.

2. Battalions will march independently as per table attached. O.C's. Bns. will ensure that they start at the exact times ordered. Correct time will be obtained from the Signal Section. Starting point in every case is present Battalion H.Q. The usual hourly halt will take place.

3. 1st Line Transport and Baggage Waggons will march with units.

4. Refilling point to-morrow will be LA COURONNE.

5. Vouchers for fuel will be given by the Supply Officer at Refilling point on the morning of the 17th. Units wishing to draw coal will receive it on presenting the vouchers on the same day at the GAS WORKS, BAILLEUL.

6. The 81st Field Ambulance will leave its present billets at 9 a.m. and move to its new billets via LE VERRIER.
A horse ambulance will report at O.C. 1st Royal Scots at 5-25 a.m. at FORT ROMPU to follow that battalion.
A motor ambulance will collect sick unable to walk at billets of other 4 battalions at 7 a.m. Sick will be left at their old billets to be called for.
A horse ambulance for these 4 Battalions will follow the 1st A & S H. It will join the column at STEENWERK CH. at 7 a.m.

7. Brigade H.Q. will be at STEENWERK CHATEAU until 5-30 a.m. at which hour it will move to MARIE, VIEUX - BERQUIN.

Issued at 12-45 p.m.   *[signature]* Captain.
16.9.15.   Brigade Major, 81st Infantry Brigade.

        Copy No. 1. War Diary.
           "   " 2. File.
           "   " 3. 1st Rl. Scots.   by Cyclist.
           "   " 4. 2nd Gloucesters.   "   "
           "   " 5. 2nd Camerons.   "   "
           "   " 6. 1st A. & S. H.   "   "
           "   " 7. 9th Rl. Scots.   "   "
           "   " 8. 81st Fd. Ambulance.   "   "

MARCH TABLE.

UNIT.	HOUR OF START.	DESTINATION.	ROUTE.
9th R.Scots.	5-15 a.m.	between LA COURONNE & VIEUX BERQUIN.	STEENWERK—LE VERRIER.
2nd Camerons.	5-25 a.m.	road S of LA COURONNE—BLEU Road.	STEENWERK—LE VERRIER.
1st R.Scots.	5-30 a.m.	WHITE RUE.	BAC ST MAUR—CROIX DU BAC—LE PT MORTIER—DOULIEU—LA COURONNE.
2nd Gloucesters.	5-30 a.m.	CARDESQUER.	STEENWERK—LE VERRIER.
1st A.& S.H.	6-5 a.m.	BLEU.	STEENWERK—LE VERRIER.

APPENDIX IV
War Diary.

Copy No. 1.

SECRET.

81st Infantry Brigade Operation Order No. 58.

18.9.16

Reference. HAZEBROUCK Sheet 5A. and AMIENS Sheet.

1. The 81st Infantry Brigade will entrain on 19th and 20th as per table attached.

2. Blankets will be picked up by Battalions at HAZEBROUCK STN. Lt. Wakefield, Cyclist Company will point out at the station where they are stored. The same officer will also shew units where they draw straw.

3. Captain Burke, 1st Royal Scots will be in charge of the entrainment.

4. The composition of trains is as follows :-
   Each Infantry Battalion.
   1 Officers coach.   25 trucks for men.   9 trucks for horses.   12 trucks for waggons.
   Each waggon truck holds 1 G.S. Waggon and 1 two wheeled Cart, or two limbered waggons complete, (ie. 4 half limbers)

5. Units will be met on arrival by the Staff Captain or the representative of their unit, who will lead them to their billet. They will send a cyclist to the detraining point, (GUILLAUCOURT) to meet the 12.31 train on the 20th to guide the rear platoons to their billets.

6. Units should enquire from the Staff Captain on arrival where the new Brigade Head Quarters will be situated.

7. Rations.   Each Unit will take the unexpired portion of the rations for the day of departure of the train on the men, and one days rations in their supply waggons.
   The 2 platoons which move with the last train will carry the rations for the 20th on the men.
   The O.C. Camerons will use his discretion as to what rations, (if any) for the 20th he carries on the men in addition to the unexpended portion for the 19th.

Issued at 1 pm.

[signature] Captain,
Brigade Major, 81st Infantry Brigade.

Copy No. 1 to File.
"   "   2 to War Diary.
"   "   3 to 1st Royal Scots.   )
"   "   4 to 2nd Gloucesters.   )   by Cyclist.
"   "   5 to 2nd Camerons   )
"   "   6 to 1st Arg. & Suth.Hrs.   )
"   "   7 to 97 Coy. A.S.C.   )

81st Infantry Brigade.

UNIT.	Place of entrainment.	Time of arrival of Transport & Loaders of units.	Time of departure of train.	Halts at ABBEVILLE.	ARRIVES GUILLANCOURT.	REMARKS.
1st Rl. Scots. (less 2 platoons.)	HAZEBROOK.	15.09 19th	18.09 19th	0.41 - 1.37 20th	3.21 20th	
2nd Cameron Hghrs. (less 2 platoons.)	"	18.09 19th	21.09 19th	3.41 - 4.47 20th	6.31 20th	
1st A. & S. Highrs. (less 2 platoons.)	"	21.09 19th	0.09 20th	6.41 - 7.37 20th	9.21 20th	
2nd Gloucesters. (less 2 platoons.)	"	0.09 20th	3.09 20th	9.41 - 10.37 20th	12.21 20th	
9th Rl. Scots.	"	3.09 20th	6.09 20th	12.38 - 13.27 20th	15.11 20th	
81st I. B. H.Q.) 3rd Corps Cable Sect.) 97th Coy. A.S.C.) 2 platoons from each) Bn. except 9th R. Scts	"	6.09 20th	9.09 20th	15.41 - 16.47 20th	18.31 20th	

www.ingramcontent.com/pod-product-compliance
Lightning Source LLC
Chambersburg PA
CBHW080821010526
44111CB00015B/2588